Freedom at Work

Penelope Brook

Auckland
OXFORD UNIVERSITY PRESS
Melbourne   Oxford   New York

Oxford University Press

Oxford University Press, Walton Street, Oxford OX2 6DP

OXFORD   NEW YORK   TORONTO
DELHI BOMBAY CALCUTTA MADRAS KARACHI
PETALING JAYA SINGAPORE HONG KONG TOKYO
NAIROBI DAR ES SALAAM   CAPE TOWN
MELBOURNE   AUCKLAND
and associated companies in
BERLIN   IBADAN

Oxford is a trade mark of Oxford University Press

First published 1990
© Penelope Brook 1990

ISBN 0 19 558220 9

Cover designed by Chris O'Brien
Photoset in Times by Wright & Carman Ltd.,
and printed in Hong Kong
Published by Oxford University Press
1A Matai Road, Greenlane, Auckland 5, New Zealand

Freedom at Work

As long as it is a matter of demonstrating the ills of society and the abuses of those who abuse, he has no hesitations (except for the fear that, if they are talked about too much, even the most just propositions can sound repetitive, obvious, tired). He finds it more difficult to say something about the remedies, because first he would like to make sure that they do not cause worse ills and abuses, and that if wisely planned by enlightened reformers, they can then be put into practice without harm by their successors: foolish perhaps, perhaps frauds, perhaps frauds and foolish at once.

Italo Calvino — *Mr Palomar*

Contents

Acknowledgements

Many people have given patiently and generously of their time and advice to assist in the preparation of this book. Some will not agree with my arguments, but I have learned much from their dissent; to all I offer my gratitude. They include:

Richard Blandy, National Institute of Labour Studies, Adelaide; Richard Epstein, University of Chicago; Bob Flanagan, Stanford University; David Haarmeyer, New Zealand Centre for Independent Studies; Gary Hawke, Institute of Policy Studies, Wellington; Ed Lazear, University of Chicago; John Martin, Organisation for Economic Cooperation and Development; Scott Masten, University of Michigan; Graham Mather, Institute of Economic Affairs, London; Morgan Reynolds, Texas A&M University; Klaus-Walter Riechel, International Monetary Fund; Sherwin Rosen, University of Chicago; Ted St Antoine, University of Michigan; Andrew Sharp, University of Auckland; Rudiger Soltwedel, Organisation for Economic Cooperation and Development; Graeme Wheeler, New Zealand Treasury; Bryce Wilkinson, Jarden Morgan (NZ) Ltd., and Oliver Williamson, University of California, Berkeley.

The first draft of the book was prepared while I was employed as a policy analyst by the New Zealand Business Roundtable. I would therefore also like to acknowledge the support of the members of the Business Roundtable, and of my colleagues in the Business Roundtable office, Ann Henare, Roger Kerr and Suzanne Smith.

P.J.B. *Wellington, July 1990*

Introduction

To work, to exercise strength and intellect in creating things that will make life better, is fundamental to the nature of human beings. It is in co-operating in work, in sharing out functions according to abilities and preferences, that economic society is founded. By specializing in different tasks, individuals can together generate a higher level of well-being than they can by acting in isolation. The evolution of co-operation and interdependence between individuals, of complementarity in work, is an important aspect of human history. The history of social organization—whether that organization is spontaneous or imposed—is in part the history of attempts to discover those rules and social structures that make such interdependence both feasible and fruitful, and that encourage people to work together.

The emerging dominance of employment relationships, largely as a result of the technological and organizational innovations of the industrial revolution, is just one aspect of this history. This has perhaps made us forget that it is not payment that makes an activity 'work'—a misapprehension that leads, for example, to proposals for the state to compensate unpaid work, such as the work of women in the home. Such proposals miss the point; payment for work is simply a reflection of the fact that some work is organized through markets, where money proves an especially effective and flexible medium of reward. Not all work is best organized through markets, or rewarded through market mechanisms. But this in itself implies nothing about the intrinsic 'value' of (or real rewards to) different kinds of work.

Paid employment is, however, one particularly advanced form of interdependence between individuals. There are big potential rewards to such interdependence, as the skills and knowledge of many are brought together in such a way that all can benefit. But there are inevitably also risks, in particular the risk that the individual will be lost in the grander social organization, that his or her autonomy will be compromised, resulting in a sense of alienation, or that the rewards of co-operation will be 'unfairly' distributed. Order in employment relationships therefore depends on both facilitating interdependence—finding ways of structuring employment which make for secure, rewarding work—and protecting the freedoms of the participants.

New Zealand's system of labour market legislation – like that of many other Western economies – is based on a centralist-collectivist approach to these problems. This approach, set out in the late nineteenth century writings of the Fabian Socialists in England and the Christian Socialists in Germany in the late nineteenth century, places a strong emphasis on the wisdom and elevated intentions of those given political power as a means of creating the 'good society'. To promote social and economic organization, these writers looked to the government to order the activities of the masses and to effect 'socially just' outcomes. In so far as they were concerned with individuals, they saw them as being protected through the establishment of 'rights' to certain outcomes, and through the 'extension of democracy into the workplace' by means of the creation of unions with government-like powers.

There are, however, considerable problems, both theoretical and practical, with this kind of approach. The ability of central planners to improve on the outcomes of voluntary processes is severely hampered by their sheer incapacity to gather and utilize information about individuals' varying needs, preferences and circumstances. It may be tempting to believe that well-meaning, rational planners could improve on the apparently chaotic interactions of independent citizens, but, as Hayek expresses it, this 'overlooks the fact that the totality of resources one could employ in such a plan *is simply not knowable* to anybody and therefore can hardly be centrally controlled' (1988a, p. 501, emphasis in the original).

Quite apart from these informational problems, there are problems with the incentives of politicians and planners when it comes to respecting the interests and liberties of citizens. To say as much is neither to deny the good intentions and integrity of public employees nor to argue against any government involvement in the economy. Rather, it is to say that the incentives given to bureaucrats matter, and that failure to take account of this in designing policy has imposed high costs, not only in the extreme cases of excesses by the *nomenklatura* of Eastern bloc countries, but in the mediocre performances of the increasingly bureaucratized economies of the West. Democracy is no guarantee against the arbitrary use of bureaucratic power, or against the creation of bastions of privilege.

As applied to the labour market in New Zealand, the collectivist approach of the Fabian Socialists has been translated into a rigid, adversarial, centralized system where compulsory union membership and predominantly craft and occupational unions with exclusive (and extended) rights of coverage make for a high degree of monopoly power in labour markets. Protected unions take the role of promoting their own particular version of 'social justice' in the labour market. This role is supplemented by legislation maintaining statutory minima in wages and conditions. It is a system which functions by undermining co-operation, by limiting opportunity and by carefully balancing privileges, and it is defended by ever-more elaborate, obfuscating rhetoric. Walker's description of Australian labour law is equally applicable to New Zealand:

> This is a region where the law is binding on the weak but not on the strong, where the law exalts rather than discourages conflict and confrontation, where the decision of a tribunal does not settle a dispute but merely provides something else to dispute about, where the person most affected by the decision has no necessary right to be heard and where freedom under the law is treated almost as a superstition. (1989, p. 81)

An increasing weight of evidence bears witness to the failure of this kind of system. This failure is most often described in terms of the inflexibility it generates across all aspects of employment relationships — inflexibility in labour costs, conditions of employment, work practices, rules and regulations (including taxation), training and mobility within and between firms. (That there are a number of areas in which flexibility can be promoted should allay fears that policies for increasing labour market flexibility will inevitably be focused on wages.) The overall effect is that barriers are erected to the fruitful and co-operative use of labour, at a high cost in terms of unemployment and underemployment. The opening up of the New Zealand economy to international competition through the finance and product market reforms of the 1980s has brought into focus the costs of such inflexibility. These costs have broad economic and social implications — exaggerating the effects of economic shocks, constraining innovation, aggravating inequality of income and generally eroding the potential for improvements in the quality of life.

While the adaptability of relationships in all markets is important to economic welfare and growth, there is an increasing awareness, in New Zealand as overseas, that the adaptability of employment relationships is pivotal. Thus the Dahrendorf Report of the Organization for Economic Co-operation and Development argued that:

> [T]he operation of labour markets is of strategic importance. Labour markets are important for the growth process itself; as the level of economic activity increases, they function better, and as they function better, the level of economic activity increases further. Such flexibility then serves not only processes of adjustment, but also innovation, equity, and a higher quality

of life. It should be seen as an active agent of manpower policy which is supportive of an overall objective of increasing the level of employment. In this sense, labour market flexibility is a key to both economic efficiency and social progress. (OECD, 1986b, p. 8)

That the heavily regulated systems of labour market organization adopted in most Western economies in the twentieth century have, because of their inflexibility, imposed high costs in terms of the efficiency of resource use, equity in access to employment and income, and the potential for economic growth does not in itself imply that the philosophy that underpins them is fundamentally misguided. There is always the chance that with better models, more rational decision-making processes or better intentions more flexibility could have been planned into these systems. This, indeed, is the assumption behind experimentation with incomes policies in many Western economies in the 1960s and 1970s,[1] and behind the more recent initiatives for an 'Accord' in Australia and a 'Compact' in New Zealand.

However, the failure of this kind of enforced collectivism, both in labour markets and more generally, is rooted more deeply than in its shortcomings as implemented by 'imperfectly socialist' individuals. Rather, its failure rests in its suppression of individual autonomy and freedom (and thereby of co-operative effort). As such, it offends against any ethical standard which places pre-eminence on the individual and his or her autonomy. But this ethical failure also has important economic and social repercussions, in that individual autonomy is in essence not a barrier to, but a prerequisite for, the peaceful and successful functioning of society. By this reasoning, the case for advocating voluntary market exchanges, rather than centralized planning, as the basis for economic activity, takes its strength from its protection of individual freedom:

> The ethical argument for the market is . . . not only that it allows practitioners of different traditions and values to live in peaceful coexistence, but also that it allows for innovation and novelty in thought and practice in a way that collective decisions cannot. This is to say that market freedom protects the very basic freedom to think new thoughts and try out new practices. At its most fundamental, the moral argument for the free market is one which appeals to its indispensable role in *enabling* people to implement their ideas and realize their goals . . . . [I]t is only the institutions of the market that accord full respect to human agency, while efforts to 'empower' people through government intervention typically turn them into passive consumers of impersonal bureaucracies. (Gray, 1989, pp. 34-5, emphasis in the original)

It is perhaps ironic that in a century where increasing emphasis has been placed on civil liberties, governments have, through interventions like New Zealand's labour relations legislation, actively eroded economic liberties. Civil liberties, and the associated emphasis on 'rights' to particular outcomes cannot, however, compensate for lost economic liberties; no amount of effort to 'extend democracy into the workplace', for example, can compensate for the loss of autonomy of individual workers and employers. No amount of compassionate rhetoric can substitute for freedom.

The central theme of this study is that we cannot hope to achieve the outcomes that we desire from employment relationships — whether these outcomes are defined as the efficient use of labour resources, equity in employment relationships or empowering individual workers — if we do not return to an emphasis on the liberty of individual workers. The correct focus of labour market policy is to make this liberty 'meaningful', by protecting the rights that a worker brings to employment, and minimizing the costs of forming and maintaining productive, satisfying employment relationships. This will require a fundamental shift in philosophy from an outcome-oriented, centralist-collectivist viewpoint to an incentive-oriented, truly individualist viewpoint, and an accompanying shift from a directive to a facilitative policy.

Chapter 1 begins with a brief discussion of the evolution of employment relationships through the industrial revolution and of attempts to accommodate this process, while retaining an essentially individualistic perspective, by modifications in private and public law. It then discusses the basic tenets of the collectivist approach to social and economic policy which was gaining an increasing hold among intellectuals throughout Europe in the latter part of the nineteenth century, and which was to serve as a basis for strongly interventionist labour law throughout the Western world from the 1890s to the 1990s. While the particular manifestations of this philosophy vary across jurisdictions, they rest on common preoccupations with bargaining power, the potential for workers to be exploited by employers and the unique characteristics of labour: characteristics which led to a concern to 'take labour out of competition', and to deny the relevance of market exchanges in deciding how labour services should be used and rewarded.

Attempts to deal with these concerns led to two strands in labour policy. These are described in Chapter 2. The first was state support for labour market collectives; the creation and protection of monopoly power on the part of unions. The mechanisms varied and the models adopted in New Zealand, the United Kingdom, the

United States and Germany are compared. But the common objective was not only to ensure 'socially acceptable' outcomes in employment contracts, but to promote a sense of participation and 'industrial peace'. The second strand of policy involved direct government interventions to constrain the outcomes of employment contracting, for example, through minimum wage laws and legislation on hours and conditions. Chapter 2 concludes with some discussion of recent policy proposals in New Zealand, which, with the exception of reforms in public sector employment law, have essentially protected the existing system.

Chapter 3 looks at the effects of systems like the one adopted in New Zealand, beginning with some general comments on the methodology for testing both specific policies and the philosophical 'visions' on which they are based. The various justifications put forward for legislation in support of unions are discussed, with reference to the experience of other unionized economies. Attention is then turned to the rules surrounding union formation and union activities in New Zealand, both rules that confer extraordinary powers on unions, and rules designed to compensate for the weakness of market constraints on their accountability to their members. The argument here is not about whether unions can perform a useful role, but about whether the existing rules facilitate their formation when they can, but discourage it when they cannot. There is also some discussion of the effects of the changes implemented in the Labour Relations Act of 1987, and in particular of the extent to which they can be seen as enhancing the flexibility of employment arrangements and the freedom of individual workers. The effects of statutory minima on wages and conditions, including comparable worth legislation, are then considered.

Both theoretical argument and the empirical evidence in New Zealand and in other countries with similarly motivated labour law suggest fundamental flaws in this kind of labour legislation and in the philosophy that underpins it. This suggests that if reform of the labour market is to be successful, it must be based on a re-evaluation of the principles of government intervention.

Chapter 4 is concerned with elucidating the principles on which labour market regulation should be based if it is to facilitate fair and efficient labour market relationships (including relationships between workers and unions). It emphasizes the liberty of individual workers to use their labour as they see fit, and in particular to enter contracts with employers or unions that will be of mutual benefit — in essence, a freedom to co-operate. In this sense, individual freedom serves as a basis both for the protection of individuals and for social cohesion.

Voluntary exchange cannot, however, function in a legal or moral vacuum. Rather, it depends on the existence of mechanisms for protecting the property rights of the individuals involved and enforcing the contracts that they form with each other (except where the process by which these contracts are formed is clearly unconscionable). The central problem here is to find legal or moral means of reconciling potentially competing freedoms, for example, through the prohibition of force or fraud in the formation of contracts, or the availability of remedies where third parties are significantly adversely affected by a contract between others. There is also a need to clarify the nature of entitlements involved when we say that an individual worker is 'free' to contract both with an employer and with a union.

'Private' law, as represented by the English common law, yields the basic legal principles of property, contract and tort needed for a well-functioning body of employment (and union) law. There is, however, likely to be some value in establishing a special labour statute, specifying and to some degree elucidating the relevant principles, and offering standard forms as a means of reducing the costs of drawing up employment and union contracts. In order to handle such problems of monopoly power as might arise in labour markets, whether on the part of monopsony employers or monopoly unions, extending the coverage of the Commerce Act to the labour market is suggested.

Chapter 5 is concerned with assessing the effects of implementing a system of labour law like the one proposed. How a theory can be tested, and the relevance of empirical data from other markets and other countries, is considered. The possible evolution and outcomes of bargaining arrangements based on choice for the individuals involved is also discussed.

A case for reform along the lines suggested arises both from an assessment of the 'economic' benefits — the potential for higher living standards and greater fairness in employment relationships — and from its superior ability to protect individual freedom; to empower individuals in their work relationships. This case is summarized in the final chapter.

1
Ideology in Labour Market Regulation

In its detail the system of labour market regulation in New Zealand is largely unique. However, it is based on an ideology that has been common to the regulation of labour markets both in socialist countries and in much of the Western world. In order to understand the evolution of labour market law in New Zealand and to evaluate its effects, it will be helpful to begin by describing this basic ideology and the concerns on which it rests.

1.1 The Evolution of Employment Relationships

The employment relationship as it is currently known has its roots in the industrial revolution—in the creation of large groups of workers who did not readily conform to the traditional categories of servant, hired hand or skilled artisan. Their relationship with the purchasers of their labour was neither essentially domestic nor a matter of discrete market transactions.

For a system of law to retain meaning in the face of such important changes in the nature of relationships between individuals, it requires flexibility. In England, where these new employment relationships were first to emerge in any number, an important source of such flexibility had traditionally rested in the nature of private or 'common' law. As applied to contractual relationships of all kinds this law was not static, but rather judge-made. Essentially this was the result of centuries of judicial activism and accumulated precedent—of legal 'learning by doing'. In contrast the law of continental Europe 'tends to move more theoretically by deductive reasoning, basing judgments on abstract principles; it is more conceptual, more scholastic and works more with definitions and abstractions' (Van Caenegem, 1988, p. 88). The emphasis placed on the English common law in this study is, however, appropriate, since this is the tradition in which the legal system inherited by New Zealand was based.

A system such as the English common law is not, of course, immune to error, but its reliance on accrued wisdom—on experience of what works and what does not—is an important means of minimizing error. The ability of the law to adapt to economic change may also be aided by deliberate legislative change on the part of governments. Thus in the area of corporate law, for example, the explicit legalization of limited liability companies was an important means of forming companies which could cast widely for funds rather than relying on family wealth, and could invest and innovate in the use of capital equipment.

With the new kind of employment relationship that accompanied industrialization came a lack of clarity as to the interpretation of common law. Kahn-Freund (1977), for example, argues that well into the nineteenth century legal interpretations drew on the eighteenth century legal texts of Blackstone, leading to a view of the employment relationship in terms of domestic or family law. This view was inconsistent with rapid and dramatic changes in the nature of work. This led to an emphasis on Elizabethan and Jacobean law regarding the enforceable obligation to serve, which was in turn an elaboration of statutes enacted by Edward III in the aftermath of the Black Death as a means of ensuring service while enforcing wage maxima in the face of extreme labour scarcity. The result was that relatively little emphasis was placed on the contractual nature of the employment relationship, and more on the 'status' of the parties:

> [T]he bulk of labour law, and especially the bulk of legislation for the protection of workers, developed until our own century and partly still develops outside the frame of the contract of employment. It was only comparatively recently that such legislation began to take its effect by conferring on the workers *contractual* rights which could not be abrogated to their detriment. The normal pattern of protection was through the law of tort or through special statutory rights unconnected with the contract of employment (Kahn-Freund, 1977, p. 524, emphasis in the original).

However, at least in America which shared the same common law tradition, Dickman argues that by the late eighteenth century the contractual nature of the employment relationship was well established:

> On the eve of the American Revolution, the individual laborer's right to contract for the sale of his own labor (his right to make his own bargains) was firmly entrenched in law and custom, as was the individual businessman's right to fix prices for his own products. (1987, pp. 73-4)

In the United Kingdom, a political philosophy conducive to a contractual approach to employment relations was also well established by this time, and by the second half of the nineteenth century it was becoming entrenched in practice. There were clearly some continuing problems, for example, as a result of applying the notions of status and duty that had been central to traditional 'Master-Servant' relationships to fixed-term labour contracts.[1] However, the emerging trend was for employment relationships to be governed by common law principles of property, contract, tort and procedure.

In addition to the need for the law to accommodate the new kinds of employment relationships that were emerging, there was a need to adapt to accommodate union representation of workers. (It should be noted that at the same time as the law was required to deal with the new form of unionism that accompanied industrialization, it was also being required to deal with another, arguably more novel, kind of collective: the collective of investors, which was to serve as the basis of the modern corporation.) Collective organization of workers was nothing new. It had precedents in the medieval trade and craft guilds, which performed a number of tasks not unlike those of modern professional organizations — regulating entry, policing quality standards, setting prices, regulating the wages of apprentices and arbitrating disputes among members. Dickman (1987) instances prohibitions on carpenters from doing masonry, plumbing, daubing or tiling; on shoemakers from repairing shoes (a task which was reserved for cobblers), and, at one point, on bakers of white bread from baking black bread. Such guild activities were governed from the early sixteenth century both by regulation and by common law checks on the abuse of their monopoly power.

The unions of wage labourers that emerged in the United Kingdom in the late eighteenth century were initially concerned primarily with the provision of friendly benefits to their members. Gradually this function expanded to embrace negotiation of pay and conditions, then pressure for the broadening of suffrage and for the legal right to provide financial support to political parties. Brown writes of unions in the Victorian era that they had 'little or no apparent power to deflect or obstruct the working of market forces' (1983, p. 22), and were on the whole regarded by employers as assisting productivity by attracting skilled and responsible workers:

> The implication for the employer was not only that trade unionists were to be respected because they were personally among the most skilful and intelligent of his employees, but that the labour which received the full trade union rate was not dear, because it was highly productive. This was all the more so, because the unions actually strengthened the character and improved the performance of their members. (1983, p. 25)

In a similar vein, Brown quotes an 1889 Royal Commission in Canada which saw the effect of unions as being to inculcate a spirit of self-control, of independence and of self-reliance, and especially to promote temperance, stating that 'where organisation has made much progress the moral standing of the people is also high. No one can become a member who is not sober' (Brown, p. 24). By the turn of the twentieth century, he argues, long experience with collective negotiation at the level of the individual firm meant that 'the union appeared no less indispensable than its existence was intelligible' (p. 24). As a result, Brown argues, there was in the United Kingdom no consolidation of employers in resistance to the growth of unionism. A similar argument has been used to explain the minimal resistance by British employers to the proliferation of closed shops in the mid-twentieth century.

While there were indisputably benefits associated with the rise of unionism in the United Kingdom, particularly where it had a company basis, not all accounts are so rosy. Dickman (1987), points to violent strike activity, often involving arson, vandalism and riot, as early as the late eighteenth century. Criminalization of union activities, codified in the Combination Act of 1800, may be seen as at least partly a response to such violence.

In the United States, there appears to have been a less tolerant view of unionism than that described by Brown. This may in part have been a result of the predominantly craft (rather than enterprise) basis of unionism, and the 'ugly face' of such unionism that emerged in the latter part of the nineteenth century:

> An aura of collective protest, high-pitched emotion, and revolutionary fervour accompanied unionism everywhere. And with it came the spectre of union violence. Bombings and killings in the anthracite fields during the 1870s (attributed to the Molly Maguires), the anarcho-syndicalist flavor of the Haymarket riot in 1886, the violence of railroad and steel industry disputes, and many other incidents helped create a public image of unionists and organized workers as a threat to peace, prosperity, property rights, and liberty itself. (Reynolds, 1987, pp. 5-6)

The social acquiescence in the emergence of unionism described by Brown in reference to the United Kingdom—where union activism was also on the increase in the later nineteenth century— appears to have been rather less in the United States. Reynolds attributes this to the overriding importance attached in the United States to the ethics of liberalism and individualism:

> American capitalism was in its heyday . . . and the concepts of free enterprise and individual freedom had a grip on popular opinion that is hard to imagine

from our contemporary vantage point. The United States was not fertile ground for planting union doctrine — or for other forms of collectivism, for that matter. The main adhesive of European unions — easily aroused class resentments — was absent in America, and Marxist-style sentiments about the plight of the working class never became a dominant mood . . . . (1987, p. 6)

The approach of the courts to newly emerging unions was essentially antagonistic in both countries. In the United Kingdom, the declaration by Lord Mansfield, an eighteenth century Lord Chief Justice, that a trade union was inherently a criminal conspiracy continued to influence thinking well into the nineteenth century. However, under pressure from liberal opinion in the middle years of the nineteenth century, there was a series of moves to decriminalize the activities of unions which began with the 1824 Combination Act and culminated in the 1871 Trade Union Act and the 1875 Conspiracy and Protection of Property Act. From 1875 onwards the potency of the union immunities that these moves created was eroded as the courts again proscribed a wide range of the decriminalized activities under the auspices of tort and civil conspiracy law. Thus, for example, picketing was restricted, tort was applied to union attempts to secure breach of labour contracts, and, in the Taff Vale case of 1901, there was acceptance of the liability of a union (as distinct from its members) to be sued.

Similarly in the United States the first cases of labour law were criminal conspiracy cases over the right of journeymen to act collectively (Wellington, 1968). Later, antitrust legislation, in the form of the 1890 Sherman Act, was to be applied to the activities of unions, creating a basis for injunctions against some forms of union activity that was to stand, if in diminished form, for a further four decades.

An essential element in many explanations of the subsequent widespread legislative initiatives to redefine both the individual employment relationship and the prerogatives of unions seems to be that the common law had proved itself deficient in adapting to the new economic realities of employment relationships, or in adequately protecting the interests of the newly emerging labouring 'classes'. Thus Brown argues, for example, that:

[T]here was a basic divergence between the principles of common law and the realities of industrial life . . . . [The common law] sees only the contract of employment between the individual workman and the employer, and is not able to find a status for the combination of workmen that negotiates a collective agreement, or a place for the terms of the agreement itself. (1983, p. 29)

Brown's point is that if the notion that a combination is tainted with conspiracy is a 'prima facie assumption' of the common law, the need of workers to organize to countervail the 'economic power' of employers will inevitably bring them into conflict with the common law. He thus goes beyond the widespread agreement that it was inappropriate to apply criminal conspiracy law to the activities of unions, and asserts the inappropriateness of civil conspiracy cases and the awarding of damages against unions as entities. Wellington (1968) takes a similar view on the situation in the United States in the latter part of the nineteenth century.

Agreement that the use of criminal conspiracy doctrine was misguided as it was applied to trade unions is not limited to those who have advocated some form of statutory backing for unions. Epstein, for example, refers to the use of the doctrine as 'an unfortunate . . . flirtation' (1983a, p. 1364), while Hayek writes that American liberalism 'far too long maintained an unjustified opposition against trade-unions as such' (1948, p. 117). That the common law could permit such an 'unfortunate flirtation' does not, however, imply a wider irrelevance of common law principles to labour market relationships. Rather, the criminal conspiracy cases of the nineteenth century can be condemned precisely for their departure from common law principles protective of freedom of contract and freedom of association. (This role of common law principles will be discussed in Chapter 4.) What is clear from the circumstances that produced these cases is that the extent of social and economic change that was occurring was placing the traditional legal system under some considerable strain. An increasing reliance on legislative initiatives must certainly have been a tempting means of resolving the new situations and changing trade-offs that this system faced.

1.2 The Ideological Roots of Modern Labour Law

The wave of government intervention in labour market relationships that began in the second half of the nineteenth century and continues to the present day cannot be explained solely in terms of 'proven inadequacies' in the common law — whether in detail or in terms of its ability to adapt — or of comparable 'inadequacies' in markets. One important explanation is what has been described as a turning of the intellectual tide away from individualism and towards socialistic or syndicalistic collectivism, a movement that has its intellectual roots in the work of such writers as Godwin and

Rousseau. The ideas put forward by this movement remain important, in that they have shaped the content of much existing labour market legislation, and continue to be used to justify an activist role for governments in this area.

Friedman and Friedman (1988) put the 'flood stage', at which collectivism began to dominate opinion, at the founding of the Fabian Society in the United Kingdom in 1883 — a society which was to be greatly influenced by the writings of Sidney and Beatrice Webb, who not only asserted the benefits of unionism to society (rather than simply to workers), but also 'conveyed the impression that the unions they surveyed formed an essential part of any system of rational social administration, such as was dear to the authors' hearts' (Brown, 1983, p. 26). In the United States, a comparable date was 1885, when a group of young economists founded the American Economic Association, intending it as a means of spreading the ideas of the German Christian Socialists. This particular attempt foundered when the association proclaimed a policy of 'non-partisanship and avoidance of official commitments on practical economic questions and political issues'.

This 'intellectual tide' was based on a 'vision' of the nature of causation in society that had implications for everything from the interpretation of essential rights and concepts of equity and justice, to a redefinition of the role of the government and government agencies in all spheres of activity. There have been a number of attempts to analyse this 'vision'. It is the 'unconstrained' vision described by Sowell — unconstrained because it rests on a view of individuals as capable, if appropriately guided, of ever-increasing virtue (even if proponents of this vision sometimes showed great disdain for the 'lower' classes of their own day[2]):

> Running through the tradition of the unconstrained vision is the conviction that foolish or immoral choices explain the evils of the world — and that wiser or more moral and humane social policies are the solution. (1987, p. 37)

Hayek (1948) describes it in terms of its emphasis on the rational, and a resulting conviction that social institutions constructed and operated by appeal to rationality could improve upon the — inexplicable — operation of decision-making through markets. Barry explains it in terms of theories directed to some political 'end-state', which he describes as follows:

> First, they attribute the production of desirable outcomes to *intentional* acts of individuals (or bodies). Second, they emphasise the role of an active *reason* in the determination of social events. Third, they depend heavily on the

centralisation of knowledge. Fourth, they depend ultimately on the existence
of benevolent and omniscient dictators. (1988, p. 43, emphasis in the original)

In this view of the world, the rights of individuals are determined
not according to what will make society function as well as possible,
but in terms of personal benefit. They are rights not so much to
access to economic, social or political processes as to results. Justice
becomes not a matter of fair procedure, but 'social justice', the
notion that membership of a society carries with it an entitlement
to share in the wealth of that society:

It is maintained that the distribution of income and wealth in a community
should not be determined by the 'random' or blind forces of the market but
by 'rational' moral principles. The unpredictable and often unfortunate
outcomes of the market should be controlled and corrected by values
embodied in a more ethically pleasing end-state. Income should then reflect
desert, merit and 'need' rather than the value of labour services as revealed
in market exchange. (Barry, 1988, pp. 41-2)

Equality becomes a matter of results rather than treatment (and
'equality of opportunity' is respecified in terms of the opportunity
to attain equal outcomes). Moreover, inequalities—and the angst
that accompanies them—are seen as in some sense deliberate; the
observation that the poor are poor and the rich are rich leads to
a conclusion that the poor are poor *because* the rich are rich, that
the poor are but passive victims of the rich.

This notion of causation, and the emphasis on economic 'power'
that it embodies, increases the 'moral weight' of the notion of social
justice. Together, these concepts enable the importance of property
rights (and the incentives that they create) to be played down—a
concern with property rights being seen as representing a 'tilt against
redistribution'. It is not ownership of property that confers a right
to decide how that property shall be used, but rather excellence in
terms of 'sincerity, articulated knowledge and reason'. The pursuit
of 'social justice' thereby becomes a means of sanctioning the erosion
of the economic liberties that accompany property rights. Underlying
all this is the belief that 'the social cake can be sliced up in any way
we like without there being any "feed-back" on the way the cake
is baked or on its quality or size' (Barry, 1988, p. 42).

The result is a vision of politics as a kind of Newtonian science,
a means of systematically acting on the world. This vision of politics
is rich with engineering analogies, and assertions of 'scientific'
analysis of what is socially desirable and 'rational' pursuit of these
social goals; '[s]ocial issues then reduce to a matter of 'technical

coordination" by experts' (Sowell, 1987, p. 72). It is here that the collectivist urge described by the Friedmans arises. The role of the government becomes one not of establishing incentives for the efficient and equitable use of resources, but of elucidating and providing desired social outcomes; economic planning becomes a matter of 'articulated rationality'. The role of the courts becomes one not solely of applying the law, but of providing 'fresh moral insight', of investigating the implications not of what the law says, but of the 'values' which underly it: 'it is not simply a question of the locus of discretion, but also of the morality, reasonableness, and equality or inequality with which that discretion was exercised' (Sowell, 1987, pp. 163-4). Regulation is taken to be 'not a matter of counting economic costs and benefits, or of defending private entitlements, but part of a continuing process of deciding what sort of society we shall be' (Stewart and Sunstein quoted in Epstein, 1983a, p. 1361).

What led this view of the world to take hold in societies where essentially *laissez faire* policies had in the course of the industrial revolution generated increasing wealth – and dramatic improvements in the economic well-being of the least advantaged? In explanation Friedman and Friedman quote from the constitutional lawyer A.V. Dicey:

> The beneficial effect of State intervention, especially in the form of legislation, is direct, immediate, and, so to speak, visible, whilst its evil effects are gradual and indirect, and lie out of sight . . . few are those who realize the undeniable truth that State help kills self-help. Hence the majority of mankind must almost of necessity look with undue favor upon governmental intervention. This natural bias can be counteracted only by the existence . . . as in England between 1830 and 1860, of a presumption or prejudice in favor of individual liberty – that is of laissez-faire. The mere decline, therefore, of faith in self-help . . . is of itself sufficient to account for the growth of legislation tending toward socialism. (1988, p. 460)

In other words, it was not the demonstration of particular failures in relatively liberal policies – or that these failures could be rectified by government intervention – that led to increasing, results-oriented interventions around the turn of the century. Rather it was a change in the way that the world was viewed. And this 'new' view was one of considerable popular appeal. It offered the 'certainties' of planning in place of the inexplicable operations of the market. It promised results, and it suppressed – or perhaps failed to recognize – the costs of achieving these results.

These intellectual developments are emphasized in this study because they were to define the terms in which our present labour market legislation is expressed, and the kinds of trade-offs that continue to be deemed important when changes to this legislation are being considered. However, an explanation of how these ideas came to take hold would be incomplete without some reference to the changes that were occurring in Western political systems around the turn of the century; the emergence of universal suffrage, and with it the emergence of previously constrained interest groups as a political force. In the context of the labour market, the crucial factor was the growing importance of trade unions as a source of political pressure, both through their command of individual votes, and through the establishment of political parties rooted in the union movement. The mechanism was set for pluralistic rent-seeking on a scale hitherto unimagined; an institutional shift that in tandem with emergent centralist-collectivist ideas was to provide a potent basis for interventionist policy.

The results of this shift in terms both of policy and of judicial interpretation of policy was felt to some degree in all markets— most uniformly in the socialist nations that were to emerge in the twentieth century. Under the banner of social democracy, they have remained pervasive in various manifestations in non-socialist countries—the United Kingdom up until the late 1970s, the Scandinavian countries, post-reconstruction West Germany, New Zealand and Australia—as well as in the United States, supposedly a bastion of individualism and liberalism. But the implications of an 'unconstrained' vision have arguably been most significant where it has been applied to the employment relationship, and to markets for labour. The following section discusses its impact in terms of how employment relationships came to be perceived.

1.3   Preoccupations in Labour Market Policy

If social outcomes are thought to be determined by the morality and wisdom of those who make key social, economic and political decisions, it follows that observed disparities in income will be seen as evidence of the foolish or immoral exercise of power. This translates in the context of the employment relationship into a preoccupation with the notion of inequality of power between employer and employee, and the possibility of exploitation of employee by employer.

In other words, the emphasis is placed not on the mutual concerns of employer and employee (for the running of a successful, job-sustaining business), and the incentives that this mutual interest creates, but rather on their relative 'power'. This emphasis tends to be reinforced by observation of the unpleasantnesses of life on the production line, and the sense of alienation that this can generate:

> The production line is emasculating, and thus the quest must be to restore man to man. It is dehumanising, and thus the worker must again be made human. It is uncreative, and thus man at his machine must be given a creative outlet. (Wellington, 1968, pp. 26-7)

This provides another important rallying cry; that 'labour is not a commodity'; that the employment relationship, because of its human content and the 'power' relationships that it represents, is fundamentally different from other economic relationships. The envisaged solution is therefore not economic but political — the 'enfranchisement' of workers through 'industrial democracy' and collective bargaining, and active government support of these activities.

Is Labour a Commodity?

> Labor is a factor of production — but the worker is a human being, and his work involves social as well as technical relations. Work is not merely the way to get a living, but a way of life, a game or a thralldom, a field of conflicts and loyalties, anxieties and reassurances, prestige and humiliation . . . . The occupational and social structures are interlocked. (Henry Phelps Brown quoted in Winter, 1963, p. 24, n. 39)

The notion that labour is a commodity like any other is to many a source of abhorrence, as is the associated argument that wages, like the price of any other good or service, should be determined by competitive market processes. The problem here is to distinguish between the things that make individual workers important — and that make the quality of employment relationships important — and the problem of determining how labour is to be put to the best possible uses, and how it is to be rewarded.

The concerns underlying the assertion that 'labour is not a commodity' are important and valid ones. The employment relationship is a vital and consuming one for any worker. He or she looks to work not only for the income to meet personal and family needs but for personal fulfilment, the satisfaction of participation in a creative process, the means to self-development and improving quality of life, and the companionship and stimulation of fellow workers. A poor employment relationship can be demoralizing and alienating. The inability to secure employment can impose not only material hardship but also loss of self-regard.

Those who assert that labour must not be treated as a commodity[3] and that wages must be taken out of competition are effectively arguing that these factors make wages and conditions of employment too important to be left to the market; that there is a social interest in ensuring that work is not 'dehumanizing', not mere 'wage slavery', and that the market is either too uncontrolled or too much at the control of employers to deliver 'socially responsible' outcomes. Instead, wages and conditions should be determined by some 'democratic' process, based on 'rights' of a kind that do not accrue in other economic relationships. Thus a former Minister of Labour in New Zealand has talked of 'the extension of human rights into the workplace' (Rodger, 1989, p. 18). The New Zealand Council of Trade Unions asserts that the employment relationship should fulfil rights to 'a job, a fair income and dignity and security for [working people], their families and the communities in which they live' (1988, p. 3). Similarly, proponents of comparable worth legislation argue in terms of women's 'right' to equality of income with men.

This implies a distinction between the principles applied to the management of employment relationships and those applied in other economic relationships. It is argued to follow that employment relationships should not fall within the domain of civil law, but rather be the subject of a separate legal jurisdiction:

> Labour law must break free from the assumptions of underlying institutions of the civil law, the property rights of the employer, through which he controls work and the enterprise, the prerogative of the employer to organise and distribute work, and the status of subordination attached to the worker. The contract of employment could be retained as representing a free choice to enter an economic relationship but it must be modified, on the base rather of a realistic agreement (*un ordre concret*) than of hierarchic subordination. Above all labour law was distinguished from civil law by its collective character, its umbilical cord to the social facts. (Wedderburn, 1988, p. 222)

This kind of argument has had significant implications for government involvement in labour markets throughout the Western world. It goes a step further than saying that the 'articulated rationality' of wise and virtuous governments can generate outcomes in employment relationships that improve upon the 'circuitous and uncontrolled' processes of the common law and of markets—an argument which could 'explain', for example, government legislation for minimum wages or standards of employment in the same way that it would 'explain' such interventions as rent controls or restrictions on takeover activity. In *addition* to saying this, it says that the employment relationship is so fundamentally different from other economic relationships (between tenant and landlord, or shareholder and company) that the same principles of law cannot apply. And an important variant of this is the delegation to unions of government-like powers to determine minimum conditions and to compel compliance — though often without accountability comparable to accountability, albeit limited, of elected governments.

The critical assumption in these arguments is that if employment relationships are left to be determined by 'the market' — more accurately, by the *voluntary* decisions of workers (individually or collectively) and employers — both incomes and work conditions will be driven to a 'dehumanizing' level, and workers will be little better than wage slaves. It is further assumed that 'democratization' or compulsory collectivization of the wage- and condition-determining process can unambiguously improve on this outcome; conferring on workers wages and a working environment that are 'socially just'. It is almost as if by *willing* labour to be free from the relevance of scarcities and surpluses it can be made so; if we declare fervently enough that labour is not like other commodities, the factors that constrain the use and price of these commodities will, in the case of labour, pale to irrelevance.

To say that labour is a 'commodity' is, however, to say no more than that it is something of value; it does not imply that people are chattel, and it *certainly* does not abrogate the social maxim that workers cannot be bought and sold. Rather it reflects the right of individual workers to offer their labour *services* for whatever remuneration they can attract. As Heldman *et al.* explain it:

> [A]n employee will always be a seller of labor, an employer will always be a buyer of labor, and wages (or compensation generally) will always be the price of the commodity. This cannot be changed; at most, it might be distorted. (1981, pp. 6-7)

However, if it is believed that workers are always at a disadvantage in their dealings with employers, and that the freedom of the market is nothing but the freedom of individuals to coerce each other, it could still be conceded that labour *was* a commodity without abandoning the argument that 'market' outcomes are, in the case of employment relationships, socially untenable. This notion of inevitable disadvantage is at the heart of arguments about unequal bargaining power. And in train with this notion come arguments about the 'inevitable' exploitation of workers.

Unequal Bargaining Power and Exploitation

If differences in status, income or wealth are seen as the result of social injustice, it is a small step to attribute them to an unjust distribution of economic or political power, and an unwise or even malicious exercise of that power. In particular, authority exercised on the basis of property rights, as opposed to authority exercised on the basis of civic virtue or 'superior' rationality, comes to be seen as creating and perpetuating injustice—as exploitative. And the relationships between individuals come to be characterized in terms of their relative 'power', rather than in terms of their mutual interests.

The literature on labour market relationships is thick with the language of inequalities in bargaining power and the exploitation that might accompany them. At one end of the spectrum are arguments about a fundamental conflict of interest between capital (and increasingly transnational capital) and labour, and about an ongoing struggle over some fixed economic cake between the representatives of each. As the New Zealand Council of Trade Unions has put it, in all employment relationships 'the common factors are that capital (in the form of various companies) gets people to perform work (in various forms) and then uses its control over the production and distribution processes to make profits' (1988, p. 18). It is not the fact that companies are large relative to individual workers, or that they are observed to collude to oppress workers, that makes them 'exploitative' in such a view, but the fact that they 'represent' capital, that their efforts are directed at the creation of a profit for the benefit of the owners of capital, that it is the essence of capital to exploit labour. Wages are 'low', in this view, because profits are high.

In a late twentieth century guise, this makes for arguments of the following kind:

As a result of the gross inequalities of power in our society, the last few years have seen a decline in working people's share of the national cake. The beneficiaries of this decline are the large companies and the record profits those large companies have made in the last few years have been expended on increased dividends to shareholders and a consolidation of corporate ownership within the economy i.e. increasing monopolisation. The free market policies of recent times have accentuated this process of increased profit and monopolisation. (Knox, 1986, p. 2)

This view can only be sustained if the fundamental interdependence of capital and labour, and the answerability of both to the interests of consumers, is set aside. In other words, it involves insisting that competition in the labour market is competition *between* employers and workers, rather than between employers for workers, and between workers for jobs. And it disregards the fact that in so far as 'power' is exercised over employment relationships, it is the power of *consumers*, through their willingness to purchase the goods and services that employers and workers collaborate to produce. As Hutt puts it:

> [T]he suppliers of assets and circulating capital are just as subordinate as the workers to the power of consumers' sovereignty. Consumers are the true 'employers'. The assets of the firm are employed just as the workers are. The services of both are embodied in output. The investors willingly submit to the ruthless discipline of the market. (1986, p. 61)

However, even where it is accepted that the different participants in a firm have some common interests, it is sometimes still argued that there is room for the pursuit of interests which they do not hold in common to lead to the systematic 'exploitation' of one by the other. Such arguments hinge on the notion of a surplus that is created within a firm by virtue of the firm-specific investments (for example, in training) made by employers and workers, and that generates a degree of indeterminacy in wages. The 'worthlessness' of such investments *outside* the firm is seen as making workers vulnerable *inside* the firm, in that 'strong' employers can appropriate all the value of this investment, without risking losing their workers to other firms.

These subtly different arguments involve quite different ways of thinking about what a fair wage consists of. In the former, fair wages are seen in terms of some *intrinsic* value. The notion of a 'just price' in this sense—an absolute value rather than a value which is dependent on scarcity and preferences—has a long and rather unsatisfactory history. As Paul (1989) points out, it was exemplified by the medieval guild system, setting prices not only for the labour of members but also for their products. It was a major preoccupation of classical economists theorizing on wage funds in the nineteenth century, and central to Marx's labour theory of value. And it continues to manifest itself in vigorously defended wage-relativities, and in proposals for 'equal pay for work of equal value'. Its central tenet is that wages determined in competitive markets are inherently unfair; that 'fairness' depends on the suppression or replacement of market forces as determinants of wages.

In the latter, the argument seems to be not so much that market-determined wages — wages that depend on the scarcity of different kinds of labour — are unfair, as that market 'failures' undermine the fair (and efficient) functioning of the wage-setting process — 'failures' that are again often couched in terms of inequality of 'bargaining power' and the capacity for 'exploitation' that it creates. The concern here is not that markets are unfair, but that departures from textbook perfect competition amount to departures from fairness. 'Fairness' in this case is seen as depending on remedying these departures.

But what is the meaning of power in the context of an economic relationship? And what are the conditions under which an imbalance in such 'power' makes exploitation possible?

'Exploitation' is essentially a matter of removing alternatives, for example, denying a worker any real choice in how he or she will be employed. The wage that a worker can 'bargain for' depends on his or her access to alternatives. The worker's 'bargaining power' *vis-à-vis* a current employer is measured by the best remuneration package that he or she could attract from a competing employer; that is, by the competition that exists for his or her services. In this context, Hutt argues that notions of bargaining power can be used with consistency and meaning only in reference to the individual worker, not to workers as a mass or a class:

> We cannot talk of 'labor's disadvantage in bargaining', although we can discuss the *individual's*. The remedy for the individual's 'bargaining weakness' is to raise the value of his work. His 'bargaining power' depends (a) on his having scarce and valuable powers, which simply means that he can provide goods and services which consumers need, and (b) on his effective right to use those powers. (1973, p. 65, emphasis in the original)

Central to this argument is the notion that it is the presence of competition that 'empowers' workers in their relationship with employers — that ensures remuneration commensurate with their contribution to the company. (Correspondingly, it is the presence of competition that protects employers against abuse by workers or collectives of workers.) Competition *precludes*, rather than creates, the possibility of exploitation of one party by the other. Concerns about bargaining power will by this reasoning only arise in situations where the threat of competition is removed, or perhaps greatly subdued. One source of concern in this regard is the presence of sustainable monopoly power in the market for labour services — a monopsony position on the part of an employer, or a monopoly position on the part of a union or professional organization.

'Monopsony' exists where a single employer is the sole purchaser of labour. Just as in output markets most producers have some degree of monopoly power — that is, they could raise their prices somewhat without losing all of their customers — most employers have some degree of monopsony power. But their ability to abuse this power is in most cases limited by the realization that sustained abuse, for example, in continuing to pay below market wages or provide work conditions below the 'market' level, will mean that they lose employees to other employers. Such factors as their geographical isolation and the quality of information flows about other prospects for employment will clearly determine the extent to which the pay and conditions that an employer offers will differ from those established elsewhere in the market. Thus there was a legitimate concern with the ability of employers to 'exploit' workers in, for example, isolated single-company towns in the nineteenth century, when the geographical mobility of workers was low. But unless an employer can actively restrict mobility over time, his or her monopsony power will not be sustainable.

The resources that a worker can fall back on may be important, at least in the short term, to an ability to exercise his or her employment options — to quit and go in search of alternative employment. Arguments about the exploitability of workers in the late nineteenth century frequently turned on the assumption that, lacking reserves of wealth or alternative income, workers were in fact unlikely to take the risk of resigning to go in search of better employment (or of striking), whereas companies had large resources to fall back on.

Such arguments are less sustainable in the late twentieth century, with wider recourse to savings and the availability of unemployment benefits reducing the costs of periods out of employment. Moreover, it is important to recognize that severing the employment relationship also imposes costs on the employer, who in practice may not have significant resources on which to draw while seeking a replacement. For small employers, loss of an employee may lead to the loss of customers as orders are not met, or the overdrawing of overdrafts. In the case of larger employers, particularly those using continuous production processes, deficiencies or undue turnover in manning can also impose severe losses. There may also be a detrimental impact on the employer's reputation, which raises the future costs of employment. So in terms of his or her ability to bear the costs of severing the relationship, the employer may be as 'shut in' as the employee.

Exploitation of workers by shutting them into a particular and unremunerative category of employment – the abuse of monopsony power – is rare in practice. While most employers have some degree of monopsony power, their ability to abuse it is limited by the threat of competition from other employers. The potency of competition between employers as a means of protecting workers' interests, even where specialist skills are being developed, has long been underestimated or ignored by those using bargaining power arguments as a justification for collectivization of labour markets.[4]

Similarly ignored is the role of unions acting, typically with statutory backing, as monopoly suppliers in exploiting workers by shutting them out of employment. Unions are usually advocated as the means of protecting employees from exploitation, predominantly through the use of strike threats ('industrial muscle'). But in practice they readily become means by which one group of workers can exploit others, by which insiders – those in employment – can exploit outsiders.

Even in periods of high unemployment it is common for union officials to pursue pay increases that will benefit their members while pricing the unemployed out of access to jobs. Similarly, male unionists may defend conditions of work or work practices that make their occupations inaccessible to the majority of women (in particular women with children). And unionism can also be used to perpetuate racial income differentials, as in the case of white unionists in South Africa pursuing minimum wage policies designed to close off competition from black workers.[5]

For this reason, state protection of unions is a poor cure for those occasional instances of exploitable monopsony power as do occur. The usual justification for answering monopsony with a state-backed monopoly union is to create a 'balance of bargaining power'. In practice, it is not possible to say anything definite about where this balance will lie – or whether it will be endowed with any stability. What is relatively certain is that a fair portion of the surplus over which a company and union are bargaining is likely to be consumed in negotiation costs (including the costs of industrial disruption), leading to an overall reduction in the resources available for investment in productivity and the prospect of better wages in the future. As Simons wrote in 1944:

> The skin disease of monopsony is certainly a poor excuse for stopping the peaceful and productive game of free enterprise and free exchange in favor of the violent contest of organized producer minorities. (p. 7)

And there is a simple test of whether what a union is doing is countering an employer's abuse of monopsony power:

> If a strike-threat or a strike has had the effect of raising the wage-rate in an occupation to the 'free-market' . . . level, no additional worker will be found who is prepared to accept this wage-rate (or less). If a union insists, in these circumstances, that would-be interlopers shall be refused access to the bargaining table to offer less than the wage-rate conceded, it is admitting that, in its judgment, its forcing-up of the wage-rate was *not* a countervailing of monopsonistic exploitation by employers, but a (presumably justified) exploitation of investors or others. (Hutt, 1975, p. 101, emphasis in the original)

The second version of the bargaining power argument asserts that, while it may not be possible for an employer to capture an entire labour market, he or she can exercise power within the firm to the detriment of employees. In the absence of an external market for the firm-specific skills developed by employees, wages become to some degree 'indeterminate'; both employer and employees hold 'hostages' against each other, in the form of the costs that each would bear were the relationship to be severed. This 'indeterminacy' arises not from uncertainty over the relative power of the employer and employees, but from the high information cost of matching rewards to inputs out of the context of a broader market. It may give rise to power games, but such games are strictly constrained. As Epstein puts it:

> The whole question of bargaining power arises in the bounded context of how much of a supracompetitive wage the worker will obtain. At the very worst, the worker will get the amount that is offered in some alternate employment where he has built up no specific capital. (1984, p. 976)

In practice, few employers are likely to risk paying this minimum, and it is for this reason that large employers in particular invest in job evaluations to supplement the wage information that they can obtain from the market. Investments in employment are almost always shared between employer and employee; both lose if the relationship sours. The 'balance of power' in such relationships is indeed likely to be fluid. As Barker and Chapman argue:

> [W]here both sides have hostages, bargaining power depends on hostage exposure. The party with the lower hostage exposure has a clear bargaining advantage in holding up the other party. However, this bargaining advantage is not likely to remain fixed over time. (1989, p. 324)

There are various means by which the parties to such relationships can contract beforehand to control the sorts of problems that interdependence creates—for example, access to grievance procedures, or contract renegotiation triggers. Union representation *may* be one means of reducing the costs to both employers and workers of negotiating and maintaining such mechanisms. However, as in the case of 'classic' monopsony power, state-backed monopoly unionism is likely to be about as helpful as a spanner in the works.

Moreover, even where there is a substantial degree of interdependence, the threat of competition is unlikely to be absent. Most 'firm-specific' skills have some market value, in that they indicate a capacity to *learn* skills that may be more important to other employers in an environment subject to ongoing technological change than the *possession* of particular skills.

To talk in these terms presupposes some acquiescence in the relevance of 'the market', and this is precisely what a significant proportion of proponents of state collectivism would disallow. Just what would be used in place of the market was a matter of considerable debate and disagreement at the turn of the twentieth century when the basis was being laid for present-day labour law in many Western countries. The one point that does not seem to have been a matter for debate, whether the response being espoused was syndicalism or socialism, arbitration or 'industrial federation', was that the replacement of the market with a pseudo-political process for determining wages and conditions of employment would bring an unambiguous improvement in social justice and social well-being.

Whether or not state-sanctioned collectivism can—and, in the New Zealand case, does—improve on market outcomes is the subject of Chapter 3. Chapter 2 sets out the details of the system that has evolved in New Zealand, drawing parallels with the experience of other Western countries. It is not possible to draw direct comparisons between systems of labour market regulation. But a common basis in results-oriented, collectivist ideology, and common preoccupations with the 'social' aspects of the work relationship, and with 'bargaining power' and 'exploitation', all mean that they can be used to provide insights on the system that has evolved in New Zealand.

2
Current Labour Market Policy

2.1 Legislating for Collectivism

A belief that employment relationships are better directed by collective decision-making than by being left to the individual initiative of firms and workers does not in itself imply that union activities should be protected or supported by the government. (Nor, as will be argued in Chapter 4, does an emphasis on individual liberties *preclude* an acceptance of collective organization.) For example, socialism, with its emphasis on subordinating individuals to society, would also seem to require the subordination to society of such associations as unions—at least where these are free and independent. Thus socialist writers at the time when major pro-union legislation was being formulated in New Zealand and elsewhere tended to see the kinds of unions that existed under capitalism as temporary, and primarily destructive rather than constructive in purpose. Some were more strongly opposed to unions in their role in collective bargaining, seeing this as a form of class collaboration, a means of co-opting workers out of the revolutionary struggle.

In contrast, some argued that collective action and collective bargaining by union organizations was a step towards usurping the 'power' of capitalism, and ultimately overthrowing the capitalist system. Others saw private collective agreements, given the force of public law, as a means to social peace. In both cases, the interests of unions, like the interests of workers, were seen as subordinate to the interests of society as a whole. And in both cases, legislative suppression of the freedom of the individual worker to contract for the sale of his or her labour services was a crucial element.

It is this emphasis on government intervention in the process by which employment relationships are formed and maintained, effectively attempting to outlaw the market in favour of pseudo-democratic but non-governmental decision-making, which has set labour law apart from other bodies of economic law in Western economies. This is not to say that governments in these economies have not attempted to intervene directly to affect labour market outcomes; they have, and their attempts to do so through minimum wage laws, restrictions on work conditions, occupational health and safety regulations and the like are the subject of the following section. But in no other area of policy have they moved to confer government-like powers and immunities on non-governmental organizations to the extent that they have conferred them on trade unions.

Legislating for Unionism in New Zealand 1894-1987

New Zealand was among the first countries to introduce formal legislation in support of unions, in the form of the Industrial Conciliation and Arbitration Act of 1894, 'an act to encourage the formation of industrial unions and associations'. While a humanitarian concern to assist a dispersed and lowly resourced workforce was clearly important to the introduction of this legislation, a more immediate cause rested in the events of a general maritime strike in 1890.

The central features of the legislation were provision of compulsory arbitration of disputes in a specialist Arbitration Court, and the ability of unions to extend the coverage of wage agreements to employers and workers who had not been party to their initial negotiations. The latter was to establish the legal basis for unions to act as the exclusive representatives of jealously demarcated groups of workers — effectively enabling them to compel industry- or craft-wide collective bargaining. This was principally justified on the basis of the dispersed nature of the New Zealand working population, but it was also seen as a means of overcoming employer resistance to collective bargaining. (This resistance was not especially strong, extended agreements having the 'virtue' of reducing competition between employers to contain labour costs.)

The legislation also prohibited strikes and lock-outs both during arbitration and after an 'award' — an arbitrated agreement — had been made. Up to around 1900 this earned New Zealand a reputation for industrial peace. This 'peace' was aided by the ingenuity of the Arbitration Court in resolving the issue of compulsory as against voluntary union membership by establishing the notion of a preferential union shop. Unions could demand a clause in their award compelling employers to hire union members in preference to non-union members wherever equally qualified union members were available. This 'qualified preference' system was not the same as compulsory unionism, but it did provide a very strong incentive for unionism.[1] Any resistance by employers to such compulsion was weakened by the ability of the Arbitration Court to order reinstatement of workers dismissed on account of their union affiliation (damages being paid to the union, not the worker).

There have been numerous changes to labour market legislation since 1894. Compulsory arbitration was abolished in 1932, and reintroduced along with compulsory unionism legislation in 1936 by the first Labour Government. National governments marginally weakened compulsory unionism in 1961 and again in 1976 (essentially through provision for secret ballots among workers for the retention of 'unqualified preference' clauses — clauses that effectively created a 'post-entry' closed shop, as distinct from the kind of 'pre-entry' closed shop that has, until recently, operated on the New Zealand waterfront, under the auspices of the Waterfront Industry Commission). General labour market policy was recast, but not fundamentally altered, by the third Labour Government in the Industrial Relations Act of 1973. In 1983, under a National government, unionism was made voluntary; in 1984 with the return of a Labour government it was made compulsory again, but arbitration was made voluntary.[2]

However, neither these changes nor the changes embodied in the 1987 Labour Relations Act have reflected or instigated any major changes in the general approach to labour market regulation that was adopted in 1894. The present system of labour relations is very much the product of the early institutionalization of arbitration, extended agreements (or 'blanket coverage') and a degree of compulsion in union membership.

This system has laid the basis for national, occupation- and craft-based 'awards' which set out minimum wages and conditions. A formal union registration process, the ability in law to extend coverage to the employers of all workers whom the union claims to represent and compulsory membership combine to confer on unions the 'right' to make these minima binding on workers and employers across a significant portion of the economy.

The registration system is intended to promote the formation of unions and to minimize disputes over demarcation. Registration is not compulsory, but is heavily favoured by unions both as a means of securing membership and because the agreements made with employers by unregistered collectives of workers lack legal force. It confers on a union the right to represent all workers deemed to be 'conveniently covered' by it, usually on an occupation or craft basis, and to require employers to enter negotiations over the wages and conditions to apply to these workers.

The technical purpose of registration is to bring unions, and in their wake employers, into the formal industrial relations system — into the mysteries of award rounds and tradition-steeped arbitration processes. Their primary economic effect is to confer quasi-monopoly status on existing unions, an effect that is reinforced by the ability, upon a ballot, to include a compulsory membership clause in awards. The rate of new union formation is low, as the coverage 'rights' of existing unions are jealously guarded. However, union amalgamation is not uncommon, and has been spurred on by the introduction of a minimum union size of 1000 in the 1987 legislation.

The power conferred on registered unions is not untempered. Rather, the same legislation which gives unions 'rights' over workers, transferring from worker to union the right to contract with employers over how (and effectively also whether) that worker's labour will be used, seeks by various means to make unions 'good' representatives of workers. It does so through a complex mass of legislation setting out acceptable union objectives and codes for their internal management, and constrains their activities and the course of the negotiation process. Such legislative attempts to ensure that unions treat their members 'fairly' (if within a sadly limited notion of fairness) are primarily necessary because of the inability of workers to opt out of a union that treats them unfairly – other than by opting into unemployment.

Negotiation between employers and unions can only be initiated by the creation of a 'dispute'. This may be a dispute of 'interest' involving wages and conditions of employment and necessary to the establishment or renewal of an award covering the union's members. Or it may be a dispute of 'right', involving the interpretation of an award or the implementation of a personal grievance procedure. The creation of a dispute opens a process of conciliation, assisted by a government-funded conciliation and mediation service. Where conciliation is fruitless, the process can move to arbitration.

Under compulsory arbitration (1894-1932 and 1936-1984), either party could force the other to the Arbitration Court for a settlement. The initial intention behind compulsory arbitration seems to have been to prevent the strikes and lock-outs which occurred when collective bargaining either was rejected by employers or broke down. The effect, however, was not to complement collective bargaining, but rather to undermine it by reducing the incentive for serious bargaining. Thus Holt argues that the results of compulsory arbitration foreseen by the Webbs were to be broadly fulfilled in New Zealand:

> Once [a state] tribunal existed, weak trade unions would inevitably refuse
> to accept a hard bargain and would turn to the tribunal or court for an award.

The end result would be an end to collective bargaining and the regulation
of wages and working conditions by the state. This was roughly what was
to happen in New Zealand. (1976, p. 105)

It is in this sense that compulsory arbitration was referred to by
some New Zealand unionists as 'labour's leg-irons'.

The reintroduction in 1984 of voluntary arbitration, under which
the agreement of both union and employer representatives is required
before a dispute can go to arbitration, did not in practice bring about
any immediate changes. Union support for the Arbitration Court
had fallen off since it supported a nil wage order in 1968. From
that time until its replacement with a Labour Court and an
Arbitration Commission in 1987 it received little use other than in
arbitration over general wage orders.

National awards on an occupational and craft basis present the
makings of a particularly rigid system. This rigidity was enhanced
in the inflationary environment of the 1970s; the government
periodically applied wage controls in an attempt to rein in inflation,
while in periods in which controls did not apply there evolved a
pattern of award rounds in which relativities between unions were
adhered to closely. This emphasis on relativities on the part of unions
was a means of reducing the potentially uneven impact of periodic
wage controls.

From 1973 to 1987 some flexibility was added to the underlying
system by provision for 'second-tier' bargaining — bargaining at a
more disaggregated level after an award had been settled. This was
primarily a means by which the wages and conditions of workers
at, say, an enterprise level could be adjusted upwards — there was
little if any scope for using second-tier bargaining to 'undercut'
national awards in cases of hardship. From 1980 it also became
possible to negotiate composite agreements, in which a number of
unions negotiated a package with an individual employer that would
supersede national awards for his or her work-force. This was a
potentially important development in terms of facilitating enterprise
bargaining, but was not widely adopted.

Until the 1970s, the government had little direct involvement in
the bargaining process, although in individual instances (such as
the 1951 waterfront dispute) it had intervened heavily. This changed
with the emergence of inflation as a major economic problem and
the government's attempts to tackle it by means of wage controls.
In the early 1980s, there was a move to attempts at tripartite
(government-employer-union) wage-fixing, also involving
negotiations over a wage-tax trade-off. This was somewhat

overwhelmed by the imposition of a wage-price freeze from 1982 to 1984. In 1984 the incoming Labour Government introduced a revamped Tripartite Wage Conference. The main function that has emerged for this conference has been to serve as a vehicle for the government to communicate its assessment of the state of the economy and the implications for (mostly annual) award negotiations of developments in economic policy. The period 1984-1990 has in practice been notable for the lack of any direct input to the negotiation of awards by the Minister of Labour.

The Labour Relations Act 1987

At the end of 1985 the government initiated a general review of labour relations legislation, on the basis that the thorough-going reforms that had been instituted in other areas of economic policy made a reconsideration of regulation in the labour market necessary. At the economic summit of 1984, which was called to debate the future direction of economic policy in New Zealand following the election of the Labour Government, there had been general agreement among both unions and employers as to the need for greater flexibility in the labour market—for example, a union submission to the summit said that:

> [T]he unions would like to see the old system modified so that more consideration could be given to factors that could be specific to an industry or occupation, and a good deal less to entrenched relativities. (Quoted in Blandy and Baker, 1987, p. 20)

The review process was guided by a Green Paper that raised questions on all aspects of the existing legislation with the exception of compulsory unionism. However, there was no clear analytical framework underpinning these questions, and the principles and objectives on which New Zealand's labour market regulations and institutions are based were left unchallenged. In this, it differed fundamentally from the review processes and reforms that the government was undertaking in other sectors. The result was that, despite a prolonged review process, the new Labour Relations Act 1987 adhered closely to the objectives and procedures of pre-existing legislation.

Under the 1987 Act, compulsory unionism was retained, but responsibility for enforcing it was shifted from employers to unions, and provision was made for a ballot among members for the retention of an unqualified preference clause in awards once in every three award rounds. There was some provision for changes in union coverage, but the process involved was tightly regulated, and the right to initiate changes was restricted to existing unions. The minimum size for unions was raised to 1000, supposedly as a means of ensuring that unions were not too small to exercise 'bargaining power'.

The Act also altered the basis for making agreements outside the national award system. In place of enforcing the results of second-tier bargaining, it made provision for unions to cite an employer out of a national award where they wished to negotiate a separate agreement (which would then be legally binding in the way that second-tier agreements had previously been legally binding). There was, however, no corresponding provision for an employer to opt out of a national award.[3]

Finally, the Act made some changes to the mechanisms for negotiating and enforcing awards and agreements, splitting the Arbitration Court into an Arbitration Commission and a Labour Court. The Commission serves as an industrial body, charged with considering disputes of interest — matters arising in the course of negotiating awards and agreements. In practice, it is principally concerned with issues surrounding the registration of awards and agreements. The Court deals with legal matters arising from labour disputes, demarcation disputes and personal grievances.

The 'essentials' of the system established in 1894 remained, however, largely untouched. Reforms in financial markets, in protection for domestic producers and in the state sector in the 1980s have fundamentally altered the principles on which these sectors operate — and the principles underlying the government's role in regulating them. The crucial feature of these reforms was a belief that government or bureaucratic manipulation of outcomes in these sectors, altering and confusing the incentives under which their participants made economic decisions, had been at the expense of the wealth and welfare of New Zealanders; the reforms reflected an abandoning of a centralist-collectivist ethic. In the labour market, by contrast, the emphasis was on streamlining and a bit of mild give-and-take in an attempt to balance out the 'interests' of unions and employers. The assumption that monopoly unionism, supported by the state, was the way to go about promoting the interests of workers in employment relationships went largely unchallenged — as did the more fundamental socialist assumption that these relationships were basically adversarial. Labour remains 'different'; wages remain largely 'out of competition'.

International Comparisons

The New Zealand system has not been without its admirers, and even its imitators. The 1894 legislation inspired international interest. In the United States, it was championed by the socialist reformer Henry Demarest Lloyd, who particularly favoured the idea of blanket coverage. This device was to be introduced in a somewhat modifed form in the National Recovery Administration in the United States in 1933. He was also a strong advocate of New Zealand's system of compulsory arbitration, seeing it as 'the instrument through which democracy equips a majority to maintain its welfare against the attacks of an anti-social minority'. By contrast, Dickman (1987), quotes the American labour leader Samuel Gompers as likening compulsory arbitration to slavery. There was a similar resistance to compulsory arbitration by unions in the United Kingdom, as Holt explains:

> To a trade union [compulsory arbitration] meant surrendering control of its own destiny to an unpredictable and untrustworthy judge who would almost certainly be a man of upper- or middle-class background. Successful trade unions had only achieved power through years of bitter struggle. They would not willingly throw away their right to strike for better conditions. Only weak trade unions were attracted to the idea of compulsory arbitration. For them it might bring recognition, or at least legally enforced common rules for the trade. (1976, p. 106)

The qualified preference form of closed shop which prevailed in New Zealand up until 1936 was incorporated in the 1910-1916 'Protocol of Peace' established in the garment industries of New York and Chicago after a period of heightened and destructive strike activity.[4] Ironically, by this stage the belief that the New Zealand system would usher in industrial peace was being severely tested in its homeland, as the economic situation deteriorated and the Arbitration Court increasingly ruled in favour of employers.

The system of exclusive representation created in New Zealand in 1894 also had its imitators, most importantly in Australia, but also in Germany in the early days of the Weimar Republic, although in this case it was on a more 'corporativist' (industry rather than occupational) basis. On the whole, however, while evincing enthusiasm on the part of moderate unionists and popular socialists, the New Zealand system was not widely copied, and in terms of labour law New Zealand and Australia remain oddities among OECD nations.

On the other hand, the concerns underlying the New Zealand

legislation were widely shared — concerns about the dehumanization of workers should their labour services be treated as a commodity like any other, or should they be subjected to Taylorist management practices, and concerns about workers' weak 'bargaining power' and the power (and will) of employers to exploit them. The growing acceptance around the turn of the century of a collectivist vision of society, and in particular of the merits of 'industrial democracy', whether inspired by Fabian Socialism or German Christian Socialism, eased the way for a government role in facilitating the formation and activities of unions — which themselves were beginning to take on a deliberate role as political pressure groups. But the form taken by government involvement varied.

In the United Kingdom, the development of unionism was supported not so much by positive legislation as by the extension of important immunities to unions, a key piece of legislation being the 1906 Trade Disputes Act. This Act effectively swept away the application of civil conspiracy law to union activities. The Royal Commission established to develop legislation saw these immunities as justified not because unions should not be held accountable for their actions, but because accountability within unions might prove too weak:

> [T]he members' painfully accumulated funds were at the mercy of the consequences of some rash step taken, it might well be without the knowledge of any union officer, by any one of scores of thousands of members scattered across the country. (Brown, 1983, p. 36)

However, the legislation went further than this, protecting unions from any tort liability, including for libel, negligence or procuring breach of a contract (in the case of strike activity). The extent of these immunities was at least in part a reflection of the growing success of trade unions in exerting electoral pressure.

In contrast to the New Zealand system, in the United Kingdom there was no legal basis for exclusive representation and no compulsory arbitration. Collective agreements were never enforceable by law; rather, the relevant terms of collective agreements were read into individual employment contracts, which were legally binding. (Proponents of a more strongly collectivist approach, uneasy at this distinction, have in some cases argued for an abandoning of the notion of an employment contract altogether, and its replacement with an employment 'status' to which various rights are attached.[5])

At least until the 1970s the strength of the immunities conferred on unions provided a basis for high union membership, widespread collective agreements, and, particularly after the second World War, widespread use of closed shops. From 1979 Margaret Thatcher's Government introduced a series of pieces of legislation aimed at individualizing the rights of workers, enforcing ballots and reducing union immunities. A Green Paper entitled 'Unofficial Action and the Law', released in October 1989, proposed extensive changes aimed at making unofficial strikes more difficult, making it easier for employers to dismiss workers involved in unofficial strike action, outlawing all secondary action and abolishing pre-entry closed shops. However, a hard core of immunities remains: even in essential services, for example, it is still possible for unions to strike with immunity.

The use of immunities as a tool in labour market legislation is widespread, if more often implict than explicit, but it is in the United Kingdom that this tool was used most comprehensively. This comprehensiveness has been admired by New Zealand unionists, despite the more extensive positive protections that they have received. Thus in its submission on the 1985 Green Paper the Federation of Labour argued that:

> The existence of 'common law' procedures in injunction and damages should be abolished. The emphasis should be on defining what rights trade unions have and the right to strike should not be artificially restricted by the existence of the common law . . . [T]he concept of an industrial code implementing the immunities contained in the UK Trade Disputes Act should be put in place. The High Court should have no jurisdiction whatsoever in industrial matters. (Knox, 1986, p. 12)

Immunity from injunctions in the case of strike activity was also a burning issue in the United States. The Clayton Act of 1914 had reduced the applicability of the antitrust principles embodied in the Sherman Act to labour monopolies, but some injunctive powers remained. These were largely eliminated by the Norris-La Guardia (Anti-Injunction) Act of 1932, an Act somewhat similar in function to the Trade Disputes Act in the United Kingdom. It declared 'yellow dog' contracts (contracts requiring an employee not to join a union) unenforceable, relieved unions from liability under antitrust law, and nullified the 'equity' powers of the federal courts in labour disputes, thus removing a significant injunctive power against picketing and strikes.

It was the depression of the 1930s which was to provide the necessary boost for legislation positively supporting union structures in the United States. As in other countries, the push for such legislation reflected a loss of faith in the ability of markets to self-regulate or to self-correct, and a growing belief that workers were by definition vulnerable to exploitation, a vulnerability that could only be mitigated by means of union representation. Moreover, it was believed that only unions could deliver the high wages on which a return to prosperity was expected (if mistakenly) to be grounded. This belief system was, naturally, reinforced by the leaders of organized labour both inside and outside the political system. As elsewhere, support for pro-union legislation went hand in hand with a belief that self-reliance and voluntary self-help were socially redundant concepts; that the welfare of individuals was ultimately the responsibility of the government. As Dickman explains it:

> The intellectual relationships between industrial democracy, the mixed economy and the welfare state spring from their common anti-capitalistic heritage; the political relationship was, and is, a close one: most mixed economy and welfare state legislation has for half a century worn a union label. (1987, p. 258)

The parallels with New Zealand are obvious.

The major piece of labour market legislation to be introduced in the United States was the National Labor Relations Act (the Wagner Act) of 1935. This Act created a National Labor Relations Board (NLRB) to be appointed by the President, charged with enforcing majority elections at any workplace for union representation, determining who was eligible to vote in such elections, enforcing the monopoly bargaining rights of the union representatives that it certified as a result of these elections, and enforcing union pay scales for all the workers that they were certified to represent (including non-members). In addition, it specified 'unfair practices' on the part of employers, and required that they bargain with certified unions in 'good faith' — refusal to do so constituting an 'unfair' practice.[6] This has to some extent been matched with a judicially constructed requirement that unions represent fairly the workers over whom they have coverage (irrespective of union membership), and direct statutory control over the activities of unions under the Labor-Management Reporting and Disclosure (Landrum-Griffin) Act of 1959. These latter requirements were justified in terms of their prospective contribution to 'industrial peace'.

There are parallels here with the legislative basis for union registration in New Zealand, though the details of both legislation and bureaucracies differ. As in New Zealand, and in contrast with the United Kingdom, a collective agreement negotiated by a certified union is enforceable in the courts. The requirement to bargain in good faith is a rather litigious substitute for the New Zealand system of compulsory arbitration. In practice, it appears to have been interpreted to require not simply a willingness to communicate, but a commitment to the 'right' results and the 'right' frame of mind, as evidenced by a willingness to make concessions:

> [O]ne is led to the inescapable conclusion that the regulation of bargaining works in such a way as virtually to require that employers start with the least expensive compensation proposal which it can reasonably justify (to the examiners, hearing officers, and members of the NLRB or to the courts), while the union forsakes important dynamic advantages if it fails to launch the bargaining process with a set of demands which, in the aggregate, could be considered objectively as predictably unacceptable. (Heldman *et al.*, 1981, pp. 60-1)

This is, of course, as good a way as any to make the employment relationship look and feel adversarial.

Union membership cannot be required in the United States. Some states reinforce this with 'right-to-work' laws, outlawing requirements for employees to either join a union or pay union dues. In other states, agency shops are possible, through the requirement that non-unionists in enterprises with union coverage pay some form of dues to the union. It is in this, and in the absence of provision for 'blanket' or extended coverage that the United States system primarily differs from its New Zealand counterpart.

In Germany, the 1919 Weimar Constitution guaranteed workers the right to join and organize unions and prohibited discrimination against unions. Closed shop agreements were, however, regarded as anti-constitutional. The Constitution also laid the basis for the kind of tripartism that was to become a significant aspect of European labour policy after the second World War. Legislation introduced in 1920 introduced a system of works councils with rights of bargaining and consultation, in parallel with regional and national employers' associations. These laid the basis for a reorganization of the entire economy along corporativist lines — though this was not implemented in the lifetime of the Weimar Republic.

The institutional framework for employment relationships in postwar Germany was set out in the Collective Bargaining Act (*Tarifvertragsgesetz*) of 1949, which was based on an acceptance of the collectivist principles that had been set out in 1918. It conferred on unions the sole right to enter collective agreements on behalf of employees, either with individual employers or with the confederation of employers. As under second-tier bargaining in New Zealand, any employer is free to offer above-agreement conditions, but agreements constitute binding minima for wages and conditions. Something like blanket coverage can be obtained for a contract negotiated between a union and an employers' federation if either or both apply to the Minister of Labour for this. Soltwedel and Trapp (1987) record increasing use of this provision.

The justifications for this kind of system are familar ones:

> This collectivist system has been justified – and that since the early 1920s – on the grounds that the provisions are necessary to avoid 'wage dumping' (*Lohndruckerei*) and 'dirty competition' (*Schumtzkonkurrenz*). This has been the standard argument, is still the prevalent opinion, and can be considered as the backbone of the German collectivistic labor law. (Soltwedel and Trapp, 1987, p. 197)

A further significant feature of the current West German system is legislation for codetermination of enterprise policy. Beginning with the Montan Act of 1951, a series of codetermination laws was introduced which required parity between worker and shareholder directors of companies in the mining and steel industries. In other industries, there is a requirement for minority worker representation on company boards. Concerted avoidance of this legislation led to the introduction of 'Codetermination Protection Acts'. This experience, and the experience of other European and Scandinavian countries under systems similarly designed to promote tripartite management not only of employment relations but of broader economic decisions, is relevant for New Zealand in that similar urges appear to underlie proposals for 'industrial democracy' legislation and a 'Compact' between unions and the government (with or without an employer input).[7]

2.2   Legislating for Outcomes

Government policies in support of unions may be seen as having two primary objectives. One is the creation of 'democracy' in the workplace, whether this is seen as a means of eventually breaking down capitalism, or as a means of combatting the supposedly dehumanizing practices of capitalism. It is an objective of politicizing an economic relationship.

The second objective is to assure certain outcomes for workers in terms of remuneration and work conditions, by countering the 'bargaining power' of the employer (or employers as a class) with the 'bargaining power' of a monopolistic union. By conferring a degree of monopoly power on unions by statute, the government effectively delegates to unions its own power to 'set' outcomes in labour market relationships; unions, rather than the government or its bureaucracies, are seen as the 'rational', 'articulate' and 'wise' replacement for the 'uncontrolled' processes of the market.

The alternative, of course, is to legislate directly for these outcomes. And in practice, even where the powers conferred on unions are extensive, as in New Zealand, governments do take on a substantial role in attempting to set pay and work conditions directly. This role would seem to indicate at least an implicit acceptance that unions are in fact not a very good way of protecting the most vulnerable members of the workforce; their *forte* lies rather in bolstering the position of the middling strong. This is made explicit in Dickman's description of the agenda of union leaders in the United States earlier this century — an agenda combining support for pro-union legislation (syndicalism) and direct intervention in outcomes (statism):

> For the unorganized and what they saw as the unorganizable classes of labor (women and children), many trade union leaders favored laws that would either directly fix wage contracts (minimum wages) or remove the contractors from the market entirely (abolition of child labor, immigration restriction). But for organized or easily organizable workers, their agenda was more syndicalist and less statist — an approach which one scholar has aptly summarized in another context as a policy of having the government become 'the ally of the labor organizations against the employer, supplying the power' to override individual rights, but 'not dictating to what ends it shall be used'. (1987, pp. 224-5)

Similarly in New Zealand legislated minimum conditions are seen as underpinning the award system, and becoming more significant with any weakening of that system:

> A national Minimum Wage, set at a realistic level, would underpin the award system. It would provide a level below which awards could not fall and a moral incentive for the parties to award negotiations to settle above the statutory minimum. (Brosnan and Wilkinson, 1989, p. 16)

Union support for direct intervention to fix outcomes for the 'unorganizable' was and is not, of course, a matter of pure altruism. Intervention to set a floor on wages or conditions reduces the ability of workers outside unions to compete with union members for jobs, for example, by providing an incentive for employers to change the nature of production or their entire business to substitute workers outside a unionized occupational category for workers inside that category. Thus wage restrictions in South Africa have been an important means of protecting white workers from competition by blacks.[8] Intervention to limit market entry altogether is an even more sure way of limiting competition and bolstering union power. This was arguably a motive behind the Factory Acts in England (that limited the employment of women at a time when factory conditions were becoming less, not more, arduous),[9] and behind shop trading hours legislation in New Zealand.[10] More recently, it has surfaced as an explanation of the support given by relatively wealthy members of the European Community to harmonization of labour legislation covering everything from codetermination to comparable worth:

> In some member-states . . . an argument has surfaced and received a good deal of sympathy that without a strong social action programme the wealthier countries in the Community will suffer from social dumping, namely, that Greece, Spain and Portugal, and in the future possibly Turkey, which have lower labour and social costs, will enjoy an advantage under the [Single European Act]. In other words, unless the comparative cost advantages of these countries are harmonised by a common level of social costs they will gain at the expense of the more industrially advanced countries. This is a classic protectionist argument . . . . (Roberts, 1989, p. 45)

On the other hand, the extension of government involvement in legislating for outcomes also serves to weaken the case for supporting collective bargaining in an era in which the notion of a fundamental capital-labour struggle — and hence the 'need' to politicize the employment relationship — is losing its edge. As unions are increasingly justified in terms of the economic benefits that they can win for workers, their position could be argued to be weakened by direct legislation for such 'benefits'. The regulations that they have nurtured have, by their coverage of workers irrespective of union membership, reduced the incentives for membership, and thus the dominance of collective bargaining.

There has been a strong belief within the union movement in New Zealand that there are certain things that should not be negotiable, regardless of the power of unions to negotiate for them. These take on the character of 'inalienable' rights of workers, unionized or non-unionized, and they range widely. There is a 'right' to a forty-hour week, a 'right' to strike and a (more ambiguous) 'right' against 'unjust' dismissal, for example. Similarly there is a notion that occupational health and safety should not even be seen as an 'industrial' issue (that is, as an integral part of the employment relationship), and that related work conditions should be non-negotiable.

Minimum wage law is perhaps the most significant means of directly regulating the outcomes of employment relationships. New Zealand has had a statutory minimum wage since 1942, introduced to 'protect' the wages of workers directed to essential industries because of wartime conditions. A Minimum Wages Act was passed in 1945. Since 1948 it has not been necessary to amend the Act to adjust the minimum upwards; this is achieved instead by an Order-in-Council. The relative value of the minimum wage has fluctuated considerably over time. In 1948 it was 78% of the average wage. It fell below 60% in the mid-1960s, and below 40% by the beginning of the 1980s. When the Labour Government came to power in 1984 it was 30% of the average wage ($84.17 per week), but it was subsequently adjusted upwards to 53% of the average wage ($210 per week) in 1987. Increased again in dollar terms at the beginning of 1988 (to $225 per week, or 51% of the average wage), it was effectively higher than the minima established in 20% of awards then prevailing.[11]

It is not uncommon for an economic gloss to be put on the 'case' for a minimum wage. For example, Brosnan and Wilkinson in their defence of minimum wages in New Zealand argue that:

> Besides the effect on living standards, cheap labour brings with it a clear cost in economic terms. Within the workplace, it is a cause of low morale, poorer standards and higher labour turnover. At the level of the individual firm, reliance on low pay as a competitive strategy reduces the incentive to innovate and invest. At the industry and sector level, low wage competition produces uncertainty for individual firms, destabilises the business environment and hinders economic growth. At the macroeconomic level, low pay also results in reduced demand for goods and services. Finally, from the taxpayer's point of view, low pay increases dependence on social security, resulting in higher levels of public expenditure. (1989, pp. 91-2)

The justifiability of this reasoning is considered in the following chapter.

A wide range of regulations other than the minimum wage affect the conditions of employment and the cost of employing labour. The eight-hour day/forty-hour week, statutory vacation requirements, requirements for maternity/paternity leave, occupational health and safety regulations, accident compensation levies and industry training levies all determine the conditions under which an employee can be taken on, and the cost of employing him or her. They make voluntary agreements to do things differently, where this is the interest of both employer and worker, impermissible—the implication being that society knows better.

Another range of interventions similarly affecting the nature of employment relationships involves those dictating how the relationship between employer and worker can be conducted (as opposed to specifying minimum conditions directly). Into this category fall such interventions as legislation against discrimination on the basis of sex, race or disability where this is irrelevant to the job. It also includes legislation on the conditions under which an employee can be dismissed — legislation against 'unjust' dismissal, redundancy requirements or plant closure laws — each of which indirectly raises the costs associated with employment, and the incentives for job creation.

The emphasis here can extend beyond outcomes to defining permissible procedures — further 'usurping' the role of unions and legislation establishing bargaining procedures in unionized firms or occupations. This is increasingly being reinforced in judicial practice in New Zealand and overseas, as the courts tend towards a 'substantive' approach to justice, for example, looking beyond formal contracts in an attempt to discover whether they are the outcome of 'real' bargaining processes.[12]

2.3   Recent Initiatives

Since the passage of the Labour Relations Act in 1987, there have been a number of significant policy issues raised in the area of labour market regulation. These include the reform of labour relations in the state sector, the establishment of a state- and employer-funded Trade Union Education Authority, proposals for 'employment equity' (affirmative action and comparable worth) and 'industrial democracy' legislation, a proposal to bring some independent contractors under the Labour Relations Act, proposals for levying employers to support training, proposals for the reform of shop trading hours and occupational health and safety regulations, as well as attempts to establish a 'Compact' between unions and the government with a view to a more co-ordinated union influence not only in labour market issues but in general policy formation.

The state sector reforms were particularly significant in that they represented a far greater shift away from the traditional system of labour market regulation than the reforms contained in the Labour Relations Act. In other cases, most notably the 'employment equity', independent contractors and 'industrial democracy' proposals and negotiations towards a 'Compact', the tendency has been towards a more collectivist approach; a reinforcement of the traditional system and the ideology underpinning it. This reflects a view that more reliance on voluntary exchange — 'the market' — in other areas of economic activity, rather than increasing the pressures on employers to upgrade their employment relationships, has rendered workers *more* vulnerable. Thus the Royal Commission on Social Policy in 1988 (apparently labouring under the misapprehension that 'freedom' in labour markets is all about driving wages downwards) reported, with approval, that:

> The free market model is argued by some as not being appropriate for New Zealand conditions. That model is argued to be based on 'Western European values of freedom and individual rights and a belief that active pursuit of these will result in the greatest good for all' . . . [It is argued that] this approach is monocultural, taking no account of collective values, ignoring existing structural inequalities, and creating greater inequalities. Similarly . . . the free market ethic [is viewed] as resulting in a society 'which serves the needs of those who command power and financial resources: in New Zealand this group is predominantly white, middle class, middle aged, able-bodied and male'. The Commission is broadly in agreement with these criticisms. (1988, p. 512)

Late nineteenth century concerns with 'bargaining power' and exploitation, and a belief in the comforts of coerced (as opposed to voluntary) collective responses, are clearly alive and well in late twentieth century New Zealand.

Independent Contractors and the Labour Relations Act
In 1988 a Committee of Inquiry was established to consider whether independent contractors who were 'substantially dependent' on a single firm should be brought within the jurisdiction of the Labour Relations Act. While this matter remains unresolved, it is an important one, in that it turns on the fundamental differences between the law applying to employment relationships and the remainder of commercial law in New Zealand. A contractor who is deemed 'independent' is free to structure his or her relationship with a firm on his or her own account and in accordance with his or her own interests; within the broad constraints of commercial law, the voluntary exchange principles of the market apply. If, on the other hand, that contractor is deemed to be an 'employee', for example, on account of a heavy reliance on a single firm for contracts, the conduct of that relationship would become the prerogative of a union.

From one perspective, this can be seen as an argument about 'exploitability'. If the employment relationship is regarded as *fundamentally* exploitative, it is not surprising that the relationship between a small contractor and a large company will similarly be regarded as exploitative. If the power of the union to exploit the employee is ignored, so too will be the power of the union to exploit a contractor.

In essence, however, it is an argument about territory. Independent contracts have been used increasingly by employers and workers alike to avoid the constraints imposed by a centralized system of collective bargaining, presumably because it is in the interests of both to do so. The drive by the central union hierarchy to have these contracts relabelled as 'dependent contracts' (Knox, 1986, p. 24) was in this sense primarily a move in defense of the award system, at a time when increased pressures on individual firms to improve their international competitiveness were raising important questions about the compatibility of this system with their survival and the security of employment. (In this regard, the increasing importance of independent contractors in New Zealand is matched by the rise of self-employment in the United Kingdom. Mather (1987) reports increases in self-employment between 1979 and 1987 ranging from 24% in the worst-performing region, where paid employment fell by 17%, to 78% in the best.)

'Employment Equity'

New Zealand has had equal pay legislation since 1972, and anti-discrimination legislation (in the form of the Human Rights Commission Act) since 1977. The essential concern of these two pieces of legislation is with fair treatment in employment relationships. In 1988, the Working Party on Equal Employment Opportunities and Equal Pay put forward proposals for 'employment equity' legislation, combining target-based equal opportunities and comparable worth ('equal pay for work of equal value') legislation (Wilson, 1988). The emphasis here is not on equality of treatment, but equality of outcomes (or 'intrinsically just' relativities).

An Employment Equity Bill, providing for mandatory, results-oriented equal employment opportunities programmes (that is, affirmative action) and comparable worth, was introduced late in 1989. This was despite widespread opposition from the business community and from government officials concerned about incongruities between the Bill and at least the announced intentions of the Labour Relations Act, and about the likely costs of comparable worth, both fiscally and in terms of unemployment. The government, however, regarded itself as having made a strong electoral commitment to the policy, and the Bill was passed into law in July 1990.

The key assumptions underlying the Act are familiar ones: the concentration of women in a limited range of occupations and a gap between the average wages of women and men are seen as reflecting discrimination; discrimination is seen as inherent in market relationships (according to some, markets are little more than a tool of white male oppression), and the only means of countering this 'discrimination' is thought to be the creation of a rational, wise and caring 'gender-neutral' bureaucracy, charged not with uncovering and penalizing discriminatory behaviour, but with promoting equal outcomes, whether in paid rates or in the distribution of women and cultural minorities across jobs and job hierarchies.

The 'employment equity' proposals increase in significance once they are placed in the broader context of a strongly collectivist labour relations system. This system already serves to equalize wages and conditions across broad categories of workers and establish fairly rigid relativities between categories. Notions of 'just price' and comparable worth are in a sense already strongly enshrined in this system, and 'the market' is already substantially squeezed out. In so far as discrimination is a problem, it must therefore be seen as enshrined not in the market but in the system that has sought to replace it.

The Employment Equity Act provides for these policies to be implemented by an 'Employment Equity Commissioner', given extensive powers both to set and to enforce policy, allowed considerable information-gathering and entry rights, and subject to minimal appeal rights. The resulting combination of virtually unlimited power over employers and workers with very limited accountability is noticeably at odds with attempts in other areas of government activity to separate policy advice from policy implementation, and to increase bureaucratic accountability.

The part of the Act dealing with 'equal employment opportunities' is highly prescriptive. Detailed programmes are required for a wide range of 'designated groups' — women, Māori, Pacific Islanders, workers with physical or mental disabilities, and any other group of workers that the Commissioner might decide to designate. (It could be assumed that some means would be found of excluding white, able-bodied men from these designations.) The Commissioner is also given the right to set minimum standards for programmes (including for the required 'targets'), and to require amendments to programmes, both when they are first being prepared and after they have been in force for two or more years — without any right of appeal.

The part of the Act concerned with comparable worth (under the misnomer 'pay equity') is even more cumbersome and reliant on bureaucratic intervention. One notable feature is the effective exclusion of women not represented by a union or represented by a union unwilling to take a comparable worth claim, as claims could only be implemented through the existing award system. Another is the minimal provision for recognition of 'economic factors' in assessing and implementing claims. A third is the direct conflict between some provisions of this Act and the Labour Relations Act. In particular, comparable worth claims will be based on paid, not award rates, thus reintroducing a form of the second-tier bargaining which was removed by the Labour Relations Act. Further, the Act provides access to compulsory final offer arbitration for the settling of comparable worth claims, a move that is in conflict with the removal of compulsory arbitration in 1984.

Overall, the Employment Equity Act represents a significant reversal on at least the rhetoric which accompanied the Labour Relations Act. It can be expected to reinforce the centralization of wage determination and the preoccupation with relativities that have long characterized labour relations in New Zealand.

'Industrial Democracy' and the 'Compact'

In 1989, a Committee of Inquiry was established to consider legislation for 'industrial democracy', which was defined as 'meaningful participation' by workers in the decisions affecting their working lives, at the workplace, enterprise, industry and national level. This task was subject to widely varying interpretations, and was only partly limited by the requirement that such legislation should be consistent with the intentions of the Labour Relations Act. But one important motivation appears to have been an interest in the applicability of the 'corporativist' models of Germany, Austria and the Scandinavian countries to the New Zealand labour market system, with 'codetermination' at the company level, industry-wide planning, and participation of union officials in economic planning at a national level — an interpretation that has been adopted with some enthusiasm by the Council of Trade Unions (Douglas, 1989).

'Codetermination' would represent a significant development in shifting decision-making power away from shareholders and the managers who represent them, and thus away from those individuals who bear the key risks associated with a company's activities. It is a logical extension of the argument that the 'bargaining weakness' of workers can only be overcome by the politicization of the employment relationship — and ultimately a grasping by 'labour' of the decision-making prerogatives of 'capital'. A similar notion is at work in negotiations towards a 'Compact' between the Council of Trade Unions and the government (employers' organizations having declined to participate).

The report of the Committee of Inquiry was released late in 1989. It recommends highly prescriptive legislation for participatory councils to be established within enterprises, a move towards more industry-level consultation, and an expansion of national tripartite initiatives.

The Committee's report reinforces the concerns about the direction of labour market policy which were created by the likes of the 'employment equity' initiatives. It is a strange mixture of assertions of pragmatism and rather crude pseudo-Marxist ideology, of logical inconsistency and confused empirical reference. It illustrates the conviction that competition in the labour market is between employers and workers. And its recommendations are both highly prescriptive and biased in favour of reinforcing the position of the existing union hierarchy. The one strong impression that it creates is of a will to legislate, contrary to the Committee's own asserted preference for voluntary solutions. Indeed, the Committee's approach was nicely summarized in its own assertion that: 'Our approach is pragmatic. We do not intend to embark on philosophic, academic or broadly principled analyses.' (Horn *et al.*, 1989, p. 26)

State Sector Reforms

The state sector in New Zealand accounts for around 25% of the work-force. The system of collective bargaining that applies to this work-force has from the beginning differed fundamentally from that operating in the private sector. In particular, registration has not been required for unions to be recognized and the awards they negotiate to be legally binding. In some instances union membership is voluntary, including in the Public Service Association which is the dominant representative of state employees.

On the other hand, wages and conditions in the state sector have tended to be more susceptible to direct intervention than those prevailing in the private sector. This in part reflects the practice of setting wages by reference to a set of relativities with the private sector and within the public sector where comparable jobs cannot be found in the private sector. But the practice is reinforced by the notion that public sector pay, conditions and practices should set an example for the private sector, for example, with regard to equal pay and the rights of women and minorities.

The activities of government departments were subjected to increased competition with the move to corporatize their trading activities through the formation of state-owned enterprises (SOEs). This in turn created a need for greater flexibility in employment contracts. Provisions to enable collective bargaining on an enterprise basis were included in the SOE legislation which came into effect in April 1987.

A concern to reform 'core' (non-trading) government activities similarly brought renewed attention to public sector labour relations, and to proposals to change state sector pay-fixing mechanisms. The State Sector Act passed in 1988 sought to reduce disparities between the private and state sectors, for example, applying union registration requirements to state unions, and abolishing the special appeals procedures. It also introduced fundamental changes in personnel arrangements; heads of departments were replaced with chief executives appointed (with a Ministerial right of veto) for a maximum of five years, who were to be responsible for all other appointments within their departments. Automatic wage adjustments applying across the state sector were abolished.

The flexibility of arrangements now possible in the state sector is notably greater than in the private sector. There have been important moves in the direction of enterprise bargaining, both in the SOEs and through a move (advocated by the Public Service Association) to department-by-department agreements. The parameters of union coverage have also become negotiable, so that there are effectively no legislative constraints on the nature of representation.

The result is a system which is more responsive to worker and employer needs than the private sector system under the Labour Relations Act. However, it remains in essence a similar system. It takes its justification from the same sorts of concerns about the potential for exploitation of workers by a powerful employer (the government manifesting a profound distrust of its own bureaucracies in matters of employment policy), and it answers these concerns with the same policy prescription: collective bargaining and 'good employer' requirements that shape both the contents of employment contracts and the processes that determine employment relations.

2.4 Summary

Throughout the Western world, the law that surrounds employment relationships has differed in important respects from the law governing other economic relationships. In both, the twentieth century has produced increasing government involvement in these relationships, sanctioning procedures and setting constraints on outcomes. But in employment relationships to an extent not found elsewhere there have been attempts to introduce 'democracy' into an economic relationship, through the promotion of unions with powers not unlike those of governments themselves.

The general trend to replace or modify the voluntary exchanges of 'the market' and the operation of the common law with government interventions and statutory law, plus support for collective governance of employment relationships, all reflect an earlier tide of intellectual opinion: an emerging vision of the world less trusting of individuals and market relationships than of 'rational' government and 'wise' bureaucracy. They reflect a growing preoccupation with planning for 'desirable' outcomes and for 'social justice'; a faith that engineering analogies can be applied to society with benefits for all. The result is an approach to political economy which is by virtue of its distrust of individual economic liberties highly tolerant of pressure group attempts to pursue political interventions in favour of their members.

The values and concerns that underpinned this vision — and that underpin the arguments of its modern adherents in their proposals for 'employment equity' or 'industrial democracy' — are not themselves in question. There may be disagreements, for example, over just what 'exploitation' consists of, how great a problem it poses, and how it should be countered, but there could be no disagreement that the defence of the vulnerable is a proper concern of any society. Similarly, there may be disagreement over how productivity and innovation are to be fostered, but there would be little disagreement that a proper function of labour market law is to facilitate employment relationships in which they can be fostered.

In considering the New Zealand labour relations system — and other systems constructed on similar ideological premises — and the case for reform, the question to be asked is not whether the values that motivated our labour law were desirable values, but whether the system that emerged was the best one for serving those values. To answer this question, we must first consider the effects of the existing system. We must then consider what a feasible alternative would look like, and what it could be expected to deliver. The first of these tasks is taken up in the following chapter.

3

The Effects of New Zealand's System of Labour Market Regulation

Questioning the virtues of the organized labor movement is like attacking religion, monogamy, motherhood, or the home. Among the modern intelligentsia any doubts about collective bargaining admit of explanation only in terms of insanity, knavery, or subservience to 'the interests'. Discussion of skeptical views runs almost entirely in terms of how one came by such persuasions, as though they were symptoms of disease. One simply cannot argue that organization is injurious to labor; one is either for labor or against it, and the test is one's attitude toward unionism. (Simons, 1944, p. 1)

3.1 Introduction: Testing Policies and Testing Visions

At least in New Zealand, the debate on labour market arrangements — in so far as discussion on these arrangements can be glorified with the description 'debate' — has not moved very far from the state described by Simons in the 1940s. The notion that in the 1890s New Zealanders were social pioneers is fondly cultivated, and to question the continuing relevance of the labour market and welfare state institutions which emerged in this 'pioneer' period is readily cast as an attack on all that our ancestors stood for — for all that the present system differs dramatically from that which they had envisaged.

In this sense it has been argued that the reforms promoted by the Labour Government between 1984 and 1987 in fact constituted a return to the philosophy of the purportedly 'socialist' reformers of the 1890s and 1930s, rather than a radical departure from this philosophy. Ormond Wilson, a member of the first Labour Government (which came to power in 1935), records the statement of his fellow Member of Parliament Morgan Williams that 'I am by nature a conservative and an individualist' as representative of the entire Labour caucus at that time (1982, p. 71). With regret, Wilson also comments that partly as a result of his government's initiatives in introducing compulsory unionism and the five-day week, the present-day union movement is now out of touch with the real needs of the work-force:

> The trade union movement was born out of the struggle against oppression, and the oppressor was the capitalist boss. Its unity is preserved to this day only by clinging to this sense of oppression. In New Zealand in the eighties the capitalist boss has almost vanished from the scene, but the myth remains, and is the stock-in-trade of all those trade union functionaries whose livelihood and *raison d'etre* depend on keeping it alive. (1982, p. 62)

There is an urgent need to shift the debate on labour market policy, to re-establish its roots in the experience of the workplace. When a problem is perceived, we must not leap to conclusions about its causes or how it should be resolved, but rather test both the problem and the merits of different ways of resolving it. Correct identification of a problem is an essential step towards finding a solution that will work. Assessment of the costs as well as the benefits of different ways of resolving it is essential if unexpected and adverse side effects are to be avoided. The purpose of this chapter is to consider whether the current New Zealand system of labour market regulation is based on a correct perception of the problems to be tackled, and whether it is the most effective and efficient way of dealing with these problems.

Underlying greatly differing visions of how society works and the role of government in society, there are important common objectives. In the area of employment relationships, the primary objective is one of making these relationships work well; 'working well' will be widely agreed to embrace both notions of the efficient or wise use of labour resources, and notions of fairness. However, what is thought to be an acceptable test of the quality of employment relationships will depend on how the world is thought to work, and how 'fairness' is defined. It is thus impossible to escape from the problem of making general judgments about the appropriateness or otherwise of what Thomas Sowell has called visions — visions of society, and visions of social causation.

One way of dealing with this problem is to consider how well the New Zealand labour market system works, in theory and in practice, in terms of the vision in which it is couched. It can then be asked whether there is any feasible way of dealing with the deficiencies that emerge while staying within this general, collectivist vision, or whether it is a vision that is fundamentally flawed in terms of its ability to deliver the kinds of labour market outcomes sought by its adherents and its critics alike.

This raises questions as to what has motivated, and what continues to motivate, the collectivist vision in New Zealand. As Buchanan (1986) points out, advocates of collective (or 'anti-capitalist') solutions to economic problems fall into two broad camps; those with a basically individualistic philosophy, and those whose basic philosophy demands subordinating the interests of individuals to the interests of society as a whole. The former will support widespread government intervention to the extent that they believe that voluntary exchange and market processes fail to work in the interests of individuals. They are concerned at the apparent arbitrariness of market processes (the power of the 'robber barons' and the 'gnomes of Zurich') and at the potential for markets to 'fail' at the expense of the interests of *individuals*. The latter, whom Buchanan describes as 'anti-libertarian socialists', do not place this emphasis on individuals:

> The anti-libertarian socialist . . . could never have written, or sympathised with, the slogan of the American revolutionaries, 'don't tread on me'. His initial anti-market or anti-capitalist mentality stems not from anger, rage, or loathing at the arbitrary powers that others seem to exercise over him, and not from any apparent limits placed on his own liberty by others. Instead, this person opposes the market order for a much more basic reason. He does not think that individuals *should* choose their own destinies. He objects to the market just as much if he knows how it works as he does if he remains ignorant. And he objects just as much to a market that works well as to a market that fails. (1986, pp. 5-6, emphasis in the original)

The 'anti-market' individualist is likely to be more open to conviction by the arguments of this chapter (and this study) than the 'anti-libertarian socialist'. This is in one sense utterly appropriate, in that the labour market legislation of 1894 was motivated primarily by a concern about the impact of 'unfettered' markets on *individuals*, and in that support for the current system is phrased primarily in terms of the need to protect vulnerable *individuals*. For better or worse, New Zealand society remains dominated by the individualistic traditions it inherited from England. However, the arguments used against applying 'Rogernomics' to the labour market are seldom couched in terms of fundamental flaws in any economic policy focused on individual incentives and individual initiative. Rather, it is argued that the labour market is too special, too complex or too imperfect for the straightforward application of individualistic principles to work.

There have also, of course, been elements of quite potent anti-individualism in the debate on labour market issues in New Zealand. A relatively recent manifestation is the proposal for comparable worth legislation, in which the (supposed) collective good of women is placed above the interests of those women whose employment opportunities would be reduced by such legislation. The analysis presented here will speak less immediately to these elements, but is not without relevance to the sustainability of a social vision fundamentally at odds with an emphasis on the individual. Individualists and anti-individualists alike base their appeals for support on claims to deliver a wealthier, fairer society. In comparing the capacities of markets and bureaucracies (or monopoly unions) to deliver wealth and 'fairness', and in comparing the real-world experience of systems that subordinate the individual interest with systems that promote it, it thus becomes possible to compare the merits of competing 'visions'.

This chapter sets out firstly to consider whether the kind of labour market system that has been developed in New Zealand is particularly well-designed in terms of meeting the concerns that have been raised about the fate of individual workers in relatively open labour markets, drawing both on theory and on the experience of other countries. There is then some discussion of the effects of the changes embodied in the Labour Relations Act of 1987. Direct government intervention to set the parameters of employment contracts is also considered. The broad conclusion is that the retention of this system could be expected to act as a barrier to efficiency and equity in employment relationships; that there is something about a collectivist approach to labour market relationships that is fundamentally flawed.

Starting Out: Equity and Efficiency in Labour Markets

As discussed in Chapter 1, the role of any system of labour market regulation is to facilitate good employment relationships. 'Goodness' in this context has two key components; in the jargon of economics, these are 'efficiency' and 'equity'.

Efficiency is about using labour resources as well as possible; about ensuring that labour services are used in the way which has the highest value to consumers, and thus yields the best possible return to the worker. It is a dynamic concept. It doesn't just mean making the best use that we can of labour now: it also means planning to make ever-better use of it in the future, which involves such processes as investing in training, planning career structures and developing personnel policies conducive to trust and to co-operation.

Equity is about fairness in employment relationships, and the perception of fairness. While there is debate over what equity consists of — in particular whether it relates to outcomes or to opportunities or equality before the law — there is general agreement that an employment relationship is only sustainable, and in a sense only socially admissible, if it measures up to what those involved regard as fair.

The arguments that have motivated comprehensive systems of labour market regulation in New Zealand and elsewhere contain elements of concern about both the efficiency and the equity of employment relationships where these are formed on the basis of voluntary contracting (that is, in 'the market'). As described in Chapter 1, these concerns are usually formulated in terms of 'bargaining power', the potential for exploitation, and the alienation or dehumanization of workers. On a surface level, concerns about 'exploitation', 'bargaining power' and the need to 'humanize' the work relationship seem to be concerns about equity – about the 'inherent unfairness' of a system where wages and conditions are determined by competition. Market solutions are seen as unacceptable because they are thought to facilitate the oppression of the weak by the strong, or at least to 'fail' periodically, to the disadvantage of the weak. But the collective solutions that are proposed are typically 'justified' not only in terms of their greater 'fairness' – less dispersed outcomes – but also in terms of their greater efficiency. Thus Brosnan and Wilkinson(1989) write of the supposed role of the minimum wage in forcing employers to be more efficient, and a burgeoning literature has emerged on the contribution of unionism to productivity.[1] (That unions *can* promote efficiency is not at issue here; the question that must be asked, however, is why, if this is so, there is a need to enforce unionism by law – why employers would not actively encourage unions if they aided employment relations.)

In so far as arguments about 'exploitation' or 'bargaining power' have economic meaning, they are primarily arguments about the ability to reduce employment options by some artificial and unacceptable means – about the abuse of monopsony or monopoly power. Again there are implications for equity in the sense that the deliberate (and economically unjustified) closing off of employment options offends against equality of opportunity. Further, an employer in a monopsony position is arguably in a position not only to drive down the wages of his or her entire work-force without risking resignations, but also to systematically discriminate, for example, on the basis of sex or race. In either case, however, the abuse of monopsony (or monopoly) power offends against *efficiency*; it means that the labour services of workers are not being used as well as they could be, and thus that workers are receiving lower wages or worse conditions they would in a competitive situation. Efficiency and equity defined as fair treatment are thus intertwined.

The difference here from the kind of argument espoused by Brosnan and Wilkinson is that the achievement of *both* is seen to rest on the existence, rather than the suppression, of competition or the threat of competition.

If, as is argued in this study, it is competition which creates the conditions for both efficiency and fair treatment in employment relationships, the primary concern of labour law must be with those situations in which competition breaks down or is absent. This does not mean conditions in which the mythical beast of 'perfect competition' is absent; rather it means conditions in which an employer can drive down the wages or conditions of his or her work-force without fear of losing them to competing employers, or in which an association of workers can effectively debar other workers from competing with them for employment.

This holds both in the market for employment and within the confines of the firm and of ongoing employment relationships. In the latter case, many of the conditions of employment may be left unwritten (complete contingent contracts tend to be inordinately costly in something as complex as an employment relationship), and there may be no 'market wage' for the task performed. However, the presence of information costs does not equate with the potential for 'exploitation', and 'indeterminacy of wages' is not indicative of a 'power vacuum'. Long-term employment relationships typically involve investments on the part of both employer and employee, and both stand to lose if the relationship is severed. Monopsony power will typically be weak in a relationship whose continuation is a matter of mutual concern. Williamson (1982) argues that for this reason a strategy of exploiting the firm-specific investments made by workers will effectively be restricted to 'fly-by-night' firms, or firms playing 'end-games'. Instead, the norm is for employers to avoid such behaviour, if only in order to protect their reputation in the labour market.

3.2   Justifications for Supporting Unions

It will be generally agreed that, to function well, employment relationships require some form of legal backing, and that this may well involve some statutory intervention over and above the support and protections provided by the common law. Accordingly, government support of union activity could be seen as justified if it could be shown that this made employment relationships work better — more efficiently and more fairly — and that the benefits of such support outweighed the costs.

There are four main ways in which unions have been argued to contribute to good employment relationships:
— by countering monopsony power on the part of employers;
— by reducing the cost of forming and maintaining employment relationships (in acting as an agent on behalf of employees and/or in providing employees with collective goods);
— more generally by enhancing productivity and economic performance, and
— by promoting 'industrial peace'.

The case for government intervention in support of unions or their activities would not, however, follow directly from proof of the capacity of unions to perform such functions. The concern of the policymaker should not be with whether unions *can* perform a useful function, but with the general conditions under which unions will survive (and prosper) if they are useful to workers and employers and wither away if they are not. A case for active support for unions will only follow if it can be shown not only that unions can improve upon the employment relationships negotiated on an individual basis, but also that under normal conditions of voluntary exchange there are (inefficient) barriers to union formation.

Unions and Monopsony Power

> Collective bargaining is often justified in part as a device for curing alleged imperfections in free labor markets, but it is hardly designed to eliminate these directly. It does not generally increase the mobility of employers and employees or improve the channels of communication so that information is more accurate and plentiful. As far as employer collusion is concerned, collective bargaining may well mitigate its harsh effects, but it surely does not purposely prevent the act itself, as the familiar institution of multi-employer bargaining amply demonstrates. (Winter, 1963, pp. 17-18)

Arguments that workers must be represented by unions if they are to withstand the 'superior bargaining power' of employers are essentially arguments about the capacity of employers to systematically abuse monopsony power, and the ability of collectives of workers to counter this power in a meaningful way.

As was argued in Chapter 1, 'bargaining power' is determined by the options that are available to a worker. It is thus meaningful to talk of the bargaining power (or exploitation) of individual workers but not of groups of workers; it is individuals, not groups, who have alternative sources of employment. The merit of proposed solutions to 'weak bargaining power' will correspondingly be decided by their capacity to enhance the options of the individual worker. In this sense, 'bargaining power' can be equated with 'bargaining freedom'—with the existence of options, knowledge of these options, and the ability to act on them. A union may be able to enhance bargaining freedom, for example, by enhancing the information available to workers, but may also act to constrain it. Thus Hutt argues that 'bargaining freedom' requires that a worker be able to offer his or her services for whatever remuneration he or she believes to be appropriate; 'bargaining justice' requires that:

> [W]hile a union should retain the right to *advise* an individual against what is thought to be his wrong judgment of the value of his services, that word *advise* should not be allowed to be interpreted in the way in which the words 'persuade' or 'induce' have come so often to be interpreted, namely as synonyms for 'intimidate' or 'coerce'. The individual's 'bargaining power', means, indeed, his 'bargaining freedom'. (1973, p. 72, emphasis in the original)

Where a union is involved in bargaining for wages and conditions that represent the averaged interest of their members (or of union officials), the bargaining position of workers who differ from the average in skills or abilities or preferences will inevitably be compromised. Where the union is in a position to impose the wages and conditions that it negotiates on all workers in a workplace, an industry or a craft, the result will be an effective *reduction* in the options of all but the 'representative' worker (or, more probably, the 'representative' union official). Workers whose productivity exceeds the average will be limited in their ability to seek remuneration that recognizes this. Workers whose productivity is substantially below the average may find themselves priced out of employment. Workers whose preferences (for example, with regard to the flexibility of hours) differ from the average will be less able to negotiate employment packages that reflect those preferences. Whereas the employer with (substantial) monopsony power may be in a position to exploit workers by shutting them in, a monopoly union established to 'countervail' this power, by shutting workers out or restricting their contractual options, can also perpetrate exploitation.

As has been argued above, sustainable monopsony power is in practice rare. The nineteenth century experience of workers spending most of their lives within a few kilometres of their birthplace—of low mobility, poor information flows and remnants of Master-Servant allegiance—is far less relevant in the late twentieth century.

This does not mean that the potential for exploiting workers has disappeared, but it does mean that it is unlikely to be so pervasive that blanket monopoly unionism — with its own attendant exploitation — will be an appropriate response.

In everyday argument, the concern expressed about the 'weak bargaining power' of workers is generally not so much a concern with the options available to workers (and thus their 'bargaining power' proper) but a concern with the relationship between wages and profits — a concern to achieve what is construed to be a 'fair' relationship between the returns to work and the returns to investment. Underpinning this is at least a hint of the notion that competition in the labour market is competition between employers and workers, rather than between employers for workers, and between workers for jobs.

Freeman and Medoff, for example, regard union confiscation of the returns to capital as acceptable because it 'reduce[s] the exceedingly high levels of profitability in highly concentrated industries toward normal competitive levels' (in Reynolds, 1987, p. 155). This in part reflects the simplistic notion that 'the poor are poor because the rich are rich' — that 'the visual is causal' (Minogue, 1989, p. 7). However, wages and profits are in any event not directly comparable, wages being a return to a factor service, and profits being a residual income after all factor inputs have been paid for — a reward for bearing risk which Hutt has described as 'the most important form of social security for the workers that society provides' (1986, p. 61). Attempts to redistribute income from shareholders to workers through the institution of monopoly unionism will as a result be counter-productive:

> [T]he proper correction for inordinate rates of return is not higher wages but larger investment, larger employment, larger output, and lower relative product prices. If the large earnings reflect monopoly restraint upon output by enterprises, as they occasionally will, measures should be taken to extirpate such restraint; monopoly in the labor market will only aggravate and consolidate restriction. Temporary increases in relative wages are justified if necessary to attract additional supplies of labor from other industries. If attained by collusive, collective action of workers where supply is adequate or redundant, increases will serve, not to facilitate expansion of output, but to prevent it. (Simons, 1944, p.16)

Union monopoly gains are, moreover, highly unlikely to be limited to such enterprises as are capable of acquiring and abusing market power. Particularly where unions operate on an industry or occupational basis, they will be made at the expense of many small companies with strictly limited market power — and ultimately at the expense of employment by these companies.

Unions as Agents and Suppliers of Collective Goods

An employment relationship is, by definition, more complex than a simple market exchange. The very existence of employment relationships springs from the fact that it is simply too costly for consumers to deal directly with each of the individual workers involved in producing everyday goods and services; it is more efficient for these workers, either as employees or as contractors, to be co-ordinated through an intermediary such as the firm, which the consumer pays, directly or through a distributor, for the final product of their labours.

The sorts of costs that make it inefficient for consumers to deal individually with everyone involved in producing the good or service that they want to purchase also arise within firms. Tasks must be co-ordinated, good performance elicited, risks managed. In a dynamic context, means must be found of innovating not only in what the firm produces, but also in how it is organized, and how its members interact. The shape of the individual employment relationship will be a product of these circumstances. In particular, it will depend on how readily the contribution made by a worker can be measured and controlled by rules or by incentives (and thus how much scope there is for opportunistic behaviour), and how much the firm and the worker invest in each other, developing firm-specific skills.[2]

Williamson (1982) shows how these two factors — the ease with which a worker's contribution can be measured and the extent to which he or she has invested in skills specific to the firm — can, in different combinations, lead to fundamentally different relationships between the worker and the firm. If the worker's output is readily measured, incentive or authority structures aimed at monitoring his or her inputs will not be required. If, in addition, the worker has made no firm-specific investments (and the firm no particular investments in the worker) there will be little value to either the worker or the firm in developing complex contractual mechanisms for perpetuating the relationship; termination of the relationship will be the best way of resolving dissatisfaction on either part. If instead some firm-specific skills have been developed by the worker, both the worker and the firm will have an interest in sustaining the relationship, and will look to establish safeguards against the arbitrary termination of their relationship.

If it is difficult to measure what the worker produces, the firm must find some way of controlling his or her output indirectly, for example, through supervision or incentive structures. In the absence of firm-specific skills, there will be no great emphasis by either party on perpetuating the relationship, but the relationship will be more complex than the simple, market-like relationships that arise where measurement problems are also absent. If, however, the worker's output is difficult to determine *and* he or she has invested in firm-specific skills, the relationship between the worker and the firm will require quite complex contractual support, promoting good performance through incentives and inculcation of team spirit, and providing significant guarantees against arbitrary termination.

If a third factor, uncertainty, is added to these two, the costs of establishing a well-functioning relationship increase. No contract can account for all possible contingencies; significant trade-offs emerge between dealing with the problems of opportunism that arise wherever measurement of workers' contributions is difficult and skills are firm-specific, and leaving space to deal with changes in the broader economic environment. Crocker and Masten summarize the trade-offs in this way:

> Generally, the value of a flexible, more relational exchange is enhanced the more difficult it is to devise definitive obligations due to the complexity of the transaction or its environment. Conversely, environments where opportunism is expected to be rife or where economic conditions are relatively simple and static will tend to favor more precise agreements. (1988, p. 7)

The general result is that some of the elements in an employment relationship will not be written into the actual employment contract, rather being left implicit. Whereas the explicit elements of contracts are readily administered by outside parties such as the courts, the implicit elements may be better handled by internal negotiation, perhaps with the assistance of a mediator. This can lead to an emphasis in actual written contracts not so much on the terms of the contract as on procedures, for example, for renegotiation and for handling of grievances; 'a more general statement of the process of adjusting the terms of the agreement over time—the establishment, in effect, of a 'constitution' governing the ongoing relationship' (Goldberg, 1976, p. 428). But an emphasis *purely* on procedures is unlikely; typically there will be a combination of explicit and implicit mechanisms for enforcing contractual relationships. Some elements will be specified explicitly, and thus be open to enforcement by third-party arbitrators or the courts.

Others will remain unspecified, and ultimately be enforced by the implicit threat of terminating the relationship (Klein, 1984).

Within a firm, the most appropriate kind of contract is likely to vary among workers, according to the tasks that they perform, the responsibilities and risks that they bear, and the extent to which they are required to invest in skills of little value outside the firm. However, just as specifying all aspects of an individual employment relationship or contract is costly, so that there are economies in leaving some options open and some conditions 'implicit', so tailoring of contracts to individual workers is costly. Thus even where workers differ in their capabilities and preferences, and the circumstances in which they work change, the least costly way of managing their relationship with the firm — for both parties — may be through standardized contracts and/or the use of codes, rule books and personnel policies of quite general applicability, with a degree of discretion left for dealing with 'out-of-the-ordinary' situations.

The cost of excessive standardization will be an inability to meet preferences and draw on the abilities of workers who differ from the 'average', or to adapt to changing economic and technological circumstances. The cost of insufficient standardization will be the diversion of resources into developing and maintaining contracts that could be used more productively elsewhere. In either case, the firm will under-perform, and workers' options will be reduced.

This raises questions as to the role that unions might perform in reducing the costs of developing and maintaining good employment relationships. In particular, can a union, acting as an agent for workers in a common situation, facilitate their relationship with their employer(s) by acting on their behalf in negotiating employment contracts and acting as their representative in their ongoing relationship with the firm? Or, more generally, can unions supply workers with collective goods relevant to this relationship? In each case, the benefits of union involvement must be set against the costs — not only the direct costs to workers (for example, in the form of union dues) but also any costs arising from over-standardization of employment relationships and from problems in aligning the interests of union officials with those of workers.

Where a number of workers are in a broadly similar situation, and where their relationship with their employer is made complex by such factors as problems in measuring their contribution to the firm, their investment in skills specific to that firm, or general uncertainty, there may well be advantages in selecting an agent to work on their behalf. Use of a single negotiator can enable them to take advantage of economies of scale in establishing and renegotiating contracts, and of specialization in the skills and knowledge that this requires. For example, individual workers will in many cases be poorly placed to assess workplace health and safety hazards, and thus to negotiate with their employer over how these should be handled. By employing an agent with specialist information about such hazards, they can increase their ability not only to improve workplace safety and health, but to do so as cost-effectively as possible. Williamson (1982) argues that an agent such as a union may also assist in assuring the continuity of employment relationships where workers and firms have 'invested' in each other, lowering the costs of bargaining and assisting the employer in rationalizing the firm's wage structure according to the characteristics of tasks.

A related argument is that not only does the introduction of a union to an employment relationship facilitate that relationship by overcoming informational problems, but in addition there is a collective good element to reducing informational problems, both from the point of view of informing the worker, and from the point of view of providing the worker with a collective 'voice'. What is meant by 'voice' is communication between worker and employer with the goal of improving their relationship; it serves as an alternative to quitting (or firing), an alternative that will be particularly important where the worker and the employer have made investments in each other. Thus Williamson (1982) ascribes to unions a role in encouraging what he calls 'consummate' (as opposed to 'perfunctory') co-operation, and facilitating firm-specific investments by reducing the risk that they will be intentionally or mistakenly 'exploited'. The point argued by writers such as Hirschman (1970) and Freeman and Medoff (1979) is that the individual voice of workers is weak, and that a union can provide them with a 'collective voice'. It will be seen that this is a variant of the argument that an individual's 'weak bargaining power' can be bolstered in collective action. But the emphasis of writers such as Freeman and Medoff is as much on the benefits to the *employer* as to the employee of the exercise of such 'collective voice'. The most tangible result, they argue, is a reduction in 'quits' and hence hiring and training costs, and the ability to approach investments in 'human capital' and the development of career paths with greater assurance.

Implicit in such arguments is the acceptance that a union can supply workers with collective goods — goods or services from which it would be impossible to exclude non-members — and that there are

advantages in jointly producing these goods. It is argued that such services include:[3]
— higher wages and/or fringe benefits;
— assistance in settling grievances;
— better working conditions;
— insurance;
— sponsorship of social events, conventions, union newspapers and the like;
— social services such as medical centres or retirement homes for former members, and
— charitable contributions; support for political candidates and pro-union legislation.

It is clearly possible to exclude individual workers from the consumption of such things as insurance, social events, conventions, newspapers and social services. It is feasible (and may be desirable) for individual workers to be able to dissociate themselves from a union's political activities. In other words, if a union were to provide such services to a subset of workers in an enterprise or occupation, 'free-riding' by non-members may not prove to be a problem.

The remuneration (both wage and non-wage) and the conditions that a union can negotiate in a collective bargaining process and the assistance that it can offer in settling workers' grievances are more commonly thought of as collective goods; goods which if offered to one worker can be consumed by all, and which therefore pose 'free-rider' problems. This is of crucial importance to labour market regulation, as the case for compulsory union membership and agency shops (in which membership is not required but non-members must still pay union dues), is based on the assumption of inevitable 'free-rider' problems; on the assumption that unions in fact supply collective goods. In this regard, Barker and Chapman (1989) note the importance of defining collective goods in terms of the administrative as well as the technical costs of excluding individual workers.

In the case of union assistance with grievance cases, Moorhouse argues that the reason why unions do not put a price on such assistance, and deny assistance to workers unwilling to pay this price, is not that they *cannot*, but that they *choose* not to:

> The reason unions do not charge a grievance procedure fee is not that the service represents a public good, but because it allows the union to discriminate among employees and to discipline those out of favor with the union leadership. (1982, p. 623)

Posner, similarly arguing that a union structure is not a

prerequisite for grievance procedures, asserts that '[p]robably the real reason that unions press for grievance machinery and job security is to make it harder for the employer to get rid of union supporters' (1973, p. 306). The implication in both cases is that the role of unions in grievance procedures is not a reflection of the 'public good' nature of such procedures but of the necessity of some degree of union control over these procedures if their cartel status is to be protected.

In the case of working conditions, too, Moorhouse argues that the case for treating union services as collective goods is not robust:

> (1) the benefits attributable to union action are likely to be trivial; (2) at most, it makes a case for minimum health and safety standards, not compulsory unionism; (3) union job assignment discretion [at least in the United States] whereby workers are assigned to newer, easier to operate, and safer machines, vitiates the argument that such benefits are available to all workers; and (4) competitive market pressures tend to ensure that the employer will install equipment and maintain general working conditions that are optimal from the employee's viewpoint. (1982, p. 624)

And on whether unions provide a collective service in negotiating higher wages and fringe benefits than would be available to workers negotiating individually, he argues that unions legally represent all workers over whom they have coverage not because excluding individual workers from their coverage is technically infeasible, but because that coverage is mandated by law, and that '[t]he free-rider rationale of compulsory unionism fails if it is a problem born of law and not economic conditions in labor markets' (1982, p. 624). In other words, individual labour contracts are not infeasible; in many firms, in New Zealand as elsewhere, they coexist with collective bargaining. Unions in practice operate as cartels because of their legal status; they are not cartels as a result of overwhelming economies of scale in coverage.

Whether unions do in fact, in the long run, improve the remuneration and conditions available to workers is the subject of a considerable literature, particularly in the United States, where the coexistence of large bodies of unionized and non-unionized workers in similar employment affords a substantial basis for testing this proposition. There are, of course, difficulties in making such comparisons. For example, Reynolds (1987) points out that some non-unionized employers may pay union wage rates to discourage unionization, and that there may also be a two-way relationship between unions and high wages, given the origins of unionism in relatively well-paid crafts rather than in relatively lowly paid occupations. Similarly, Parsley, in a survey of the literature of the role of unions in securing wage gains for workers, argues that:

> [I]t appears that wages affect unionization to a greater degree than unionism influences wages, but paradoxically workers presumably become union members because they believe that the latter causal direction predominates. (1980, p. 29)

The implication of studies of the union/non-union wage differential appears to be that unionized workers *do* receive higher wages than their non-unionized equivalents, but that the size of the differential varies across occupations and industries and over time. Reynolds (1987) cites a finding that union wages exceeded non-union wages in the United States by an average of 14-15% between 1967 and 1979, but that union wages were also less flexible than non-union wages, so that this difference fluctuated on an annual basis between 11 and 18%. The difference also varies between industries. For 1984, he records a gap between union and non-union wages as high as 62% in mining, and as low as -1% in the service sector. In the United Kingdom, the average wage premium for union membership is around 10%, but the premium ranges from 6% in the absence of a closed shop (but where the union is 'recognized' by the employer) to 14% where there is a pre-entry closed shop (as, for example, on the waterfront).[4]

The impact of unionization on wages also differs according to the age of workers, as a result of unions averaging wages across their membership. Thus the union/non-union wage differential in the United States is greatest for the youngest, otherwise lowest paid workers. In the United Kingdom, Metcalf (1988) estimates that union activity narrows the female-male wage differential by 1%, the black-white (male) differential by 5%, the unskilled-skilled (male) differential by 2% and the manual-non-manual differential by 9%.

The involvement of a union does not 'take wages out of competition', thus making them independent of the forces of supply and demand. Rather union involvement creates a permanent differential between the wages of unionized and non-unionized workers. In other words, the establishment of monopoly power on the part of a union creates a structural shift in the labour market in which it has coverage, jacking up union wages. This 'union' element in wages is, however, a one-off gain, so that the differential between union and non-union wages (absent any change in the nature of the union's monopoly) thereafter remains more or less constant.

It is important to recognize that the ability of unions to deliver wage differentials does not constitute evidence of provision of a collective good in the traditional sense of the term — or, correspondingly, of the likelihood that 'free riding' by non-members will be socially destructive. Rather it reflects the power of a cartel or monopoly (typically with some form of regulatory backing) to raise its price and restrict its output. In such a situation, the 'free rider' is *constructive*, not *destructive*. Epstein illustrates this neatly by comparing the situation of the union seeking compulsory membership with that of a collection of landowners with claims over a shared oil reserve. As the individual property rights of these landowners in the oil are likely to be difficult to define, co-ordinated action and statutory prevention of free-riding may be essential to the efficient use of the oil resource. The situation of the union is, however, fundamentally different:

> [S]o long as each laborer owns his own labor, these rights are well-defined. The free riding problem here is not the one which owners of oil face when the oil is in the ground. It is analogous to the problem that the owners of oil face when they try to organize a cartel to exclude competition and divide markets. (1987a, pp. 27-8)

It is perhaps only in the area of working conditions that real collective-good problems can arise — and even here, as Moorhouse argues, there is some scope for exclusion of workers who do not contribute to a union's efforts to secure better conditions. There is also a possibility that work conditions will be pushed beyond the socially efficient level by a union endowed with monopoly power, at the expense of employment for some workers. The rules under which unions operate will therefore be crucially important to the efficiency with which such potentially collective goods are delivered.

This question of rules serves to draw our attention to the broader question of whether the benefits that may be ascribed to the use of an agent or intermediary in employment relationships are in any event best supplied by unions as we know them, or whether they might more efficiently be supplied by some other kind of organization, or even a group of organizations. It is possible to imagine, for example, workers in an enterprise or workplace commissioning information on workplace health and safety from one organization, assistance in mediating grievances from another, advice on standardized employment contracts from a third and provision of insurance or medical services from a fourth. The current grouping of functions within a single union may well be a function more of legislation and tradition than of particular expertise or the

economies of jointly performing these functions — just as the choice
of a conventional union as an agent in facilitating relationships in
the workplace may be a matter more of legislation than of
organizational merit.

Unions and Economic Performance
It has been argued that by placing pressure on wages and conditions
unions promote efficiency, productivity and profitability — that
unions deliver benefits more generally than to their members and
are, in fact, 'the best thing ever to have happened to capitalism'.
The notion that unions and the conditions that they impose are
beneficial to both workers and employers has a long history.
Dickman (1987) reports that as early as the 1840s it was argued that
shortening the working day while holding gross wages constant 'paid
for itself' by enhancing efficiency in the workplace. He quotes the
German social liberal Lujo Brentano as concluding that increases
in labour productivity in the European coal industry in the 1870s
were the result of 'an increase in the average output of the workman
which was itself due to the increase of his wages' (p. 162, emphasis
in the original).

One notion underpinning such arguments is that the pressure
imposed by unions on production costs forces employers to be more
efficient — to invest in better capital goods and employ more workers
at a higher wage, to the benefit of both workers and society as a
whole — this is referred to as 'shock' theory because employers are
'shocked' into higher productivity. Similar arguments are used to
justify direct intervention by governments to raise wages or control
hours and work conditions (as in Brosnan and Wilkinson, 1989).
The other main theory underpinning the idea that unions enhance
economic performance is the theory of 'collective voice' put forward
by such writers as Freeman and Medoff (1979).

The empirical evidence produced to support the claim that unions
enhance efficiency, productivity, growth or profitability is at best
ambiguous,[5] and the methods of assessment used have proved highly
controversial, by omission as much as by commission. For example,
there has been a tendency to emphasize cross-sectional studies that
attribute productivity gains to unions that may instead reflect the
fact that employers, faced with higher wages, seek more productive
workers (at the expense of employment for the less productive). There
are also problems in accounting for firms that go out of business
because they cannot survive union wages and work rules; omission
of these cases from statistical studies has in some cases biased results
in favour of linking union coverage with productivity gains.

Where attempts have been made to take account of such factors, at least in a static setting, the implications of the existence of a union for economic performance remain ambiguous. Addison summarizes this ambiguity as follows:

> As I read the evidence, the static effects of unionism are not necessarily detrimental to productivity and may in certain cases be favorable to productivity. This is not an unimportant conclusion for those who view unions as 'always and everywhere' a collective 'bad', even if the causation issue has yet to be satisfactorily addressed. Where positive productivity effects are observed in the industry-level studies, there is the suggestion that these are most pronounced where the union wage differential is largest and where firms appear to be under the most competitive pressure. . . . At the aggregate level, however, the union effect on average is just as likely to be negative as it is positive. As for the source of productivity improvement, where this is observed, it would appear to owe more to a traditional shock-effect model than to the expression of collective voice. (1985, p. 136)

Once the need for firms to adapt to changing technologies and changing consumer preferences is taken into account – once unions are considered in a dynamic setting – the evidence so far seems to weigh less ambiguously against the benefits of unionization, with the presence of a union making for greater rigidity and, by reducing profitability, discouraging the investment by shareholders that may be necessary for adaptation or expansion.[6]

Considerable care is needed in dealing with such results, and with the theory on which they are based or which is used to explain them. First, it is necessary to assess the quality of the theory. Secondly, it is necessary to consider how far the empirical results, in so far as they might accurately illustrate the effect of unions, in fact illustrate the effect of particular *statutory protections* for unions that may be at odds with economic performance objectives, rather than the effects that might be expected of unions in, say, a more liberal statutory environment. Thus Metcalf (1988), for example, cites British research showing that the presence of a union can lead to significant *reductions* in productivity where a closed shop is operating.

Both 'collective voice' theory and 'shock' theory afford valuable insights. The idea in the former case that a union operating as an agent, channelling information between employer and workers, can make the employment relationship more efficient and in this way enhance performance is an idea of some merit although, as has been suggested above, it is unclear to what extent the service that a union can offer is a 'collective' one.

With regard to shock theory, it is a basic tenet of economics that individuals, be they workers, employers or consumers, react to changes in the conditions under which they operate; that they make the best of necessity. However, in applying this notion to the reaction of employers to increases in employment costs, it is important to consider both the options available, and the trade-offs involved in exercising these options. For example, it is important not to confuse the reallocation of capital between sectors as a result of wage pressure with a net increase in the capital stock (and associated productivity gains). Similarly, higher wages in unionized sectors imply no special 'free lunch' for workers if the fact that they can be sustained simply reflects employers' ability to find means of cutting back employment (most importantly, substituting capital for labour), demanding more effort, reducing fringe benefits, costly work conditions or training, firing relatively unproductive employees and hiring more productive ones, or simply scrapping capital and liquidating their businesses. As Reynolds puts it:

> [F]ew professional economists that I am aware of, past or present, contend that the actions of unions raise the standard of living for working people as a whole. Instead, the quarrel is over how much unions reduce national income. Unions reduce the real national income for the same reason that other cartels and monopolies do: they restrict supply, distort the structure of relative prices, and produce a misallocation of resources. . . . Union actions reduce both output per person and total employment, especially over the business cycle, thus helping to spread poverty. (1986, pp. 234-5)

Industrial Peace

As noted in Chapter 2, one of the early attractions to overseas observers of the system of labour market regulation established in New Zealand under the Industrial Conciliation and Arbitration Act of 1894 was its apparent ability to promote 'industrial peace' — more bluntly, to reduce the incidence and severity of strikes. Early British unions were admired for their role in promoting stability and sobriety in the workplace, and the 'vision' of industrial democracy that motivated the late nineteenth century social reformers in England was, at least in part, a vision of social cohesion achieved through an extension of 'democratic' rights into the workplace. In the United States, justifications for the Wagner Act drew heavily on the 'industrial peace' that such elements as the 'duty to bargain in good faith' were expected to engender.

Two threads run through these arguments. First, there is the notion that by at once legitimizing and controlling union power, violent or disruptive abuse of that power will be reduced, and that by limiting employers' 'power' to 'exploit' the occasion for adversarial confrontation will similarly be reduced. Second, there is the notion that by 'elevating' the bargaining position — and status in general — of the worker through participation in a union, his or her sense of belonging to and participating in society in general will be enhanced. This second thread has a number of variants, ranging from a commendable concern to 'humanize' the employment relationship and reconcile the worker to his or her labour, to a concern to foster pluralist democracy. Thus, for example, Winter argues that:

> Collective bargaining performs far more than the negative, but nevertheless important, function of blunting the impact of the unorganized labor market's imperfections by providing a rough balance of power and a relatively orderly means of reaching economic decisions in what would be an otherwise chaotic market. As it has developed, it plays a positive role in educating and preparing the employed worker for participation in the democratic process and in providing a device through which he can seek a bigger share of the 'social sovereignty'. If it has done nothing else, collective bargaining has gained employee consent to the system as a whole, and that is no small achievement. Further, these achievements have been reached through institutions composed largely of private groups engaged in private ordering, a process consistent with notions of diffusion of power and pluralism. (1963, p. 28)

The contribution of unions to 'social cohesion' and 'industrial peace' will clearly depend on the rules under which they operate. A degree of cohesion between some unions and employers in Victorian England appears to have been achieved in the face of judicial antipathy, and absent special statutory protections for unions, because of a sense of interdependence and an appreciation of the mutual benefits involved:

> At a time when institutions were on so much smaller a scale than now, and more relations were face to face, many an employer would have seen the union as a natural enough development among men with whose working lives he was closely acquainted. (Brown, 1983, p. 24)

But this kind of 'cosiness' between employer and union was to be deliberately resisted in the United States, where the establishment of company unions became an unfair practice under the Wagner Act, a clear attempt to delineate 'employer' and 'worker' interests — purportedly as a means to then reconciling them. The task of encouraging cohesion is instead generally placed on a body of legislation aimed at making employers and unions behave reasonably with each other through requirements placed on, or mediation of, the bargaining process. However, as Wellington points out with regard to the legal duty to bargain in the United States:

> [I]t is questionable whether one can assert with assurance that substantial progress toward agreement without warfare will be made by requiring employers and labor organizations to behave toward one another in a fashion deemed reasonable by the government. (1968, p. 57)

More fundamentally, the question of whether unions (and more particularly labour market law supportive of unions) can contribute to 'industrial peace' rests primarily on an underlying assumption of industrial conflict — on a belief that the interests of employers and workers are inherently opposed. This is at odds with the view of employment relationships as the product of voluntary exchanges, undertaken to the mutual benefit of employer and worker, and the related expectation that it is in the interest of both to make that relationship work as well as possible — which may or may not mean using a union as an agent or an intermediary. (This would seem to have been the basis of the kind of worker-union-employer relationship described by Brown.)

The notion — implicit in labour market law in much of the Western world — that 'industrial warfare' is to be primarily avoided not by sanctions against disruptive activity (such as the application of tort law in cases of strike activity) but by the concession on the part of employers of a 'right to strike' (which is then in some way limited) similarly reflects this notion that the employment relationship is both fundamentally adversarial and weighted in favour of the employer. Achieving 'industrial peace' is therefore seen as a matter of redistributing rights from firms and workers (and ultimately consumers) to unions (and in particular union officials) — and, in some views, tolerating 'warfare' on the part of unions that would not be permitted anywhere else in society. Thus Reynolds writes of the United States that:

> A century of intellectual effort has promoted the idea that the noble purposes of unions justify their means. If A threatens to strike B on the head with a baseball bat to take $20 from B's wallet, it is a crime. However, if A is an organized worker wielding the bat on a picket line to prevent B — legally hired to fill a position voluntarily abandoned by A — from peacefully going to work, then the NLRB and the courts often declare it 'picket line horseplay' or 'exuberance short of coercion', despite the fact that access to employment opportunities is worth thousands of dollars to B. (1987, p. 27)

More generally, it may be argued that the existence of regulations that constrain the bargaining process or its outcomes (or both) will itself inevitably be a source of conflict:

> Regulation . . . consists of a foreclosure of options imposed externally upon a market by political authorities. This indicates that exchanges in a regulated market are fewer, less flexible, less mutually satisfactory to the principal exchange parties, and the result of a lengthier bargaining process. This strongly suggests, in turn, that exchange agreements in a regulated market are preceded by greater levels of conflict as the parties attempt to bargain under conditions which are more hostile, *net*, to the exchange than would be the case in an unregulated market. (Heldman *et al.*, 1981, pp. 143-4)

This is not, of course, an indictment of the organization of workers into unions, but of overly restrictive legislation intended to direct the relationship of unions with workers and employers. More broadly, it is indicative of the incapacity of politicized arrangements to deliver such a social good as harmony in employment relationships. As Kukathas has argued in the context of political attempts to deal with racial conflict:

> Politics cannot create community or fraternity . . . . However fine may be the rhetoric of political actors, the 'solutions' arrived at in politics are invariably compromises—among parties of varying strength—to ensure peace. While politics may deliver us from violent conflict, it is unlikely to give us 'social justice' or foster community or bring about the 'common good'. . . . Moreover, it ought to be recognised that politics can sometimes serve to divide rather than to reconcile by creating public issues—which in turn generate competing interests and opinions. (1989, p. 9)

Summary

The employment relationship is a complex one, and substantial costs may be incurred by both worker and employer in attempting to make it function well—in negotiating and renegotiating contracts, and in developing and maintaining mechanisms for dealing with the inevitable (and desirable) gaps in these contracts. An agent such as a union may well be in a position to assist in reducing these costs, for example, by specializing in information-gathering and negotiating skills. If it takes a role in informing and advising individual workers, it may also help to forestall what Williamson (1982) refers to as 'mistaken' exploitation.

It is less evident that the services that a union can supply qualify as collective goods—goods from which it is possible (at little or no cost) to exclude non-members. The strongest candidate for the status of a collective service is the improvement in working conditions that unions may be able to negotiate, although even here exclusion of non-members is not infeasible. However, the achievement of such goods can be at the expense of simultaneously producing a collective 'bad' in the form of reduced employment opportunities for relatively unproductive workers and reduced options for all workers. Similarly, unions acting as monopolies are a costly (as well as a mistargeted) means of tackling monopsony power on the part of employers.

As for the notion that unions can contribute to 'industrial peace', it is unclear why in the absence of coerced unionism and tort immunities there should be any expectation of 'industrial warfare'.

3.3   The Effects of Regulating Union Activities

Much of the discussion in Section 3.2 attempted to abstract from the effect of the rules surrounding union formation and union activities. In practice, the protections and constraints placed on unions will have a profound effect on what they do and on whether they can live up to the expectations on which the legislation supporting them is based.

It was suggested in the previous section that unions are a poorly targeted — and potentially harmful — means of handling monopsony problems. Their effects in terms of broad economic performance are at best ambiguous. Whether they can enhance performance, and at a more disaggregated level improve the quality of individual employment relationships, will depend on their success in the role of an agent of workers — which need not have any substantial 'collective good' element.

If unions as agents of workers can make employment relationships operate more efficiently and/or more fairly, it might be expected that workers and firms would seek out union involvement of their own volition.[7] Special legal protections for unions would be redundant. If, however, such protections are imposed, their effects may be actively harmful. This section considers the effects of the kind of protective legislation that has operated in New Zealand; legislation that through its registration and compulsory unionism provisions gives legal force to monopoly unionism, that through its provision for blanket coverage makes for a substantial degree of centralization of this power, and that attempts to promote 'fairness' through set procedures and rules.

The Effects of Statutory Monopolies

The monopoly power which the Labour Relations Act 1987

effectively confers on registered unions has typically been justified by reference to the 'bargaining power' that is thus conferred on workers and by the collective nature of the benefits that can be achieved through the exercise of such 'power', and by the related concern that unless membership is compelled, some workers will 'free ride' on the services provided by unions.

It has been argued here that these justifications are on the whole difficult to substantiate. However, to the extent that there is a collective element to the services provided by unions, it will be useful to consider whether compelling membership is justified as a means of overcoming such 'free rider' problems as might arise and, more generally, whether the benefits of giving unions a monopoly on 'voice' in employment relationships exceed the costs.

The benefits of belonging to a union will differ among workers. The less homogeneous the workers' capabilities and preferences of workers, the more likely it is that they will differ in their assessment of such benefits and of the costs of being 'represented' by some majority — or possibly minority — view within the union. If membership is compelled in some way (whether directly through legal provision for compulsory unionism; through the government turning a blind eye on union coercion of non-members; or through prohibition of contracts proscribing union membership, as in some states in the United States) any 'free rider' problem may be avoided but at the expense of creating a 'forced rider' problem — the problem created where some workers are made *worse off* by being obliged to join a union.

Just who become the 'victims' of forced riding will depend on how decision-making within the union is organized. If the tendency is to represent the interest of the average worker, workers whose productivity or preferences differ from the average will be penalized. If the tendency is to represent the interest of union officials and their immediate peers, the victims will be those whose interests differ from these officials — who may in practice 'represent' only a minority of their membership. Thus, for example, even in unions with a growing female membership, 'union' attitudes to such issues as flexible working hours, job-sharing and part-time work or creche facilities may be the attitudes of a progressively outnumbered élite of male unionists with an interest in maintaining a 'male-oriented' *status quo* as a means of minimizing competition from such groups as working mothers. At the extreme, rather than facilitating the relationship between the employer and the worker, a wedge may be driven in this relationship by a union unresponsive to the interests of the worker, but abrogating that worker's right to articulate these interests directly to the employer.

The problems that arise where interests are 'averaged' arise in any collective organization. However, where association with such organizations is voluntary, they are kept in check: dissatisfied members can leave. This provides strong incentives for the union to represent the interests of members as accurately as possible, and developing broadly accepted rules for decision-making:

> When collective organizations form voluntarily, we can generally expect that appropriate steps will be taken to reduce conflicts to a tolerable level. To some extent, individual workers can protect themselves by contract when the group is formed if they believe that their interests are at variance with those of the group at large. Key workers can demand that certain organic elements in the operation of the union be approved by a supermajority vote, or that positions on a governing board be held by members of certain trades. Finally, the power of individual workers to withdraw also acts as a check against abuse. (Epstein, 1985a, p. 146)

In the absence of this ultimate ability to 'quit' the union, more reliance must be placed on its constitutional framework. However, a reliance on balloting and other procedural rules is in itself no guarantee of 'worker sovereignty'. In the case of national governments with coercive powers, democratic voting procedures can produce 'public choice' problems and the redistribution of income in favour of minority interests. Similar problems will arise in unions that are able to compel membership. The result will be a misdirection of union efforts and the dissipation of their resources (at the extreme, in the maximization of political power at the expense of the wider interests of their members). The potential for such behaviour would be greatly reduced where unions were obliged to compete for members.

Also at issue here is the question of union registration: the administrative process by which the right to cover workers is conferred. Where this process is complex or of long standing, even the possibility of voting a union out, or choosing to change union coverage—what has come to be known in New Zealand as 'contestable unionism'—may in practice not help an individual worker to exercise control over his or her relationship with a union. In the United States, workers in an enterprise or workplace may vote a union out through what is referred to as a 'decertification' process. However, Heldman *et al.* argue that:

> While decertification movements have been increasing in number (and have been increasingly successful), it remains true that such petitions touch only an extremely small proportion of bargaining units. Whereas some would say that this is the case because most employees are satisfied with their union

representation, it is also possible that this situation occurs because certification, once obtained, is difficult to reverse for a variety of structural and procedural reasons, regardless of employee opinions on the matter. (1981, p. 65)

A similar argument may be made with regard to the provision in New Zealand for a ballot once in every three award rounds on the retention of a compulsory membership clause. In ballots conducted to date, the voting rate has been very low,[8] and the results quite at odds with the consistent results of national opinion polls showing a clear majority of union members to favour voluntary unionism.[9]

Where a union is operating 'successfully' as a monopoly supplier of labour there will be a second and important class of 'forced riders', in the form of those workers altogether excluded from employment by the employment costs that it imposes on employers, through wages and minimum conditions. This has important implications for efficiency—the labour of some workers is wasted either in unemployment or in being diverted to an occupation where wages and job satisfaction are less than they could attain given more freedom in their work relationships. There are also likely to be significant equity costs, in that those 'shut out' of employment when a union raises employment costs will be the least productive workers—those with little or broken work experience and low skills; in other words, those whose 'bargaining power' is weakest. This gives the lie to the notion that monopoly unionism is a means to 'bargaining power' for the more vulnerable members of the work-force.

Blanket Coverage and the Tendancy to Centralization

The concept of extended agreements or 'blanket coverage' introduced in New Zealand under the 1894 Industrial Conciliation and Arbitration Act has had important implications for the level at which monopoly unions operate. (Comparable effects may be seen in West Germany as a result of an ability to extend the coverage of an agreement to all firms in an industry.) It has generated a predominance of national unions, defined over crafts or occupations. Current Council of Trade Unions proposals would see the national basis of awards retained, but shifted to an industry basis, resulting in fourteen mega-unions modeled on West German lines.

The distance between the union leadership and the workers that they are entitled to represent, created by aggregation of bargaining to a national level, makes for considerable problems in representation, if only because it is difficult to ensure that union officials are informed about the situations of workers in different and potentially diverse firms. This creates difficulties even in defining what is expected of officials, let alone in holding them accountable for their performance. Some of the smaller unions eliminated as a result of the 1000 member minimum had been regarded as relatively democratic and efficient.

The result may be a conflict between the interests of union officials at a national level (and in particular their interest in maintaining the status of national bargaining) and the interests of workers in individual enterprises or workplaces. The poor accountability of unions has been graphically illustrated in a number of recent incidents. In 1988, for example, the refusal of the national printers' union to accept an agreement negotiated between the workers and management of Independent Newspapers Limited for the introduction of new printing technology resulted in a strike against the *union* by the workers involved. In the same year, the Equal Opportunities Tribunal, after a lengthy investigation, found that female Air New Zealand stewards had had their aspirations for promotion frustrated by their (male-dominated) union as well as by their employer. In 1989, the Labour Court struck down an agreement between the workers and management of an engineering company in Auckland to waive penalty wage rates for weekend work as incompatible with wider labour relations policy.

The predominance of occupation- and craft-based unions may also substantially raise the costs faced by employers, as it means that most will need to negotiate with more than one union. This can make it more difficult to calculate labour costs, making planning difficult — although this may be offset by the maintenance of tight relativities between awards. It also serves to raise the overall costs of negotiating and enforcing awards. The potential magnitude of these costs, as well as the frustrations of a highly regulated bargaining process, have led to the widespread delegation of responsibility for bargaining to central employer organizations. However, this is likely to have reinforced the perception of the employment relationship as something to be fought out between big employer and union organizations. It is also likely to have been harmful to productivity and innovation, reducing the scope for creative responses at the enterprise level to both technical problems and employee relations.

A significant side effect of such centralization is innovation in the organization of work so as to avoid employment relationships altogether. In particular, the 'all-or-nothing' nature of national awards is likely to have generated a degree of reliance on self-employment and independent contracts far greater than would have occurred were it easier to negotiate employment relationships at a more disaggregated level. Union opposition to the exemption of labour-only contractors from union coverage and attempts to bring homeworkers and some categories of independent contractors within the ambit of the Labour Relations Act may be seen as one indicator of the extent to which external contracts are being used to escape the restrictions imposed by the Act.

Rules About Bargaining

One important effect of conferring on a union the exclusive right to negotiate with an employer or group of employers, and restraining competition from other unions or from individual workers, is to reduce direct communication between employers and workers. Thus Heldman *et al.* argue:

> While it is often true that unions are more likely to be successful against a backdrop of poor employer-employee communications, it is more often true that the advent of unionization not only freezes that condition but also acts to prevent any significant improvements. (1981, p. 56)

This can have adverse implications not only for the ability to tailor employment relationships to the preferences and skills of individual workers, but also for the quality of workplace relationships. At the worst, a relationship that is by nature premised on the mutual benefits that it yields to the firm and to the worker is transformed into an adversarial one, antagonistic to the development of trust and co-operation that are important factors in productivity improvements and innovation.

The response, in New Zealand and elsewhere, has been to attempt to legislate for a good relationship between unions and employers. There are two main approaches. The first is to define and restrict the ways in which bargaining can take place, as, for example, in the distinct and ceremonial procedures established in New Zealand for the resolution of disputes of 'interest' and of 'right'. The second is to maintain some bureaucratic or judicial jurisdiction over the 'fairness' with which these procedures are enacted, and of the outcomes that they produce, as in the National Labor Relations Board's oversight of duties of 'good faith' bargaining and 'unfair labour practices' in the United States. In New Zealand this takes the form of the prerogatives accorded the Arbitration Commission and Labour Court.

If the relationship between a union and an employer is regulated by statute, alternative arrangements will inevitably be squeezed out. Antagonism may increase, and increasingly be resolved through litigation. Thus the very description of labour market relations in New Zealand in the neoclassical legal terms of 'disputes' that must be resolved under the watchful eye of the state — rather than in terms of the free pursuit of mutual advantage in a market context — sets the stage for a legalistic, adversarial contest. In this context, '[t]he parties will play "noncooperative" games with each other; their bluff and bluster will increase the chances of a strike, even if both sides would have been better off with some agreement sparing them the expensive costs of strikes' (Epstein, 1983a, pp. 1396-7).

The greater the level of aggregation of employers and employees covered by a negotiation process, the more such effects will be aggravated. Not only is the control over negotiators by individual employers and workers reduced, weakening their ability to ensure that their interests are accurately represented, but the incentives to negotiators to avoid imposing costs on those they represent, for example, in the form of strikes and forgone income, are also reduced. The primary benefits would seem to accrue to officials with skills in stylized combat, and the bureaucrats who mediate and regulate their tussles.

The incremental role for the state — either through its bureaucracies or through the judiciary — in overseeing the 'fairness' of behaviour and outcomes in the bargaining process produces even more vexed problems, a more stylized process and the likelihood of outcomes even further removed from the realities of the workplace. As Freed *et al.* argue with regard to the notion of a 'duty of fair representation' on the part of unions (an argument which can be extended to any proposition for oversight of fairness in other aspects of the employment relationship):

It may well be that in any particular setting there does not exist as a matter of natural law a 'most fair' way to slice the pie, or at least a set of fair ways which can be identified and distinguished from a set of unfair ways. The question that still must be asked is how a judge is supposed to know unfair distributions when they appear. The judge's problem here is similar to Hamlet's, who believes in ghosts without necessarily being able to distinguish real ghosts from diabolical impersonations. It would be idle to imagine that Hamlet's problem could be made easier by bucking it to, let's say, a Council of Spectral Ascertainment, unless the Council had some expertise in the matter that Hamlet lacked — a *Geistlitmus* of some sort to guide its inquiry. Unless it had such a *Geistlitmus,* the Council's problem would simply mirror

Hamlet's, and nothing but extra transaction costs would result from soliciting its opinions. Similarly, unless a reviewing court has some fairness divining attributes that unions lack, the judicial search for fairness in distributions is unlikely to be helpful whether or not one believes in the reality of fair distributions. (1982, p. 494)

Analogous problems would arise in bureaucratic attempts to define such matters as 'fair' relativities between men's and women's pay, as in the provision in New Zealand for an 'Employment Equity Commissioner' charged with assessing comparable worth claims.

They are also central to the issue of whether 'just cause' should be proved before dismissal of a worker is allowed. Support for judicial oversight of the justifiability of dismissal is typically based on arguments of industrial harmony or enlightened personnel relations as much as of 'fundamental fairness'. However, such oversight can in practice come at the cost of these goals. In discussing 'just cause' cases, Epstein argues:

They introduce an enormous amount of undesirable complexity into the law of employment relations; they increase the frequency of civil litigation; and over the broad run of cases they work to the disadvantage of both the employers and the employees whose conduct they govern. (1984, p. 953)

In so arguing, the importance of fairness in employment practices is not denied; rather it is asserted that judicial (or bureaucratic) determination of the 'fairness' of outcomes is in practice a poor means of achieving it.

Summary

The overall result of labour market regulation as it has evolved in New Zealand is a highly centralized system, in which the options available to workers and employers as to how to conduct their relationship with each other are greatly restricted. Predominantly national settlements can lead to problematic inconsistencies between wages and conditions and the needs and preferences of actors in individual workplaces.

At a microeconomic level, this system has resulted in inequities and inefficiencies — effort has been inappropriately rewarded, signals about how best to use labour resources muffled or distorted, and the scope for the development of career paths or encouraging investment in skills has been reduced by compression of remuneration around the national average. Competition between employers for workers is reduced by a degree of artificial uniformity in wages and conditions. Competition between unions to serve workers is effectively precluded. In each case, discrimination is fostered; employers have been able to get away with poor or discriminatory personnel practices, and union officials to protect work rules that are inconsistent with the needs of workers who do not happen to be white or male. Productivity gains and innovation have over a long period been sacrificed in the interests of a quiet life.

The progressive opening up of the economy to competition in the 1980s, in particular through the reduction of protection in output markets and reform in finance markets, has reduced the scope for under-performance in the labour market. The increased pressure to compete for consumer dollars and for investors' funds has inevitably created pressures to reconsider how employment relationships are managed. It has also arguably reduced the scope for exploitation and discrimination that is present where competition is unduly restricted.

However, the scope to reform employment relationships so as to enhance productivity has been limited by the restrictiveness of labour market legislation. One important result has been that flexibility has in many cases been achieved by means of redundancies and substitution of capital for labour rather than by innovation in work practices or the organization of workplace relationships. The resulting unemployment has been borne most heavily by relatively vulnerable groups of workers — women, school leavers, Māori, the low-skilled, and workers in relatively depressed regions such as Northland and the East Cape.

The 1987 Labour Relations Act was promoted as a means of increasing the scope for flexibility in employment relationships to accommodate the 'new world' that was being created by liberalization elsewhere in the economy, while preserving what were seen as fundamental protections of the interests of workers. The following section considers the justifiability of this claim.

3.4 The Effects of the 1987 Reforms

The Labour Relations Act was in no sense an attempt to break the mould established by the Industrial Conciliation and Arbitration Act of 1894. In particular, it retained an emphasis on the role of unions as primary protectors of workers' interests, and a view of the employment relationship as an employer-union, rather than employer-worker, matter. However, it was also regarded in some quarters as a means to increased independence from bureaucratic involvement, and greater flexibility. This view is summarized in a 1989 Department of Labour paper:

> The objective of the Labour Relations Act 1987 is to facilitate the formation of effective union and employer organisations which will be capable of negotiating awards and agreements relevant to the conditions in the industry or workplace concerned. Participants in the industrial relations system are therefore encouraged to conduct their affairs independently of legislative support.
>
> At the same time, the Act recognises that certain minimum levels of protection should be in place in order to ensure that society's preferences for equity are maintained . . . . It is, however, the responsibility of unions to negotiate remuneration and conditions of employment above the statutory minimums and to protect the rights of employees through the statutory procedures provided. (1989, pp. 1-2)

The Act does appear to have successfully performed the function of maintaining the pre-eminence of unions over workers. Whether it has succeeded in promoting flexibility is more doubtful.

In the area of worker representation, the Act involved minor changes to the processes for maintaining compulsory unionism and for determining union coverage. There was provision for periodic ballots on the retention of a compulsory unionism clause in awards and agreements, and responsibility for the enforcement of these clauses was shifted from employers to unions. Only a handful of ballots have been conducted so far, with compulsory unionism clauses being retained. Voter turnout in these ballots has been low. There is some suggestion that the requirement that unions, rather than employers, enforce membership has led to some decline in membership in small towns, where policing is relatively costly. However, the continuing willingness of employers to deduct union dues from employee pay has probably dampened this decline.

The procedure for changing union coverage must be initiated by the unions involved (rather than by employers or workers). Only existing unions can compete for the coverage of workers, and balloting is on a union-by-union basis. At the time that the Act was passed, the Federation of Labour (now absorbed into the Council of Trade Unions) passed a resolution that its members would not contest coverage. In practice there have been only two attempts to use these procedures, both of which have lapsed.

Only two new unions have been formed since the Act was passed, one covering Intellectually Handicapped Children's Society workers, and the other fishing industry workers. That more new unions have not been formed is not surprising, given the success of existing unions in determining 'convenient coverage' and the introduction of the minimum 1000 member rule. The latter has led to the creation of a number of relatively loose affiliations between small unions, often with little in common from an economic perspective. Thus sports bodies workers and fish workers have joined with the Allied Liquor Trades Unions, Canterbury flour mill workers have joined with the Furniture Workers' union, the very small Northern Fertiliser Workers Union has linked up with food workers, and:

> [s]hipwrights, boat builders, ship joiners, ships machinists, iron, brass and aluminium moulders, coach workers, pulp and paper workers (at Kawerau), boilermakers and optical technicians have formed an unwieldy union founded primarily on ideology. (*New Zealand Herald*, 27 March 1989, p. 9)

There have also been some moves towards the creation of 'mega-unions', for example between the Electrical Workers Union, the Printers Union and the Post Office Union, and between the Clerical Workers Association and the Distribution Workers Federation (which would generate a membership of around 10,000). Overall, union concentration has increased substantially. Whereas in 1986, 44% of union members were covered by unions with over 10,000 members, by 1989 this figure had risen to 66%. Membership fees also increased markedly over this period. In 1986, the average annual fee was $74; by 1989 it was $200. In the twenty largest unions, the average annual fee rose from $140 to $400 over the same period.[10]

While the Act was promoted as facilitating bargaining at an enterprise or workplace level, and thus agreements more tailored to the circumstances of individual firms and their workers, there has in practice been little progress in this direction. Much was made in the 1987-1988 bargaining process of moves to disaggregate the Metal Trades Award into narrower awards which could have served as a basis for industry-level agreements, but this has not eventuated. There was, however, some disaggregation of the Drivers' Award. Enterprise-level agreements were negotiated at Nissan and Mitsubishi. However, composite agreements of this kind were also possible under the pre-1987 legislation, and the costs in terms of industrial disruption of securing even partial agreement at Nissan were high. Movement towards port-by-port agreements for waterfront workers (pushed along by regulatory reforms on the waterfront) were similarly costly, not only to the port companies but to exporters and importers.[11] There has also been little use of the provision for unions to cite individual employers out of national awards, so as to negotiate separate agreements. For the most part, this practice has only been used where voluntary separate agreements existed before the Act was passed.

Section 152 of the 1987 Act made some provision for groups of workers to negotiate agreements directly with their employers. There was an attempt by workers at the Otaki abattoir to use this provision in the 1987-1988 bargaining round, but this move was effectively blocked by their union. In the 1988-1989 round, a similar attempt by Ventec workers was ruled out by the Labour Court as inconsistent with the objectives of the Act.

Within awards, there have been some attempts to promote changes in work conditions that would enhance productivity, generally in exchange for wage concessions. Claims by employers for cost-reducing measures have tended to be resisted by union officials rather more than by workers themselves — thus important changes were made to provisions on working hours and penalty rates in the retail (non-food) award in 1988-1989, with union members exhibiting little willingness to strike in protest. Similar changes have recently been negotiated in the hotel industry, partly in response to the liberalization of liquor licensing. The negotiation of productivity-enhancing measures has been more marked in the state sector, and the state-owned enterprises in particular — the Electricity Corporation, for example, developing seven separate agreements for its individual business units, with differing wage adjustments and some significant changes in conditions. Here again, there was markedly less hostility to these developments from the workers affected than from their union (the Public Service Association).

A further, potentially significant, development in the 1988-1989 bargaining round was that some awards were not settled (although individual employers independently passed on wage increases to workers covered by these awards). This led to pressure from the affected unions for a return to compulsory arbitration. The costs of non-settlement were initially muted, as an award that is not renegotiated continues in existence for a further two years. However, progress towards enterprise agreements in the brewing industry was arguably aided by union concern to reach a settlement before the two-year expiry period.

There are a number of reasons for the widespread retention of traditional bargaining structures. First, decentralization is strongly opposed by central union officials, who favour instead a shift to centralized industry-level bargaining. The combination of compulsory unionism, barriers to shifts in union coverage and the 1000 member rule strongly limit the potential for worker initiatives for decentralization. Secondly, this initiative cannot readily be taken by employers, as it is only unions who can cite employers out of existing awards. Thirdly, where there have been attempts to shift towards enterprise-level bargaining, as in the case of Nissan, the costs of making this transition have been high, for example, in terms of industrial disruption. At least in the short run, it is likely that many employers view these costs as exceeding the benefits to be gained from the transition. Fourthly, there are for some employers few incentives to push for change. As the New Zealand Business Roundtable explained in its review of the 1988-1989 bargaining round:

- they would have to give more attention to their employment relationships; at present they can coat-tail on other intermediaries;
- they would not be well-placed to compete in the marketplace with rivals who are more innovative and successful in quickly developing more productive enterprise arrangements;
- the award system in their eyes is delivering (by past standards) relatively low increases in nominal wages. Even though they may in some cases be in a position to pay their workers more under enterprise agreements, they can avoid doing so by remaining under the award;
- in some instances employers still operate in protected markets or face minimal competitive pressures and are able to pass on costs relatively easily. The retail electricity industry is a case in point;
- the current award structures allow some employers to foist wage increases which they can accept on to others who are less well placed to compete. This is particularly the case with some large companies concerned to protect their market share against incursions from smaller competitors. (1989a, pp. 11-12)

At least in the short run, the award system remains a means by which some union officials and employers can collaborate in protecting their own interests at the expense of workers and other firms.

A change in the 1987 Act which has proved significant was the separation of the former Arbitration Court into an Arbitration Commission, now primarily concerned with the registration of awards and agreements and related functions, and a Labour Court, charged with adjudicating disputes of right. The Court appears to be taking an increasingly activist role in the areas of redundancy and dismissals, establishing a body of precedent intended primarily as 'protective' of workers—rather than of the sanctity of awards and agreements. In the process, it has moved well beyond simply enforcing the Labour Relations Act.

In the area of redundancy, Labour Court cases suggest that there is now no clear right on the part of employers to transfer staff to a new employer when a company is sold, without the consent of those staff, unless this is specifically provided for in the employment contract. Where there is no such specific provision, workers who refuse to transfer are held to be technically redundant, and the seller is liable for redundancy compensation. In one case, the seller was held liable for redundancy compensation when the buyer made two workers redundant eight months after purchasing the company.[12] If this case is adopted as a precedent, the effect will be to impose a liability of unknown magnitude on any employer selling his or her business as a going concern.[13]

In another recent case, an employer was taken to the Labour Court for attempting to replace an employee cleaner with cleaning contractors, a change which would have afforded an annual saving of around $5000.[14] The employer claimed that this was a redundancy, necessitated by a downturn in its business. The court, deciding that it was instead an unjust dismissal, claimed that it saw insufficient evidence to show that the company was in need of financial restructuring—that redundancy was not commercially necessary. The implied readiness of the Labour Court to interfere with commercial decisions must be a cause for concern.

The 'justice' of dismissals has traditionally been a matter encompassed by disputes of rights under awards and agreements. The applicability of 'unjust dismissal' concepts outside of the award structure has been less clear. However, prior to the passage of the Labour Relations Act in 1987 there were a number of significant 'unjust dismissal' cases in the general courts. In *Marlborough Harbour Board* v *Goulden* (1985), for example, a precedent was established for bringing senior public employees within the range of 'unjust dismissal' decisions. In the same year, *Auckland Shop Employees Union* v *Woolworths (NZ) Ltd.* effectively extended the ambit of 'unjustifiable dismissal' to include 'constructive dismissal'— the situation that arises when an employee's resignation is induced by 'unfair' conduct on the part of the employer. More recently, Chief Justice Cooke of the Court of Appeal argued that refusal to renew a fixed-term contract should be able to be construed as an unjust dismissal in some circumstances (Cooke, 1989). A 1989 Labour Court decision has taken precisely this line. Commenting on his decision,[15] the presiding judge asserted that:

[T]he simple fact that a contract had expired was not sufficient reason for not renewing it. There must always be an inquiry into whether the termination of a contract was justifiable, even though the contract was determinable at will and expressed to expire at a fixed date . . . . An employer may not, without good reason, impose a fixed term contract of employment on a worker, and this court is entitled to examine those reasons. If not satisfied by the employer at the very least that the reasons are such as might prevail with a reasonable employer giving due consideration to award obligations, then we are entitled to say that from the start the employer has set the stage for a dismissal which in the end will turn out to be unjustifiable. (*The Evening Post*, 27 December 1989)

The possible adverse implications for employers seeking to increase the flexibility of employment by relying more extensively on fixed-term contracts, and for workers using these kinds of contract to escape some of the strictures of the labour relations system, are substantial.

The separation of the Labour Court from the Arbitration Commission was arguably a step forward in that it placed the adjudication of disputes over the implementation of awards and agreements in what was ostensibly a branch of the civil court system. However, this does not appear to have been translated in the Labour Court into a concern to uphold the law and contracts made according to the law; rather the court has taken upon itself a role not unlike that of the earlier Arbitration Court of deciding cases according to its own notions of bargaining power and substantive justice, and of providing a kind of paternalistic running commentary on the relationships of the parties who come before it, rather than testing the legality of their actions.

Overall, there is little evidence that the new legislation is a means to the kind of rapid evolution in employment relations made necessary by fundamental restructuring in other parts of the economy. In particular, it does not appear to be accelerating moves towards enterprise- or workplace-level bargaining, and thereby to workplace resolution of workplace issues. Most employers must still negotiate with several different unions. Workers must rely on increasingly concentrated unions for representation of their interests. A considerable distance can therefore persist between the requirements of individual firms and workers and the parameters within which their relationship with each other must be conducted. The resulting inflexibility, and its costs in efficiency and equity, can be expected to be reinforced by the maintenance of generally rigid relativities between awards. It is unlikely that this situation will be eased by the 1990 Labour Relations Amendment Bill, which would allow employers to opt out of the award system in certain restricted circumstances. The Bill's provision for compulsory final-offer arbitration in some circumstances would be an unequivocably retrograde step.

3.5   State-Imposed Minimum Wages and Conditions

The manipulation of individual prices is neither an efficient nor an equitable device for changing the distribution of personal income. (George Stigler quoted in Parsons, 1980, p. 1)

Unions with monopoly power effectively set minimum wages and conditions for the workers over whom they have coverage. Direct government intervention setting lower bounds for remuneration and work conditions has typically been advocated as providing a 'safety net' for workers not covered by unions, and for 'weaker' unions — thus Brosnan and Wilkinson (1989) note (with apparent approval) that the raising of New Zealand's minimum wage to 51% of the average wage in 1988 placed it above the minimum established in 20% of the awards then prevailing.

Minimum wages are promoted first of all as an instrument against poverty — enhancement of wages being seen as more conducive to self-worth than, for example, supplementation of income through the benefit system. By some writers it is seen as a means of restoring 'wage justice'. Comparable worth policies, which are in effect a kind of minimum wage policy for women, are thus advocated as a means of redressing 'discrimination' in the determination of wages. These 'humanitarian' concerns are in some cases supplemented by the argument that minimum wages — and more generally all minimum conditions — will also enhance economic performance; like the wages and conditions negotiated by monopoly unions they will 'shock' employers into greater productivity. Thus Brosnan and Wilkinson argue that:

[R]aising the Minimum Wage would have numerous beneficial effects for workers, employers and the state and provide a significant contribution to the basis for economic recovery. It would raise the pay of many thousands of workers. It would reduce the substantial gap between the average earnings of women and men. It would reduce the cost of state welfare payments and would increase state revenues from taxation. It would boost confidence in the economy by raising consumer demand. It would give greater stability to many sectors and could provide the base for innovation and greater exports . . . . [T]hese beneficial effects could be obtained with virtually no increase in prices and would produce a modest, but significant, reduction in employment. (Brosnan and Wilkinson, 1989, p. 15)

It was argued above that the wage premia secured by unions can lead to reduced employment opportunities and wider income disparities. In the same way, the 'benefits' of minimum wages will come at a high cost if employers' response to increased employment costs is to substitute capital for labour or highly-skilled for low-skilled workers, or to accommodate increased wage costs by reducing non-wage remuneration. At best, the result may be a redistribution of poverty. At worst, there may be an overall decline in productivity and economic welfare as labour resources are wasted.

There have been a number of attempts, particularly in the United States, to quantify the effects of minimum wage laws, both in terms of their general impact on employment, and in terms of their specific distributional effects. Minimum wage legislation was first introduced in the United States in 1938, setting a minimum rate of 25 cents per hour. The Bureau of Labor Statistics estimated that the cost was between 30,000 and 50,000 jobs, around 90% of which were in low-wage, labour-intensive industries in the (relatively depressed) southern states. The employer response in these industries to the minimum wage was to substitute capital for labour.[16] The imposition of a minimum hourly wage of $1 in 1956 had a similarly significant effect; Heldman et al. (1981) cite research that estimates job losses of between 10 and 25% across 16 industries.

More recent research by Mincer (1976) suggests that most statistical studies in fact grossly underestimate the real disemployment effects of minimum wage legislation. He argues that the major consequence is that some workers withdraw from the work-force altogether — an effect not recorded in official unemployment statistics; 'no more than a third of the employment loss in the covered sector appears as unemployment, while the bulk withdraws from the labor force' (p. 103).

The disemployment effects of minimum wage laws are not evenly distributed across workers. A study by Moore (1971) of the effects of minimum wage laws in the United States between 1954 and 1968 suggests that non-white youth were more severely affected than all other categories of workers. Kosters and Welch (1972) confirm that young workers, in particular, were adversely affected. They estimate that by 1968 the ratio of teenage to adult employment was 15% lower than it would have been in the absence of minimum wage legislation. Together with Mincer (1976), and later Parsons (1980), they assert that the main group to benefit from minimum wage legislation were adult women, who gained higher pay at the expense of jobs for younger workers.

The costs of minimum-wage-induced unemployment for young workers (and in particular young workers from disadvantaged racial groups) are not limited to the differential between what they could earn at work in the absence of such legislation and the unemployment benefits to which they have access. Work is not solely a source of income; it is also a means to experience and to on-the-job training—training which will in turn raise productivity and income. Perhaps as importantly, it is a means of enhancing self-worth and the sense of full participation in society. Denial of work by means of restrictive wage laws—or any minimum conditions that increase the costs of employment—can thus have a high social cost, perpetuating the inequalities and disadvantage on which the 'case' for statutory minima is often based.

To the extent that increases in the minimum wage are absorbed by reducing other employment expenditures, such as fringe benefits or on-the-job training, or by requiring increased worker effort, the disemployment effect will be muted. This does not, however, imply that there are no 'losers' in such cases. Rather, it can be argued that even in this situation most workers lose, because remuneration packages become less efficient and less appropriate to the preferences and circumstances of workers.[17] And as McKenzie points out, the long-term effects may be more adverse than the short-term ones:

> The long-run effects of raising the minimum wage can actually be more perverse than the short-run consequences. This is because of the marginal reduction in on-the-job training for some workers that is likely to accompany the minimum wage increase. Because of reduced training, many of the affected workers can be expected to follow lower growth in their wage profiles over all, or some portion, of their working lives. (1988, p. 209)

At a more general level, such policies can impose significant costs in terms of reduced economic performance, as Porter argues with regard to Singapore:

> In 1979 the government of Lee Kuan Yew pushed up wages dramatically, in an effort, they said, to foster high technology and labour saving manufacturing. It was an explicit attempt to restructure the economy, and to raise (labour) incomes. The consequences, predictably, were nothing of the sort, with businesses used to competing internationally losing their edge, and with workers from Singapore crossing the Causeway to work in less regulated Malaysia. (1989, p. 9)

Some Special Cases: Comparable Worth, Occupational Safety and Health, and Shop Trading Hours

'Comparable worth' policies are a relatively recent variant on the minimum wage theme. Limited experience with such policies means that there has been little research on their employment and distributional effects. However, Australian data suggest that upward adjustments in women's wages to make them 'comparable' to men's wages have had important employment effects (discounting for women's increasing participation in the work-force). Bonnell (1987) estimates an underlying reduction in employment opportunities of around 6% for both women and men since equal pay policies were introduced in 1972. Gregory and Duncan (1981) estimate that equal pay in Australia had reduced the rate of growth of women's employment by about 1.3% *per annum*. The number of women employed may have been increasing, but some women who would have moved into the work-force *given the choice* were precluded from working. O'Neill *et al.* (1989), analysing data from the application of comparable worth in Washington State, show a decline in employment opportunities in occupations covered by the policy. They also show that the rewards to training fell. This is likely to reduce the incentive for training, and thus the prospects in these occupations for increases in income over time.

In the United States, Smith argues that comparable worth policies have squeezed women out of employment in the sectors that they covered and into uncovered activities, largely at the expense of low-income women:

> [T]he women whose wages are most likely to be adjusted by the comparable worth remedy (those in female-dominated, non-teaching, government jobs) are fewer in number, much better paid, and subject to no greater gender-related wage differentials than the women whose wages are most likely to be adversely affected (those in 'female' jobs in very small firms). Women working for large employers in the private sector, to whom the comparable worth remedy may also apply, have wages that lie between those of the groups above. In general, then, among women in female-dominated jobs, the probability of comparable worth coverage is inversely related to 'need'. It is true that the primary beneficiaries of comparable worth wage adjustments in the covered sectors . . . tend to have lower pay than women in nonsegregated jobs *within* their sectors, but the cross-sector effects of comparable will tend to exaggerate earnings inequality in society. (1988, p. 238, emphasis in the original)

There is a direct parallel here with the use of equal pay for equal work policies by white unions in South Africa as a means of protecting their jobs against competition from lower paid black workers. An apparently equitable mechanism has thus become a means of protecting, in this case racial, privilege. As Williams elaborates:

> Where black employment could be excluded in the form of outright bans or strict black/white employment ratios or by the fact that blacks did not

have the requisite skills, white workers faced little wage competition from blacks. In that case, there would be very little threat to white employment from the large racial wage differential. However, in cases where it was more difficult to restrict employment of blacks, the large wage differences for the same productivity posed a competitive threat to white employment. In those cases, apartheid supporters relied more on wage legislation as a means to preserve white privilege.

Apartheid wage legislation was based on evil intentions, but we should not be blind to the fact that the effects of wage legislation are independent of its proponents' intentions. Had apartheid supporters said—as they sometimes did—that they were supporting wage legislation to help prevent the exploitation of blacks, the legislation would nonetheless have had the effect of pricing blacks out of the market and lowering the cost of racial discrimination. (1989, p. 148)

Proponents of comparable worth policies in New Zealand have argued that any adverse employment effects will be mitigated by such 'safeguards' as a gradual phase-in process, by the fact that claims are voluntary and by the requirement that the bureaucracy charged with evaluating comparable worth claims must take some account of the economic circumstances of the firm(s) involved. However, disemployment would only be avoided were the process to prove utterly 'ineffective'. Moreover, to the extent that claims are only pursued by relatively well-resourced, articulate groups of female workers, inequalities among women workers might be expected to increase.

Occupational health and safety standards have typically been advocated as a means of ensuring acceptable workplace conditions, 'necessary' either because in their absence employers are expected to pay scant regard to the physical well-being of workers, or because workers are thought to be inevitably under-informed about workplace hazards. It is notable that until recently New Zealand unions have been unwilling to become involved in occupational safety and health issues, regarding them instead as the prerogative of central government. Workplace health and safety have tended to be regarded as absolute 'goods'; arguments about trade-offs between hazard reduction and, for example, employment have been regarded as sinister. The result has been that they have been regarded as somehow separate from the relationship between employers and workers as expressed in awards and agreements.

Health and safety standards, especially where they stipulate machinery design or workplace procedures rather than performance objectives, do, however, come at a cost. Bartel and Thomas (1985a) report studies in the United States that put compliance costs for Occupational Safety and Health Administration (OSHA) regulations at \$2.7 billion per annum. Morrall (1976) estimated the cost per life saved under OSHA regulations then in place to be as high as \$92.5 million. A humanitarian concern to avoid debilitating injuries and fatal accidents cannot render such costs irrelevant.

The indirect costs of health and safety regulations are also considerable, and appear to be unevenly distributed across firms. For example, Bartel and Thomas (1985b) find that the costs of OSHA and environmental legislation in the United States have fallen disproportionately on small, non-unionized firms in the Sunbelt, to the advantage of large, unionized firms in the Frostbelt. Gray (1987) documents the negative impact of OSHA on productivity growth, particularly for manufacturing firms. He attributes a decline in productivity growth of around 0.44 percentage points per annum through the 1970s to OSHA-type regulation. Over a decade, such a loss would reduce the potential increase in GDP per capita by over 5%. This has inevitable implications for the employment and earnings potential of workers. Nor is it by any means clear that these regulations have in practice led to lower rates of occupational injury or illness. This appears to be due not to poor compliance, but to their basic inefficacy. For example, Bartel and Thomas (1985a) found that enforcement of OSHA regulations did limit violations, but had little impact on injury rates.

Since 1892 New Zealand has had legislation restricting the hours that can be worked by shop employees. The initial legislation limited the hours that could be worked by female employees and male employees under eighteen years old to fifty-eight hours each week (with a compulsory half-day holiday). While doubtless humanitarian in purpose, this legislation may also have served to limit competition against male workers by women and young people. Subsequent legislation has limited shop trading hours directly, while awards covering shop workers have maintained penalty wage rates for work in the evenings and weekends.

Unions in the retail sector have been at the forefront of attempts to resist the liberalization of shop trading hours, arguing them to be harmful to the interests of workers. In particular, it is argued that an extension of hours would lead to the 'casualization' of employment in the retail sector – a proportional increase in the use of part-time, relatively lowly-skilled labour. (It may be noted that, even with compulsory unionism, this would be likely to lead to a reduction in union coverage – perhaps a key motivation for union resistance to the idea.) However, 'casualization' is not inevitable, and, if it were to occur, could indeed prove beneficial to the extent that part-time work is particularly desirable to relatively disadvantaged sectors of the work-force. It may be expected that some workers will actively prefer to work unconventional hours, as a matter of taste, or because of the way in which this fits in with studies or a spouse's work patterns, or because the wage premia that they can earn in odd hours more than compensate for any inconvenience in working these hours. Such workers are discriminated against by the current trading hours arrangements, and the gains that they could make given more options in their work conditions makes the pejorative use of the term 'casualization' difficult to understand.

Whether legally binding minimum wages or conditions are established indirectly by monopoly unions or by direct government legislation, they constrain the options available to workers. While some constraints on employment relationships will always be necessary to ensure that they function efficiently and fairly, constraints on *outcomes* as a rule offend against both efficiency (causing labour resources to be wasted or under-employed) and equity (shutting off options for already relatively disadvantaged sectors of the work-force). This is not to say that the intentions underlying such interventions as minimum wage laws are bad, and it is certainly not to say that 'low pay' or 'poor working conditions' are good. However, intervention in outcomes has in practice proved counter-productive to the goal of promoting well-remunerated and satisfying employment.

3.6 A Flawed Vision?

> The intellectuals' vain search for a truly socialist community, which results in the idealization of, and then disillusionment with, a seemingly endless string of utopias—the Soviet Union, then Cuba, China, Yugoslavia, Vietnam, Tanzania, Nicaragua—should suggest that there might be something about socialism that does not conform to certain facts. But such facts, first explained by economists more than a century ago, remain unexamined by those who pride themselves on their rationalistic rejection of the notion that there could be any facts that transcend historical context or present an insurmountable barrier to human desires. (Hayek, 1988a, p. 502)

New Zealand's system of labour market regulation is based on an essentially socialist, utopian vision of how the world works. Considering individual workers, it sees only weakness and incapacity; considering employers it sees primarily a power to exploit. In the subordination of individual workers and employers to government decrees on the acceptable parameters of their relationships, and to the ministrations of (preferably large) unions with state-like powers, it sees the basis for social prosperity and social justice.

This emphasis on centralization of decision-making has not been limited to the labour market. From the 1890s, and with more force from the 1930s, New Zealand governments have erred heavily on the side of distrusting the capacity of markets—of voluntary arrangements between individuals—to deliver socially desirable outcomes. The response was not to eliminate markets, but to attempt, under the label of 'indicative planning', to 'order' them through controls and incentives, and to divert an increasing proportion of gross national product (and later international debt) into state welfare and centrally organized infrastructural investments. Pseudo-Keynesian macroeconomic policies were embraced with alacrity.

New Zealand was not alone in following this course—it was adopted to some degree in most Western economies—but it did pride itself in being something of a pioneer and, with Australia and the United Kingdom, it waded rather further into central planning and protectionism than most countries outside the Soviet bloc. Policies that were barely sustainable in the 'good' years after the Second World War[18] buckled in the stagflationary environment of the 1970s. As the New Zealand Treasury's post-election briefing to the incoming Labour Government in 1984 stated rather bleakly:

> The main data on economic performance, looked at collectively and in comparison with other countries, tell an unmistakeable story. Over the ten years to 1983, New Zealand's real Gross Domestic Product grew by less than half the average for all OECD countries. For the same period prices increased by nearly one and a half times the OECD average, while the registered unemployment rate increased markedly compared with other OECD countries. This relatively poor employment and economic performance occurred despite a dramatic increase in external borrowing, which had the effect of supporting activity during this period. (1984, p. 104)

The primary insight underpinning economic policy reforms in New Zealand in the 1980s was that this poor performance was to an important degree due to the suppression of individual initiative and freedom of contract; that in most circumstances governments and their bureaucracies are not so rational, wise and benevolent that they can outperform the market. There was also a recognition that the principal effect of pervasive and at times highly innovative intervention in the economy was to create and protect pockets of privilege among those most adept at 'playing the system'. Government by planning had come to be seen as fatally flawed. It was incapable of handling the complex task of co-ordinating dispersed knowledge and divergent preferences that is crucial to the efficient allocation of resources, and was inevitably subject to abuse by the relatively powerful, at the expense of fair treatment for all.

The response was a fundamental shift in the way in which government involvement in the economy was viewed. This shift was described by Roger Douglas in the following way:

> [O]ne of the major philosophical differences in the new Government of 1984 was a change in the understanding of the roles of government and its ministers. The proper role of government is to ensure that the people get the best possible value from the country's limited human, physical and financial resources and to provide the maximum benefit for the whole population, in this case 3.3 million New Zealanders, and not just for favoured sectors or industries. Value for money from our resources and equity — basic fairness for everyone in the community — are the two basic goals of economic policy. (1989, pp. 22-3)

This role was seen as best fulfilled by a shift away from central planning, 'picking winners' and legislating for particular outcomes (whether through import quotas or through price- and wage-fixing); from attempting to replace market outcomes with outcomes judged more 'socially desirable'. Instead, the emphasis was to be placed on setting the basic rules required for markets to be able to function, and leaving outcomes to individuals to decide — replacing central planning with planning by individuals.

This shift was most clearly manifested in reduced regulation of finance markets (the removal of exchange controls, the floating of the dollar, the substantial deregulation of the banking sector and a change in the basis of prudential supervision), in liberalization of the traded goods sector (through reduced subsidies and the scaling down of border protection) and in reform of the state sector, 'corporatizing' its trading activities and restructuring the departments responsible for 'core' government services.

The central planning mentality was as well entrenched in the labour market as anywhere — even if the fact that what *was* going on was central planning was somewhat obscured by the delegation of the power to plan to central union and employer organizations. However, in contrast to the reforms introduced in other sectors, the response was not to replace centralist, outcome-oriented policy with basic rules designed to encourage individual initiative in employment relationships. Instead, the labour market reforms embodied in the Labour Relations Act 1987 involved a little tempering and a little streamlining, but basically the retention of the system set in place in 1894. Subsequent policies in the labour market area have if anything reinforced this approach. In finance and product markets regulation is now targeted at making markets work better. In the labour market it is best described as intended to make compulsory collectivism work better.

There is inevitably a tension in using one model of regulation in some markets and a second, conflicting model in others — in trying simultaneously to follow two conflicting visions, or operate in two conflicting paradigms. It is not simply that the labour market is now more heavily regulated than other markets — heavier regulation might well be justified if, for example, the costs of operating employment relationships are high and the government has a particular advantage in reducing these costs. Rather, the philosophy motivating labour market regulation, and thus the structure and intent of this regulation, is now fundamentally different from the philosophy underlying government interventions in most other markets in New Zealand.

One response might be that the philosophy applied elsewhere in the economy simply would not work in labour markets, because of the powerlessness (or ignorance) of individual workers. Employment relationships are simply too important and too complex to be left to individuals to manage. Yet, as Epstein argues:

> With employment contracts we are not dealing with the widow who has sold her inheritance for a song to a man with a thin moustache. Instead we are dealing with the routine stuff of ordinary life; people who are competent enough to marry, vote and pray are not unable to protect themselves in their day-to-day business transactions. (1984, p. 954)

The fact that employment relationships are complex is not in itself a justification for complex and paternalistic regulation. It was recognized in the process of reforming other markets that an increasingly complex society can afford *less*, not more, centralized control, as centralized mechanisms become increasingly inept at acquiring and processing dispersed information and monitoring and controlling economic relationships. Intricate, comprehensive legislation, regardless of good intentions, often exploits individuals whose abilities and interests differ from the average and reduces the welfare of those it is intended to benefit. This is very much the experience under labour market regulation in New Zealand.

The system of labour market regulation that has evolved in New Zealand is rooted in a perception of employment relationships as imbalanced, exploitative and dehumanizing. It was argued in the previous chapter that there are fundamental problems with this perception. Once employment relationships, like other commercial and social relationships, are instead recognized as basically co-operative, as relationships entered upon for mutual benefit, a quite different approach to regulation will follow, aimed not at restricting the relationship between employer and worker, but at facilitating it.

This chapter has argued that, irrespective of the philosophy on which it is based, the current labour market legislation is in practice a poor way of protecting the interests of more vulnerable employees, or of promoting 'industrial peace'. More 'effective' collectivism (like the 'truly socialist community') would not, even if it were feasible, overcome these problems. While it has been argued that there may be a role for unions in facilitating the relationship between some employers and groups of workers, it is argued that the kind of unionism that has evolved in New Zealand is inherently unresponsive to the needs that may arise in individual workplaces, and inimical to the development of the kind of co-operation and trust essential if employment relationships are to function well. The following chapter considers how an alternative might be constructed.

94

4
A Contractual Approach to Labour Market Regulation

New Zealand's existing labour market arrangements were built on the presumption that by centralizing decision-making about the permissible structure and outcomes of employment relationships, a higher level of economic and social well-being could be achieved than by placing primary responsibility for these relationships on the immediate participants. In Chapter 3, it was argued that the benefits of this programme have proved ambiguous, but with marked costs in terms of both efficiency (and in particular dynamic efficiency) and equity. These failures, it was argued, are not the result of inadequacies in the detail of our policies. They cannot be eradicated by a little streamlining or fine-tuning. To yield real and lasting benefits (rather than simply the redistribution of existing privileges), labour market reform will therefore require a complete change in strategy. This chapter suggests the key elements of a reformed strategy.

The first section describes the philosophical premises of such a strategy, emphasizing the central importance of individual liberty, voluntary exchange and a law aimed at facilitating economic and social relationships rather than dictating acceptable outcomes. In the second section, the implications of basing employment law on freedom of contract — and the limits to that freedom — are discussed, and in the third section this discussion is extended to the role of unions. The fourth section considers the elements that might be included in a reformed labour statute. Some concluding remarks are made in the fifth section.

4.1 Individual Liberty and Social Cohesion

What individualism teaches us is that society is greater than the individual only in so far as it is free. In so far as it is controlled or directed, it is limited to the powers of the individual minds which control or direct it. If the presumption of the modern mind, which will not respect anything that is not consciously controlled by individual reason, does not learn in time where to stop, we may, as Edmund Burke warned, 'be well assured that everything about us will dwindle by degrees, until at length our concerns are shrunk to the dimensions of our minds.' (Hayek, 1948, p. 32)

The writings of Adam Smith are widely agreed to provide the theoretical basis for much of modern economics. But they are also significant in that they represent an important strand of the individualist thought that was coming to full flower, in particular in English-speaking countries, in the late eighteenth century. In contrast to such European contemporaries as Jean-Jacques Rousseau, the concern of writers such as Smith was to discover the kinds of social, economic and political institutions which would induce people *by their own choice* to contribute as effectively as possible to the needs of others. In so doing, they did not rely on a hope for the perfectibility of individuals in exercising sincerity or reason. Instead, they argued that (in modern parlance), given the right incentives and institutional framework, the natural instincts of individual citizens could be directed to the social good. As Hayek expresses it:

> Smith's chief concern was not so much with what man might occasionally achieve when he was at his best but that he should have as little opportunity as possible to do harm when he was at his worst. It would scarcely be too much to claim that the main merit of the individualism which he and his contemporaries advocated is that it is a system which does not depend for its functioning on our finding good men for running it, or on all men becoming greater than they now are, but which makes use of men in all their given variety and complexity, sometimes good and sometimes bad, sometimes intelligent and more often stupid. Their aim was a system under which it should be possible to grant freedom to all, instead of restricting it, as their French contemporaries wished, to 'the good and the wise'. (1948, pp. 11-12)

The cost of restricting the right to control social processes and direct the use of resources to 'the good and the wise' was not simply a loss of freedom (and of equality of opportunity) for those deemed insufficiently virtuous to hold office. It was also a loss of overall economic and social welfare; resources, needs, interests and capacities were simply not knowable by any central planner. As present-day proponents of this kind of individualism emphasize, economic, political and legal knowledge is fragmented, dispersed and constantly changing. The ability of the individuals in whom knowledge is vested to use it to social advantage will always exceed that of any centralized planning authority. To think that a central planner can have access to all knowledge relevant to the decisions that he or she must make is, in Hayek's terms, to succumb to 'synoptic delusion'.[1]

Because knowledge is widely dispersed and fragmented, its effective use will depend on the right to make decisions being similarly dispersed. Private property — most significantly, perhaps, in an individual's own labour — is therefore seen as the cornerstone of any effective social structure. 'Social order' springs not from design but from the actions of autonomous individuals — both in exercising their rights in property of various kinds, and in developing codes of behaviour that minimize conflicts of interest between them. This is not, as is often supposed, an ideology of selfishness or egoism. Rather, as Hayek has argued:

> [T]he whole philosophy of liberalism . . . does not assume, as is often asserted, that man is egoistic or selfish or ought to be. It merely starts from the indisputable fact that the limits of our powers of imagination make it impossible to include in our scale of values more than a sector of the needs of the whole society, and that, since, strictly speaking, scales of value can exist only in individual minds, nothing but partial scales of values exist — scales which are inevitably different and often inconsistent with each other. From this the individualist concludes that the individuals should be allowed, within defined limits, to follow their own values and preferences rather than somebody else's; that within these spheres the individual's system of ends should be supreme and not subject to any dictation by others. (1944, p. 59)

And, as Murray points out, the development of community is not inconsistent with, but rather is necessary to, the pursuit of individual ends:

> Strongly bound communities, fulfilling complex public functions, are not creations of the state. They form because they must. Human beings have needs as individuals (never mind the 'moral sense' or lack of it) that cannot be met except by cooperation with other human beings. To this degree, the often-lamented conflict between 'individualism' and 'community' is misleading. The pursuit of individual happiness cannot be an atomistic process; it will naturally and always occur in the context of communities. (1988, p. 260)

Within this schema, private property is seen as providing the basic incentives for the wise use of resources. Voluntary exchange is seen as the primary means of achieving this wise use — the market, then, is a key mechanism in achieving social order. Thus von Mises writes of property in capital and physical resources:

> [I]n the frame of a market economy . . . [t]he owner of producers' goods is forced to employ them for the best possible satisfaction of the wants of consumers. He forfeits his property if other people eclipse him by better serving the consumers . . . Private property in the factors of production is a public mandate, as it were, which is withdrawn as soon as the consumers think that other people would employ it more efficiently . . . [T]he owners are [thus] forced to deal with 'their' property as if it were other peoples'

property entrusted to them under the obligation to utilize it for the best possible satisfaction of the virtual beneficiaries, the consumers . . . . Such is the real meaning and character of private property in the material factors of production under capitalism. (1978, pp. 110-11)

Voluntary market exchange is not, however, a mechanism that operates in isolation. Its effective — and just — operation depends on its being set in the context of social mores and legal rules that promote self restraint and moral probity. These social mores and legal rules — these tools of community — are themselves evolving systems, analogous to languages, rather than the product of 'rational' central planning.

Just as private property and voluntary exchange are seen as having social and economic advantages in the great majority of cases over collective property and central planning, private law — exemplified for many by the English common law system — is seen as having inherent advantages over statutory law in the governance of many day-to-day relationships. The legitimacy of such law derives not from the status of the law-maker, but from its continued acceptance, its usefulness in everyday applications:

> Common law rules rest on more than the authority of the judges. Their intellectual roots derive from the libertarian and utilitarian tradition of Locke, Hume, Bentham, and Mill. The rules on the acquisition and protection of property, the keeping of promises, the importance of telling the truth and of keeping your hands to yourself are not remote or archaic conceptions. They are the stuff of all our everyday interactions. The simplicity of these common law structures allows them to cover a wide range of legal and social issues that are otherwise treated on a wholly ad hoc basis. (Epstein, 1983b, p. 1435)

The capacity of common law principles to survive becomes a basic indicator of their effectiveness and fairness. The common law is not argued to be a 'perfect' law any more than voluntary exchanges — the operation of the market — are argued to yield the textbook outcomes of perfect competition. There are costs to using the law just as there are costs to using markets, and legal decisions like market decisions are perhaps inevitably imperfectly informed (information has a cost, too). The relevant comparison is not, however, with perfection, but with the feasible alternatives offered by centrally designed laws:

> The claim that the Common Law system is an aggregate structure of rules, the entirety of which no one person designed, and that it effectively co-ordinates the actions of decentralised agents successfully, does not imply

that it is 'efficient' in some perfectionist or 'optimal' sense . . . . But the significant comparison should be made with public or statutory law rather than with an imaginary optimum. (Barry, 1988, p. 52)

The economic or social superiority of common law rules is in part an empirical matter—recent decades have seen a growth industry in academic work attesting the efficiency of common law rules.[2] At root, however, its ability to deliver 'efficient', welfare-enhancing decisions is seen as resting on its basic respect for the autonomy of individuals and its tendency to limit the ambit of governments in favour of decision-making by individuals or voluntarily formed groups. Personal and economic freedom, it is argued, go hand in hand, and together they maximize social welfare.

An important aspect of the common law's success is its heavy reliance on what Oakeshott (1983) refers to as 'adverbial' rules; prohibitions or procedures that tell individuals not *what* to do but *how* to do things. The emphasis is thus not on outcomes (which the courts may be ill-equipped to dictate) but on just process. Accordingly, 'equity' is, in the first instance, measured not by outcomes but by treatment.

The pursuit of 'social justice' in this context is seen as at best meaningless (being the pursuit of something by definition undefinable) and at worst a means to totalitarianism. Indeed, Hayek was to argue that Nazism was the culmination of the evolving social justice theories of German socialists, thinkers whose goals were quite distinct from those of the National Socialists who were to follow them, but who laid the basis for the promotion of specific social outcomes at the expense of respect for legal rules (Hayek, 1944, pp. 167-80). As William Blake admonished in *Jerusalem*: 'He who would do good to another, must do it in minute particulars./General good is the plea of the scoundrel, hypocrite and flatterer.'

Within this general framework, rights, too, come to be conceived in terms of their role in social, political and economic *processes*, rather than of what are desired as *outcomes* for individual citizens. Rights are defined in terms of immunity from the authority of governments, and confer the legal ability to undertake various activities without regard to how others might regard the desirability of the results. Of particular significance here is the emphasis placed on economic liberties—on the 'rights' of individuals with regard to property, tort and contract. These elements are at the heart of, for example, Epstein's work on eminent domain (1985b) and Buchanan's work on economic constitutionalism (1975 and 1988). The key benefits to this approach to rights are not, however, *personal*, but *social*, in that they permit:

[A]n economic process with greater efficiency, a social process with less strife, and a political process with more diffused power and influence than that possible under centralized political control of the economy. The beneficiaries of such processes are conceived to be the population at large, and the justification or lack of justification of property rights is made to rest on that basis. (Sowell, 1987, p. 186)

The justification for a libertarian approach to law and political economy thus does not rest on a preoccupation with the outcomes that individuals can secure for themselves – on the actual satisfaction of impulses, be they selfish or altruistic. Rather, its concern is with their liberty, both for its own sake and out of a belief that individual liberty, and economic and legal structures protective of liberty, can best foster economic, social and political well-being. Constraints on individual autonomy are justified in terms of making liberty work in a world where the scarcity of resources makes for inevitable conflicts of interest, and by this means promoting cohesive social processes.

The key principle implied by this kind of approach for the employment relationship is that of freedom of contract – the protection of the autonomy of worker and employer in forming and maintaining a relationship with each other, and in forming such other associations as will help this relationship along. The following section considers the implications of an approach to labour market regulation premised on freedom of contract.

4.2   The Meaning of Freedom of Contract in Employment

As far as the great field of the law of property and contract are concerned, we must . . . above all beware of the error that the formulas 'private property' and 'freedom of contract' solve our problems. They are not adequate answers because their meaning is ambiguous. Our problems begin when we ask what ought to be the content of property rights, what contracts should be enforceable, and how contracts should be interpreted, or, rather, what standard forms of contract should be read into the informal agreements of everyday transactions. (Hayek, 1948, p. 113)

Voluntary exchanges will take place in *any* legal framework. Where the state seeks to suppress markets or raises the cost of using them by excessive regulation, individuals seek to further their interests through the informal or 'black' market, or by 'capturing' the bureaucratic process. However, the nature of such exchanges and their implications for general welfare will vary greatly according to the legal framework. The size of the benefits of voluntary exchange for individuals, groups and society depend on the quality of the legal framework that facilitates and regulates exchange.

One solution is to rely on the common law. The 'common law', however, defies precise definition; it is by nature evolutionary, the product of centuries of judicial activism, tested not by specified authority but by broad social acceptance. Quoting Lord Reid, Lord Wedderburn writes that:

> [W]e do not believe any more in the fairy tale 'that in some Aladdin's cave there is hidden the Common Law in all its splendour' and that on a judge's appointment there descends on him knowledge of the magic words 'Open Sesame'. There is such a thing as judicial creativity, even a capability in judges to move with the times — though 'their function in our society is to do so belatedly'. The 'living thing' of the common law is the judiciary; the principles are changed in application; but the underlying philosophy is not. (1988, p. 229)

This is potentially problematic, in that activist judicial decisions may acquire the status of precedent without necessarily securing social acceptance — or, more generally, promoting general economic and social welfare. There is increasing evidence throughout the Western world of 'judge-made law' moving far beyond the prerogatives of traditional common law courts. In particular, there is increasing judicial involvement in assessing the fairness of outcomes and dictating acceptable outcomes — a role not unlike that assumed by collectivist governments, and potentially as damaging. In the context of employment relationships, a significant development is the increasing role of the courts in 'unjust dismissal' cases. More generally there is an increasing assumption by the courts of their right to provide a running commentary on contractual relationships, teasing out satisfying solutions and pronouncing on fairness; bearing the banner of social justice, discovering ever-new and inalienable 'rights', and, in the process, weakening or confusing the principles that traditionally made the common law an effective means of protecting individual rights and promoting socially beneficial relationships. This may be seen, for example, in the gradual erosion in the United Kingdom of the distinction between tort and property law, and thus confusion over the relationship between ownership, control and liability. It may also be seen in periodic flirtations with the notion of defining employment as a matter of status based purely on rights and duties — not unlike a Master-Servant relationship — rather than as a contractual relationship.

This may in part be because the courts have become distant from the individuals they serve, which at once limits their accountability (in terms of social acceptance of their decisions) and reduces their capacity to amass the knowledge needed to make wise decisions about desirable social outcomes (as opposed to the basic legality of processes). In other words, a centralized court system that assumes a say in the justice of social and economic outcomes will face the same problems in doing so as any centralized bureaucracy. In short, courts seem to be increasingly intervening in private relationships in a world in which their ability to make those relationships 'better' is decreasing. Their predilection for doing so would seem to be more a late manifestation of Fabian Socialism (just as it is beginning to wash out of political manifestos) and of 'realist' legal theory (in which judges come to be seen as authors of the law), than an indication of comparative advantage in promoting the social good by this means.

The point here is not that judicial activism is 'bad' *per se*, but that its usefulness depends on the limits within which it operates. As traditional mechanisms for keeping the courts accountable have been weakened as societies have grown and become more heterogeneous and complex, this limiting role may perhaps come to be provided more effectively by formal constitutions or other binding statements of principles. The broad history of the common law, as opposed to the detail of common law decisions does, however, provide guidance as to what these principles might be. Epstein writes:

> Judges themselves often have profound disagreements as to the first premises in the legal debate, and in any event the number of decisions is simply too great to allow harmony to reign here, just as it is (*a fortiori*) with administrative actions pursuant to complex legislative schemes. In speaking of 'the' common law, therefore, I am referring to the best set of private law rules that can be devised to handle the problems of labor relations . . . [T]hese rules, like all others, must be judged . . . by the way in which they handle problems of uncertainty, error and enforcement. (1983a, pp. 1358-9)

And here he asserts an 'abiding intellectual unity' between the basic common law concepts of property, contract and tort:

> Property law governs acquisition of the rights persons have in external things and even in themselves. Torts governs protection of the things reduced to private ownership. Contracts governs transfer of the rights so acquired and protected. This trinity — acquisition, protection and transfer — exhausts the range of legal relationships between persons. It is just this universality which lends coherence and power to the legal achievements of the classical common law. (1985b, p. vii)

There will be two basic concerns in this chapter; to clarify the rights that an employer and a worker (or a worker and a union) bring to their relationship with each other, and to define any constraints that should be placed on their freedom in defining, implementing, adapting or ending that relationship.

The crucial rights of the participants in an employment relationship are the property rights that individuals hold in the various goods and services that they bring to that relationship. In the case of the worker, this is the right in his or her labour services. As Adam Smith emphasized:

> The property which every man has in his own labour, as it is the original foundation of all other property, so is the most sacred and inviolable. The patrimony of the poor man lies in the strength and dexterity of his hands; and to hinder him from employing this strength and dexterity in what manner he thinks proper and without injury to his neighbour is a plain violation of this most sacred property. It is a manifest encroachment upon the just liberty both of the workman and of those who might be disposed to employ him. As it hinders the one from working at what he thinks proper, so it hinders the others from employing whom they think proper. (1974, p. 225)

While a common law approach blocks off the imposition of slavery, this does not imply that a worker cannot submit his or her labour services to the authority of, say, a manager, who in turn acts on behalf of the shareholders of a firm. In many economic relationships it is indeed beneficial to all concerned for authority to be vested in some person or people as a means of co-ordinating the activities of others and reducing the potential for opportunistic behaviour; in particular, it serves as a means of protecting the property rights of shareholders. But submission to authority in this sense represents not an alienation of the worker from his or her work — the abrogation of a 'right' — but a voluntary decision based on an acceptance of such terms and the expectation of an appropriate reward. In principle it does not diminish the rights of the parties involved.[3]

Basic common law principles of contract provide for individuals to make whatever bargains they please with whom they please; the primary role of the state in this context is to enforce these bargains faithfully — not to try to balance up the interests of the parties involved. The freedom to form contracts is not, however, unconstrained. Rather, its effectiveness as a means of ensuring that scarce resources are used wisely and its acceptability as inherently fair depend on its being constrained. In particular, there is a role for 'adverbial' rules that make the contracting process conform with the protection of the rights of the parties to it, and for rules for dealing with contracts that have substantial effects on third parties. In both cases, the concern is not to abrogate freedom, but to make it practicable and sustainable as a basis of social and economic organization.

The grounds on which, under common law principles, a contract could be set aside because of some defect in the contracting process are as a result strictly limited, as Epstein explains:

> The classical conception of contract at common law had as its first premise the belief that private agreements should be enforced in accordance with their terms. That premise of course was subject to important qualifications. Promises procured by fraud, duress or undue influence were not generally enforced by the courts; and the same was true with certain exceptions of promises made by infants and incompetents. Again, agreements that had as their objects illegal ends were not usually enforced, as, for example, in cases of bribes of public officials or contracts to kill third persons. Yet even after these exceptions are taken into account, there was still one ground on which the initial premise could not be challenged: the terms of private agreements could not be set aside because the court found them to be harsh, unconscionable or unjust. The reasonableness of the terms of a private agreement was the business of the parties to the agreement. True, there were numerous cases in which the language of the contract stood in need of judicial interpretation, but once that task was done there was no place for a court to impose upon the parties its own views about their rights and duties. (1975, p. 293)

These provisions strongly protect the interests of parties to any contract. The primary protection is, of course, the presumption of freedom of individuals to enter any relationship that they think beneficial. In economic terms, this freedom is essential to effective competition, and it is the ability to exercise options — and the right not to be unduly hindered in exercising them — that undermines 'exploitative' or 'discriminatory' behaviour on the part of employers. Moreover, its effectiveness depends not on the prior existence of 'equality' among parties to the contract, but on the necessity of both parties' expecting to benefit from the formation of that contract.

That this protection is insufficient follows not so much from the fact that the benevolent intentions of all players can not be guaranteed, but rather from the costs of assessing and monitoring or controlling their intentions and behaviour through the market alone. There are important 'economic' checks, for example, on fraud, duress or abuse of the vulnerable position of children or the mentally infirm — including through the effects on the culprit's reputation. But these may be slow and expensive and messy given the unambiguous costs to society and the unambiguous infringement of individuals' freedoms that they impose. Legal prohibitions not only guard individual rights and promote social stability; they also serve to make the contracting process less costly, in particular where the parties do not know each other well or 'natural' moral bonds are weak.

Their ability to do so, however, depends on how sensibly they are defined. In the case of duress, for example, there has been a temptation to apply a concept of 'economic duress' to situations in which 'bargaining power' is thought to be uneven. In rough terms, the test of duress must be whether an individual is being forced to choose between two things which he or she owns, a form of coercion that offends against his or her property rights. It cannot apply, however, to the question of the 'justice' of an exchange of something owned (a unit of labour services, say) for something currently owned by someone else (the means of paying wages):

> The question of duress is not that of the equality of bargaining power in the loose sense that refers to the wealth of the parties. It is the question of what means are permissable to achieve agreement. Where, as with force, the means themselves are improper, the threat to use them is improper as well; where those means are proper, so to is the threat to use them . . . . 'Economic duress' is not a simple generalisation of the common law notions of duress; it is their repudiation. (Epstein, 1975, p. 297)

The question of whether the courts should have jurisdiction over the 'harshness', 'injustice' or 'unconscionability' of relationships is at the centre of much current debate, mimicking the debate over whether the government can, by taking command over social outcomes in the pursuit of 'social justice', consistently outperform the voluntary arrangements of private citizens. In the United Kingdom it surfaces, for example, in debate over whether the employment relationship should be regarded as contractual in the first place, or whether it should be seen as a matter of 'status' (a concept harking back to Roman law) entailing various fiduciary duties on the part of the employer and duties of obedience, loyalty and faithfulness on the part of the employee, determinable and enforceable by the wisdom of judges. In the United States it appears to be assuming increasing vehemence in the debate over whether employment contracts should be able to be terminated 'at will' by either party unless they agree otherwise, or whether instead an employer should only be able to terminate employment where he or she can show 'just cause'.

Similar debates are important in New Zealand. Sutton (1988), for example, notes signs of movement in the civil courts from emphasizing the formal standing of written or formally spoken contracts to setting aside contracts 'which are affected by defects in the bargaining process'. In particular, he cites the growing importance of two kinds of 'substantivism' (effectively a concern with content rather than adherence to rules) in judicial practice in New Zealand: a willingness to look behind the formally expressed contract 'to discover whether it is the outcome of a real bargaining process', which he refers to as 'transactional substantivism', and legal tests of the merits of any particular case, which he refers to as 'doctrinal substantivism'. In the context of employment contracts, the former presumably opens up the scope for judicial meditation on 'bargaining power', and the latter for determinations of the 'fairness' of contractual terms (where the long reach of the Labour Relations Act has not already achieved this).

Chief Justice Cooke argues that in New Zealand, as in the United Kingdom, 'employment is increasingly seen as a relationship involving status; and . . . the parties to the relationship owe duties to each other reflecting the status of each, which are at least very largely summed up as duties of fairness' (1989, p. 16). Similarly, Mulgan suggests a renewed emphasis on status (which represents at least in part a reversion to the eighteenth-century Master-Servant model), in the form of a move 'to recognise the contract of employment as *sui generis*, or perhaps more clearly to recognise that the employment relationship, although founded on contract, is not to be too rigidly confined by contract rules' (1987, p. 431).

As noted in Chapter 3, the issue of 'just dismissal' is also increasing in importance in New Zealand, including in employment relationships not covered by the Labour Relations Act. This is significant both as a reflection of the evolution of judicial activism, and as a signal of the extent to which court decisions are increasingly playing a role formerly restricted to outcome-oriented labour legislation, in New Zealand as in the United States. It raises questions about the effectiveness of reforming labour legislation to shift its emphasis to simple rules enshrining freedom of contract in reducing central (whether bureaucratic or judicial) intervention in outcomes. It may therefore be fruitful, as a case study, to explore in some detail the source of 'harm' in such developments as court determinations of the 'justice' of dismissals (or other contractual adjustments), and the implications for the design of statutory principles.

'At-Will' *v.* 'For Cause' Dismissal: The Case Against Substantivism

The argument over the case for judicial determination of the 'justice' of dismissals, and the ability to impose penalties where a dismissal is thought to be 'unjust', is not an argument about whether employment relationships exist in which the interests of both employer and employee can be best promoted by only allowing their contract to be terminated 'for cause', but about whether this should be a basic rule for *all* employment relationships, even those where the parties would not choose it for themselves. The standard that should be applied here is whether prohibiting dismissal 'at-will' would advance the mutual interests of employers and employees, and lend predictability to litigation over contractual rights.

Proponents of 'just cause' as a universal (or near-universal[4]) precondition for dismissal typically base their arguments on arguments about the weak bargaining power of workers (and a corresponding lack of symmetry between the right to quit and the right to fire) and hence the possibility of exploitative dismissals. In some cases there is an emotive appeal to the potentially traumatic effects of job loss, as in St Antoine's criticism of Epstein's support for the at-will doctrine as a rule of construction, holding in the absence of specific contractual agreement to the contrary:

> His analysis admits of no living, breathing human beings, who develop irrational antagonisms or exercise poor judgment, on the one hand, or who suffer the psychological as well as the economic devastation of losing a job, on the other. Numerous studies document the increases in cardiovascular deaths, suicides, mental breakdowns, alcoholism, ulcers, diabetes, spouse and child abuse, impaired social relationships, and various other diseases and abnormal conditions that develop in the wake of impersonal permanent layoffs resulting from plant closures. It seems reasonable to presume that such effects are at least as severe when a worker is singled out to be discharged for some alleged deficiency or misconduct . . . [I]t is this piercing hurt to individuals which justifies the call for reform of the at-will doctrine. (1988, p. 67)

St Antoine elaborates his case for requiring proof of 'just cause' for dismissals in the United States by referring to the higher productivity that can occur where arbitrary decisions are rare or absent (so that employment relationships involve less uncertainty), and arguing that 'just cause' provisions would make the law about terminations more rational and systematic, so that 'many employers would be saved the crushing financial liability incurred by companies that have felt the wrath of aroused juries under our existing, capricious, common law regime' (1988, p. 69).

Everyone agrees that the human and economic costs that can be associated with job loss, arbitrariness in potentially significant decisions and undue and costly litigation can be high, and that they should not be capriciously inflicted. But they will not necessarily be avoided by adopting 'just cause' as a rule of construction. 'Living, breathing human beings' prone to poor judgment, irrationality and despair may in fact be *better* served by a law that protects choice in the contracts that are made, and promotes competition between employers, than by a law that looks to the courts for *ex post* assessments of fairness.

A law of contract that relies on employers and employees (whether individually or collectively through an agent such as a union) to stipulate acceptable bases for dismissal in their contracts *if this is to their mutual benefit* is, in fact, more respectful of 'living, breathing human beings' and their diverse interests than a blanket requirement that may not be to their mutual benefit. This is not to say that there should be no legal constraints on arbitrary and abusive behaviour, or that these would be lacking in the absence of a 'just cause' requirement. Basic prohibitions on the use of force or fraud to obtain contractual advantages, the use of contracts to abuse third-party rights, or the abuse of minors or the mentally disadvantaged all serve this purpose. But the recent unjust dismissal cases in New Zealand do not appear to be concerned with these kinds of situation; fraud, for example, is rare in employment relationships, especially where reputations and continuing relationships matter.

Employees and employers may make 'mistakes' in negotiating and conducting their relationships with each other; 'mistakes' are inevitable in a world where information can be costly to come by and uncertainty is the rule. But requiring that dismissals be provably 'just' does not remove this uncertainty, and may create new kinds of uncertainty. In this regard, the comments of Freed *et al.* on the problems of requiring 'fair' behaviour by unions are equally applicable to the requirement of 'fairness' on the part of employers in dismissal (and other employment-related) decisions:

[B]oth substantive and procedural theories of fair distributions boil down to axiomatic judgements about fairness that are inherently controversial . . . . In the absence of any overarching theory of fairness, the duty of fair representation crosses the boundary that separates unstructured coercion from the rule of law. In doing so, society suffers not only symbolic costs, but tangible social waste in the form of worthless litigation; lawyers' fees and the expense of keeping the court and its minions represent only a part of the opportunity value of time and resources that are now spent on litigating fair distributions and that could be channeled into more productive activities. (1982, p. 464)

'Just dismissal' cases are, like 'fair representation' cases, ultimately about 'fair' distributions; 'fair' outcomes. The litigation costs in such cases will inevitably be high, as 'fairness' will seldom be simple to define, and the courts are ill-placed to define it.

A 'just cause' rule is also likely to increase the real costs of employment to firms, inducing conservatism in promotion and redundancy policies, and ultimately encouraging the substitution of capital for labour, at the expense of overall employment prospects:

> Employee suits may cripple the operation of the firm and may deter the removal of inefficient employees, thereby blocking the promotion and employment of other workers, including those unwisely dismissed by other employers. Nor is there any reason to believe that a successful suit can restore an employee's reputation . . . . In addition, a for-cause rule would influence the firm's original hiring decision, making it more reluctant to take on risky workers because of the greater implicit cost of dismissal. (Epstein, 1985a, pp. 140-1)

Instead, the justification for assuming a contract to be terminable at will by either party *unless they have agreed otherwise* rests in the freedom that it leaves to employers and employees to pursue mutual benefits. Rather than concentrating on the question of how to minimize abuses by employers, it enables a broader concern with how the sum of employer and employee abuses can be minimized. (On the part of employees, such abuses consist of opportunistic behaviour that may reduce the value of the firm.)

This is not the same as saying that dismissal or the threat of dismissal will always or often be the best way of discouraging under-performance on the part of employees, just as the threat by an employee to quit will not always be the best means of inducing an employer to improve their remuneration or working conditions in some way. Particularly in situations where employer and employee have invested heavily in their relationship with each other, the use of incentives and monitoring systems on the one hand, and arbitration or grievance procedures on the other, may prove better ways of assuring performance and resolving differences. 'Just cause' requirements may be adopted voluntarily in such situations because they promote the sense of security essential if a worker is to invest in his or her relationship with the firm, undergoing training in firm-specific skills and working through a career structure. In these circumstances, where contracts have moved a long way from simple market exchanges to become what are termed 'relational' exchanges, 'governance' of the employer-employee relationship typically moves away from both the market and the courts, and specific internal structures are developed to promote equity and efficiency and to enable the relationship to evolve away from what may have been consented to originally. MacNeil writes:[5]

> In ongoing contractual relations we find such broad norms as distributive justice, liberty, human dignity, social equality and inequality, and procedural justice, to mention some of the more vital. Changes in contractural relations must accord with norms established respecting these matters, just as they do the more traditional contract norms. (1978, p. 898)

Similarly, Goetz and Scott (1981) write of the 'more creative' control mechanisms required in relational contracts than in conventional contingent contracts, because of the evolutionary nature of such relationships. There is every incentive for the parties to such a relationship to negotiate *voluntarily* contracts that allow their relationship to change over time. This may often mean that much of contract negotiation is concerned with the procedures which will be used to accommodate changes both in their relationship and in the broader environment — including procedures for dismissals and quits. The more complex and valuable the relationship, the less likely it is that the parties will be willing to look to external parties or 'the market' for enforcement; quits, dismissals or court cases will be used only as a last resort.

The kind of 'property right in a job' conferred by a 'just cause' requirement will not always be the best way of protecting the mutual interests of employers and employees, in particular where skills are not firm-specific and career structures are of little importance. In this situation, the cheapness, for both parties, of administering an 'at-will' rule and the clarity that it gives to legal obligations will indeed facilitate the formation of employment relationships, and increase the ability of both employers and workers to diversify their employment-related risks over time — to move into new relationships when old ones prove unsatisfactory — without a heavy burden of litigation.

The 'at-will' rule is, however, constrained, both in law and in practice. As mentioned above, the use of force or fraud to procure a breach of contract is countered by common law principles. Posner (1973) argues that the common law tort of unjust determination can also apply, for example, where an employee is fired for exercising a legal right. In practice, however, commercial constraints are likely to be of far greater importance than legal ones; in particular the constraints imposed by competition for good workers and by the effects on an employer's reputation of arbitrary and abusive behaviour. If a dismissed worker's fellow workers perceive the dismissal as arbitrary, they will adjust their own expectations about security of employment; this has much the same effect as a reduction in wages in determining their willingness to stay with the employer concerned. The employer also suffers directly through the costs of finding and training a replacement, which may create a significant disincentive to dismissal, and certainly to arbitrary behaviour:

> These strong and ever-present business constraints . . . caution against the use of an absolute power in an arbitrary way: for even if absolute power may corrupt the sovereign, its use in private contexts is sharply limited. The at-will contract does not guarantee that employers and employees will make sound decisions, but it does help to stabilize the situation by creating the proper level of threats. (Epstein, 1985a, p. 137)

But the primary justification for making 'at-will' rather than 'for cause' termination a rule of construction in employment relationships — selecting a liberal over a directive requirement — lies in the freedom it confers on workers and employers to negotiate contractual terms to suit their mutual interests. In an 'at-will' regime a 'for cause' requirement can always be selected. The reverse does not apply. Foreclosure of potentially valuable freedoms is thus avoided. As Shenfield argues:

> [T]he concept of unfair dismissal is alien to the rights of free man only when it is imposed upon the employer by way of legal duty or liability. There can be no objection to the inclusion of provisions relating to unfair dismissal in contracts made voluntarily between employers and employees and/or their unions . . . . So, too, if an employer is prepared by voluntary agreement to endow his employee with any other kind of property in his job, he is clearly entitled to do so . . . . The imposition upon the employer of the concept of unfair dismissal by law, and outside the purview of the voluntary contract, and similarly the endowment of the employee with some kind of property right in a job, are prime examples of [a] reversion to the governance of status. (1986, p. 13)

The argument made here applies more broadly than to the choice between 'at-will' and 'for cause' laws of construction in the area of dismissals. The latter is but one (crucial) element in the broader debate over whether employment relationships should be defined by status or by contract — over the relative roles of politically defined entitlements and economic liberties. Governance by 'status' — definition of employment relationships not by contract but by accretion of statutory rights — confers 'status' and fulfills 'rights' no more readily than any central plan delivers what might be wished of it. This does not mean that there is no place for the courts to make use of such notions as unconscionability, which may indeed be useful in directing attention to the occurrence of force or fraud or the 'exploitation' of incompetence in the formation of contracts — grounds on which contracts can be set aside under traditional tort principles. What is to be avoided is enabling or encouraging the courts 'to act as roving commissions to set aside those agreements whose substantive terms they find objectionable' (Epstein, 1975, p. 294); to overrule what workers and employers have voluntarily and legally chosen. Rather, what is to be promoted is a system in which the activity of the courts is primarily adjudicative rather than legislative, the kind of activity described by Oakeshott in his discussion of the rule of law:

> In seeking the meaning of a law in relation to a contingent occurrence this court cannot entertain speculations about the intentions of legislators or conjectures about how they would decide the case . . . . Nor may it regard itself as the custodian of a public policy or interest in favour of which (when all else fails) to resolve the disputed obligation . . . . Nor may it consider a case in terms of so-called substantive 'rights' claimed as a matter of *jus* in some current moral opinion: the right to speak, to be informed, to enjoy an equal opportunity of the advantage of a handicap. The rule of law knows nothing of unconditional rights. (1983, p. 146)

4.3   Voluntary Association: The Role of Unions

> That, if there is to be any hope of a return to a free economy, the question of how the powers of trade unions can be appropriately delimited in law as well as in fact is one of the most important of all the questions to which we must give our attention. (Hayek, 1948, p. 117)

The key contract in an employment relationship is that between the employer and the employee. However, there will always be situations in which this relationship can be facilitated by the involvement of an agent such as a union. Voluntary contracts between employees to constitute a union, or contracts between employees and some other agent to act on their behalf in negotiations or in the administration of grievance procedures should, as a matter of principle, be accorded the same respect as contracts formed voluntarily between employers and employees and other voluntary commercial contracts, provided they do not infringe the corresponding rights of other parties. It is for this reason that the application of criminal conspiracy doctrines to unions in the eighteenth and nineteenth centuries was fundamentally misguided. As Epstein points out:

[T]he voluntary formation of labor unions need involve neither the use of force and fraud nor the inducement of breach of contract. There is therefore no need to appeal to special justification to account for the legality of labor union, as it is already accounted for by a general theory of entitlements. (1983a, p. 1366)

Unless it is supposed that the very nature of unions is to act illegally (in common law terms), voluntarily formed unions should receive under law the same protections as other voluntarily formed associations. A similar right may be asserted on the part of a worker to enter a relationship with a union unhindered as applies to his or her right to enter a relationship with an employer unhindered. An analogy may be drawn with the right of investors to act collectively; the modern corporation, owned by dispersed shareholders, is effectively just such a collective.[6]

It is the voluntary nature of employment relationships that ensures that they do yield benefits to both workers and employers and that termination of the relationship is available as a last resort if these benefits do not eventuate. In a similar way, if union formation is voluntary and dissociation is possible there will be strong checks on abuse of workers' interests by unions. Common law constraints on the use of force or fraud, undue influence and the use of worker-union contracts to abuse the interests of third parties (including employers and other workers) will serve as private law constraints on 'exploitation' within unions just as they constrain and discourage it in employment relationships.

The successful coexistence of voluntarily formed unions and employment contracts will depend on a clear delineation of the entitlements involved. The crucial entitlements in the employment relationship are those of the employer and the worker. The union may act *on behalf of* the worker, but this does not mean that the employment contract becomes one between the *union* and the employer, except in so far as the employer and union agree that the latter will perform certain functions in the maintenance of employment relationships.

Making this distinction makes it possible to clarify an approach to the long-vexed issues of what constraints may be placed on union membership in employment contracts. The next section will also consider the question of the legal status of unions as independent from the workers that they represent, the legal treatment of picketing and strikes, and the more general question as to how abuse of monopoly power on the part of unions might be handled.

Compelling and Proscribing Union Membership

> It is often suggested that the right to join a union and the right to strike
> are fundamental rights. Most who believe in a pluralist society would accept
> that the right to join voluntary organisations to bring pressure to bear on
> other sections of society and on governments is compatible with and even
> extends the democratic process. This does not mean that these rights are
> absolute, any more than the right of free speech or publication are absolute
> rights to be exercised whatever the circumstances. The rights to join unions
> and to strike are, in all democratic societies, contingent rights. (Roberts,
> 1987, p. 17)

Whether union membership should be required or, alternatively,
disallowed, is ultimately a matter for the employer and the worker,
rather than the union, to decide. It depends on their assessment of
whether or not the involvement of a union will make their
employment relationship work better (or worse), and whether this
result depends on the extent of union coverage. As in other aspects
of the contracting process, the protection for both employer and
worker in making this decision stems from the voluntary nature of
that process, and their ability to look elsewhere for contractual
partners.

There can be no objection in principle to an employer offering
only contracts that stipulate that an employee will not join a union
while in employment (what are called 'yellow dog' contracts in the
United States) unless it can be shown that in a particular instance
this involves exercising force or the threat of force against some
third party. As Epstein explains:

> A yellow dog contract could be coercive only if prospective employees had
> a precontractual right to demand both union membership and employment.
> But it is unclear how any principled account of individual rights could
> generate that set of uneven entitlements. So long as the worker owns his
> own labor, and the employer his capital, then the liberal theory of contract
> is neutral with respect to the identity of the contracting parties and to the
> terms of the agreement. No law prohibits two business partners from
> demanding exclusive loyalty from each other, nor is there any reason why
> such loyalty cannot be demanded of an employee by his employer, or of
> an employer by the employee (as in the promise not to hire nonunion labor).
> (1983a, pp. 1372-3)

A distinction must be made here between allowing employers to
require such contracts and government action to ban unions. An
employer can only require that his or her workers do not join a
union; he or she cannot require that all workers refrain from forming
unions. Similarly, an employer should not be allowed to compel

a worker to breach a contract that the latter has already entered with a union. If workers see benefits in union membership they will put a price on contracts that proscribe union membership, and wages will be higher in firms where they are required.

Reynolds argues that contracts proscribing union membership add nothing to the common law right to terminate an employment relationship 'at-will' (for example, upon a worker joining a union), although they would clearly yield more certainty and lower termination costs in such circumstances. Rather than such contracts needing to be compensated by higher wages, he suggests that historically they may have been sought actively by employees fearful of union-related conflict and violence: 'Yellow dog contracts, by this view, were the result of governments' frequent failure to protect people from union coercion and violence in labor disputes; they were not due to vicious employers' (1984, p. 100).

At the other end of the spectrum from contracts preventing workers from joining a union, there would seem to be no objection in principle to membership of a particular union (such as an enterprise union) being made a condition of any contract between an individual employer and employee, so long as they are acting in a reasonably competitive open market.[7] It is the presence or threat of competition that serves to *protect* workers' choices about union membership; the opportunity to go elsewhere, or to achieve compensation through wages for being obliged to join a union if this is distasteful to them.

It is the pressure imposed on employers by having to compete for workers that makes allowing them to offer contracts either compelling or prohibiting union membership fundamentally different from *government* compulsion or proscription of union membership—just as it is competition between employers offering different, apparently immovable, sets of wages and conditions that makes the contractual terms that they 'set' fundamentally different from wages and conditions set by the government.

It should also be recalled that the freedom of employers to offer those contractual terms, including union membership provisions, that best serve the interests of the shareholders that they represent is of no negligible importance. Removing this freedom, for example, by proscribing closed shops, is in principle no less significant than removing the freedom to determine wage offers according to what the company can manage, by imposing wage regulation. In both cases, constraints on the terms that may be offered, other than those imposed by the market, are in the long term likely to harm the interests of both companies and workers. Where competition or the threat of competition is weak, the solution is not legislation to restrict contractual terms across *all* employment relationships, but the application of antitrust. This protection is discussed further below.

The Legal Status of Unions

> Freedom of association . . . is a bulwark against the invasion of other freedoms. Freedom to associate is not enough, however. If associations are to fulfil the functions suggested, they must be recognized by the law. They must be able to own property, make contracts, and employ servants. Their funds must be protected from peculating officials, their collective reputation protected by the libel laws. The law must provide ways in which their accredited agents can appeal to the courts on their behalf; without the legal recognition of legal personality, redress would require independent action by all the associates, clearly an impossible situation for a great association. (Benn and Peters, 1959, p. 331)

Just as individuals require some form of recognition before the law in order to participate in economic, social or political activities that take place within a legal framework, so, too, do associations of individuals require some form of legal standing if they are to join these activities. This becomes important where an association of many, potentially dispersed, individuals wishes to enter legally binding contracts and, as a matter of convenience, to delegate authority to individual members to do so; it is also important in defining the liability of the organization as separate from its members.

These are both matters which have had a vexed history in the case of unions, in particular in the United Kingdom. There the 'problem' of reading collectively bargained conditions into individual contracts has been a subject of continuing legal debate. The problem of defining the liability of unions (as distinct from their members) came to a head in the Taff Vale case of 1901, but was skirted, rather than directly resolved, by the union immunities created by the Trade Disputes Act of 1906. In the United States both 'problems' were 'resolved' by ousting the common law from the sphere of union activity, most importantly by means of the Wagner Act of 1935; the legal standing and rights of unions were instead rooted in statute, generating what some writers have termed 'collective *laissez faire*'. (It is interesting to note that incorporation of unions so as to make collective agreements legally binding on either unions or workers was strongly resisted by early union leaders in the United States — Samuel Gompers argued, for example, that collective agreements should have no connection with the state or the courts (Dickman,

1987). Incorporation was also seen as threatening union solidarity by enabling minority factions to tie up their unions in the courts.) In New Zealand and Australia, by contrast, unions were given neither the extensive immunities of British unions nor the degree of statutory protection found in the United States.[8]

A significant contrast can be drawn between the evolution of law supporting 'business' transactions and confusion in the law over the legal status, rights and liabilities of unions in the nineteenth century. In particular, the nineteenth century saw significant innovations in commercial law, defining entitlements and reducing the costs of forming complex business organizations funded by widely dispersed 'collectives' of investors, perhaps most importantly through the legalization of 'limited liability' companies. The value of this law was not in prescribing a particular model for business organizations, but in reducing the costs to investors (and increasing the prospective returns) of contracting into beneficial relationships with each other. This had implications not only for the internal efficiency and equity of emerging business organizations, but also for their ability to contract readily with third parties without disturbing the rights of their members. A comparative nervousness about the role of emerging unions, which was often translated into charges of conspiracy, should perhaps be seen as one of the more unfortunate quirks of the law of the period. This 'quirk' may well have helped channel unions towards political (and often violent) rather than contractual solutions to problems in their relationships with employers.

Where unions are freely formed and are not endowed with any statutory monopoly power, their structure and the relationships both between their members and with outside parties should also, within the bounds of contract and tort law, be freely determined; there is no presumption in favour of any particular organizational form. In this sense, unions and their members should be free to choose between the various models already on offer in a developed market economy, such as the unincorporated society, the partnership or the limited liability company, or to generate their own models. Their status in contracting with other parties and liability for damages to other parties should accord with those of other organizations. It is not evident that there is a need to create a particular enabling statute (as distinct from company law and the law supporting unincorporated societies) for unions as distinct from other organizations in the absence of statutory protection of a monopoly status for unions, such as an exclusive right of representation.

With regard to the question of the relationship between collectively negotiated agreements and the contractual terms that will be taken to apply to individual workers, the key concern will be to separate out those matters which relate to the employment relationship and those things which could be seen as a matter of contract between the union (or any other agent) and the employer (rather than between the union and its members). Thus, for example, agreements about wages and working conditions would typically translate directly into workers' employment contracts. (This is already done formally by a number of large New Zealand companies.) Such issues as the automatic deduction of union dues from workers' pay packets should be seen as a matter to be decided by individual workers, rather than a union-employer matter. Union representation in grievance procedures or provision of social services would effectively be a matter of contract between the union and its members. But the union — as distinct from its members — and the employer could also be seen as having a contractual relationship, covering such matters as union undertakings with regard to dispute resolution (and in particular the use of strikes), or union-employer joint ventures in providing worker services of various kinds.

Strikes and Pickets

It is strike activity on the part of unions that has generated much of the heat in debates over the role of unions, and that has proved a major motivator of labour market legislation in Western economies. The notion of a strike is foreign to all commercial contracts with the exception of collectively negotiated employment contracts. It has typically been 'justified' in the latter as a means of exercising collective 'voice' where other attempts at resolving differences fail. The 'right to strike' has been endowed with an aura of inalienability and seen as fundamental to the protection of the interests of workers in the face of intransigent and exploitative employers — Knox (1986), for example, describes it as 'a trade union's only effective power'. That arguments about the exploitative power of employers have lost much of their force raises questions as to the relevance of this argument:

> Long familiar arguments based on the absence of independent means of workers, traditionally portrayed in socialist analysis as 'wage slaves' without resources or capital of their own, have been undermined by the spread in personal ownership of property, in their homes, pensions, equity shares, and rising incomes and standards of living. (Hanson and Mather, 1988, p. 28)

That in practice the impact of strikes is regressive, bearing most heavily on laid-off workers, those debarred from competing striking workers out of the market and consumers, seems to have gone unnoticed by proponents of this 'right'.

Strikes involve withdrawing labour services from an employer. So long as what is involved is a threat to withhold services, or the actual withholding of services, which the workers involved are not contractually committed to supply, this presents no particular problem. Whether or not employment contracts provide room for such withdrawal of labour as a means of exercising 'voice'—for example, over disputes of interest—can only be decided at the level of the individual enterprise or workplace, through negotiation with individual employers. It is, however, difficult to conceive of situations in which a strike will be the 'first-best' way of promoting resolution of a dispute.[9] Legislation stipulating conditions under which strikes will be acceptable, for example, by providing for universally applicable formal balloting procedures, will therefore be inappropriate:

> There is . . . little logic for encouraging strikes following a ballot and discouraging other strikes. A strike in a monopoly service may damage many innocent users of the service and have far-reaching effects which cannot be directly tackled by those damaged as a consequence. A ballot in these circumstances serves only to deter union leaderships from calling strikes unsupported by the union's members. It cannot validate or legitimise the industrial action itself. Yet the introduction of the democratic process of the ballot undoubtedly lends a spurious legitimacy to such action. (Hanson and Mather, 1988, pp. 76-7)

Where a strike involves the withdrawal of services that were committed by contract, the contract is breached, and may be seen as amounting to self-dismissal. The remedies available to the employer will in such cases depend on the conditions for termination (such as notice provisions) that were built into the initial employment contracts, or any undertakings that were made by the union itself. Third parties (such as other workers or consumers) who are injured in the process will in such cases have an entitlement to damages under tort law.

The enforceability of a strike depends on the ability to prevent other workers from taking on the work previously performed by striking workers. In this sense, a strike is categorically different from a 'lock-out' (in which an employer refuses to allow workers to perform their work duties), in that in a lock-out employers do not (and probably could not) close off alternative employment opportunities for the workers involved—they do not infringe the rights of competing employers in the way in which striking workers typically attempt to infringe the rights of competing workers.

The question of enforcing strikes raises questions of how the law should treat picketing. Epstein (1983a) suggests that the basic question to be dealt with here is whether the common law prohibition of the use of force extends to the threat of force that may be presented by a (non-violent) picket. The legal 'problem' is to find an approach that penalizes and discourages the use of force without penalizing pickets that do not contain any element of force. Shenfield (1986) suggests some mechanism for police authorization of pickets, with attendant penalties for 'unauthorized' pickets or the use of force by 'authorized' pickets. This seems unnecessarily bureaucratic; picketing, like striking, may be more effectively handled through contracts between unions and employers. Secondary boycotts will, however, generally be subject to tort remedies, as these by definition constitute an infringement by a third party of the contractual rights of a group of workers and their employer.

Antitrust and Abuse of Monopoly Power in the Labour Market

In an economy open to international competition and relatively free of regulatory privileges, the incidence of real monopoly power will be rare. This does not mean that there will be many competitors active in all markets all of the time, but it does mean that where, for example, a firm systematically tries to abuse consumers by pushing up its prices and reducing its supplies to the market, other players will be encouraged into the market and bid its prices down. The *threat* of such competition can be as potent as actual competition in controlling the abuse of monopoly power.

However, recognizing that there may be situations in which neither actual competition nor the threat of competition is sufficient to rule out monopolistic behaviour at the expense of consumers, most Western economies have adopted some form of antitrust law. In New Zealand this takes the form of the Commerce Act. While such legislation typically has a wide reach, covering a great variety of contractual relationships, labour market contracts have typically, *de jure* or *de facto*, been exempted from coverage.

In the United States the jurisdiction of antitrust law, in the form of the Sherman Act of 1890, initially extended to the abuse of monopoly power in labour markets, where it was used most notably in the Pullman strike of 1894. The Clayton Act of 1914 exempted union activities from coverage by the Sherman Act, but some state courts continued to bring injunctions against strike activities up until the 1930s, when the availability of this injunctive power was virtually eliminated by the Norris-La Guardia Act. The Wagner Act of 1935, while not mentioning the Sherman Act directly, effectively gave both moral approval and legal protection to union attempts to organize — to construct legally-backed labour cartels. Some scope remains, however, for applying antitrust rules and damages where employers use unions as agents in creating or abusing monopoly power in *product* markets — which is in practice behaviour that is very difficult to identify.[10] Indeed throughout the emphasis has not been on power in labour markets so much as the exercise of union power in product markets:

> Even before labor unions enjoyed a sweeping exemption from the Sherman Act, that act, as applied by the Supreme Court, was not directed at the existence of union monopoly in the labor market or at efforts by a union to achieve such monopoly by organizing substantially all of the workers producing for a given market. The act was essentially a proscription against bad practices, such as union-instigated boycotts enforced either through consumers or through employees of secondary employers. (Meltzer, 1963, p. 154)

Fervent and extreme opposition to the formation of unions and their exercise of power, exemplified by the application of conspiracy law to unions in the early nineteenth century, had given way to widespread acceptance of union power and the exercise of this power, even where it involved quite serious breaches of the peace. As Hayek put it:

> Historically liberalism, first, far too long maintained an unjustified opposition against trade unions as such, only to collapse completely at the beginning of this century and to grant unions in many respects exemption from the ordinary law and even, to all intents and purposes, to legalize violence, coercion and intimidation. (1948, p. 117)

In New Zealand, the scope for applying the principles of the Commerce Act to situations where market power is abused in the labour market, as in the United States, is limited and uncertain. The Labour Relations Act serves to enforce both union coverage and union power. Presumably the direct intention was to create socially beneficial outcomes rather than to foster abuses of power that would not be tolerated in other markets. However, the very success of unions in achieving and sustaining wages above those which would prevail in a competitive market in the short run (if, ironically, below those which could be achieved in a competitive market in the long run), which is seen by most proponents of the current system as justifying their existence in the first place, could fulfil the tests of abuse of market power that are applied in other markets. There is thus a fundamental contradiction at present between labour law and antitrust law.

In a labour market based on freedom of contract and freedom of association unions might be expected to possess a degree of monopoly power, but for the most part to be held in check by competition from non-members for employment, and competition from other unions or agents for the allegiance of workers. Their ability to abuse consumers, investors or other workers (by pushing up wages above the competitive level) or to abuse their members' interests (by failing to represent them fairly) will in most cases be minimal. However, there is a case for making labour transactions, like other transactions, subject to antitrust law as a means of controlling such abuses of monopoly power as may arise from time to time—where a union, for example, finds itself in a position of natural monopoly.

There is similarly a case for applying antitrust to genuinely monopsonistic behaviour on the part of employers, in those rare situations where there are significant natural barriers to competition between employers. In such cases, unions may be able to play a useful role in initiating proceedings before the Commerce Commission.

4.4   Constructing a Labour Statute

> The common law approach works, I believe, because it can accommodate a healthy differentiation in individual terms and conditions. [It] can accommodate the radical individuals of the New Socialist authors, the new working class. It can accommodate, also, those—be they large or small in number—for whom the rigidities of the statutory employment market deny opportunity . . . . It can accommodate industrial conflict, and allow the participants to make proper use of the market signals and costs in the resolution of these disputes. (Mather, 1987, pp. 6-7)

The argument that employment and worker-union relationships should be based on the principle of freedom of contract, hedged by traditional common law protections against the use of force or fraud, mistreatment of those incompetent to contract for themselves and significant abuse of third-party rights, does not mean that there is no place for a special labour statute, or, more generally, for some government role in the labour market. The test of a labour statute, or of any bureaucratic involvement in labour relationships, must be that it facilitates free and fair contracting. In other words, it should be a test of whether legislative clauses or bureaucratic actions can make it easier for people to make mutually beneficial bargains. It should not be concerned with constraining the content or results of those bargains, *except* where they are detrimental to the rights of others *and* the government has some advantage in remedying this. In general, the key roles that are likely to remain for the government are in the enforcement of contracts and in funding the provision of information about employment relationships in the relatively rare situations where such information has a high 'public good' content.

While for the most part free and fair contracting can be effectively promoted and protected simply by recourse to common law principles of property, contract and tort, however, there may be some value in making the applicability of these principles explicit in a labour statute, as a guide both for participants in employment and union relationships and for judicial decisions.

The key right that any labour statute should be attempting to define and protect is the property right of each worker in his or her labour services, and the right of disposition that he or she holds with regard to those services. Attempts to legislate, by contrast, for such 'rights' as a 'right in a job' (through, for example, dismissal requirements) or an absolute 'right to strike' can in practice thwart this right of disposition (as well as the property rights of the firm's other contractual partners, in particular shareholders), as can legislation for such outcomes as minimum wages or conditions. Instead, the concern of legislation should be to protect the underlying property rights of workers, and related rights of association. Where these rights are adequately protected, the detail of employment and union relationships can more confidently be left to the parties directly concerned.

In terms of elaborating on the rights that are brought to the employment relationship, there has been an increasing emphasis in capitalist economies on making explicit rights to equal treatment. It can be argued that legislation such as the New Zealand Human Rights Commission Act 1977 would in practice be largely redundant in the context of the labour market in the presence of competition between employers for workers. The market itself severely penalizes gratuitous discrimination. This means that economically irrational preferences are for the most part costly to indulge unless they are protected by legislation:

[T]he market looks at individual human beings. It does not care if a person is a woman, a Jew or a black. It cares only that the person is able to perform a particular job better than any other applicant for the job, taking into consideration the costs of finding the best applicant. To the market, people are anonymous so long as they satisfy the ultimate economic arbiter, namely the consumer. (Walker, 1984, p. 11)

There is a parallel anonymity under the principles of classical law. Thus Epstein writes:

> Legal rules do not refer to flesh-and-blood individuals, but to those lifeless abstractions, A and B, about whom nothing else is known or — more to the point — is relevant. It may well be that certain individuals will in the end assume certain well-specified roles, but if so there is no reason to have legal institutions either subsidise or penalise their efforts. (1983a, p. 1364)

In moving to a law that specifically proscribes discriminatory activity, there are likely to be problems both in defining discrimination and in limiting the law's jurisdiction to genuine breaches of equality of treatment, as opposed to attempts to 'make good' inequality in outcomes (as in the case of affirmative action programmes). If opportunities are judged primarily by outcomes — which is the case in the 'analysis' underpinning proposals for equal employment opportunities legislation in New Zealand[11] — the result will be policies focused on targets or quotas for the representation of certain groups, rather than on the existence of 'economically irrational' barriers to entry or promotion. If specific prohibitions on discrimination are to be included in the law (and the case for doing so in a generally competitive environment is by no means clear-cut), they should be clearly focused on artificially high barriers to entry — barriers to fair process.

The cost of drawing up employment contracts and testing them against the law and the interests of the parties involved will be greatly reduced where the legal regime is simple and the principles by which it operates are clear and easily understood — the merit of the traditional tort and contractual principles lies not only in their avoidance of unnecessary rigidities and prescriptiveness, but also in their capacity to lower the costs of entering transactions. These costs may, however, be reduced even further by the availability of 'standard form' contracts that can be taken 'off the shelf' and used with the assurance that they are legally acceptable and that the interests of both parties are being protected. The provision of *optional* standard forms both for employment relationships and for worker-union relationships may significantly reduce the costs of forming these relationships (including legal costs). Given that legal and other transactional costs are typically regressive (the more litigious a process, for example, the more it will create an advantage for the well-endowed over the poorly-endowed), this will be of particular benefit to the more vulnerable, poorly resourced participants in the labour market. It will also provide an important protection for workers by providing them with information about what they might expect in a contract, what trade-offs are involved when their contract differs from the standard form, and what they might expect a union to deliver where contracts are collectively negotiated.

Lazear draws an analogy here with the standard contracts used for real estate transactions in California:

> California house sales usually occur without either side employing lawyers. There are two reasons: First, realtors use so-called standard contracts. The word *standard* signifies that it has been used by the vast majority of buyers and sellers and conveys information about the reasonableness of the contract's terms. Second, the disputes are settled more quickly and cheaply by binding arbitration, a less costly court-like procedure. There is no evidence that outcomes are any worse in California, and real resources are saved on legal services. The institutions need not be governmental; the government should involve itself in these activities only if it has an absolute advantage. The coercive power of the state may provide the advantage in enforcement. (1988, p. 372)

House sales are of course not directly analogous with employment transactions, but they are similarly important to the individuals concerned. They also, like employment relationships, can involve significant information problems. The example that Lazear cites is a result not of legislative effort but of learning by doing and of an evolving social acceptance of particular contractual forms and procedures. There may, however, be some benefit in translating such standard contracts into legislation (as is typically done in company statutes), at least as a transitional measure, so long as they are made optional.

With regard to the statutory treatment of unions, there may be value in specifically providing for coverage of unions by existing commercial law, such as company law and the law covering unincorporated societies. Where unions are voluntary associations, and lack the statutory power to infringe workers' property rights — or the property rights of third parties — there will be much less need for their activities to be governed by regulations. As has been argued above, the possibility of union abuse can probably be handled most effectively through the application of traditional tort principles, with antitrust law available to handle anti-competitive behaviour that is significantly detrimental to other parties. As in the case of employment contracts, there may be some value in clarifying these jurisdictions by statute (and, in particular, questions over the 'right' of employers to require either 'yellow dog' contracts or closed shops), and offering optional standard form contracts for the relationship between unions and workers.

The matters discussed so far revolve around the role of the government in defining what constitutes an enforceable contract, and in enforcing contracts that meet its requirements. It may be argued that there is some further role for the government in the labour market, stemming from the potentially high information costs of developing and maintaining employment and worker-union relationships, where the information involved has a significant 'public good' element. In such cases, there is a need to distinguish between an information-funding role and a regulatory role:

> [T]here is a distinction between the government provision of information and government regulation. Many arguments for regulation are actually arguments for information. Consider safety regulations. The government does not prevent citizens from skydiving, rock climbing, hang gliding, or scuba diving, all of which have higher death rates than almost any work activity. There is no reason why the government should prevent workers from taking risky jobs as long as workers are aware of the danger. Rather than establishing absolute standards, the government should rate the risks, thus providing information rather than regulation. (Lazear, 1988, p. 373)

However, the fact that the information relevant to employment contracting may be difficult or expensive to come by, particularly in such areas as occupational health and safety, is not a sufficient condition for government provision or funding of information about risks. It must also be shown that the government has some comparative advantage in fulfilling this role and, in the case of funding it, that there is some significant public good element to the information. The more specific the risks to a particular workplace or worker, the less likely it is that the government can fulfil a useful information-providing role, or that the benefits of the information cannot be privately captured. However, there will be cases in which the government's providing information may still be fruitful – in particular cases where risks have long latency periods or substantial spillover effects on other, dispersed, parties.

There will be few aspects of employment relationships apart from health and safety in which the government has any particular advantage over private individuals and organizations as a provider or funder of information. The information relevant to making employment or union relationships function well is typically concentrated in the participants, and they are generally in a position to capture the great majority of its benefits. Where they can benefit from outside assistance – whether in assessing risks, recommending strategies or providing mediation or arbitration services – they are again usually in a position both to assess the best sources for this assistance and to capture the benefits. In the absence of a government monopoly on such assistance (as, for example, in the present requirement that a government mediator be used in the negotiation of awards), there is no reason why it could not be provided by competing private sector suppliers.

If the government's role in the labour market is largely limited to enforcing contracts and, in some situations, funding the provision of information that will facilitate employment and union relationships, there would seem to be little need for a specialist labour market bureaucracy. A move towards a simpler labour law, based on principles of property, contract, and tort and focusing on the fair application of the basic rules arising from these principles rather than on the manipulation of outcomes, would also reduce any need for a separate labour court.

A special labour court system has been 'justified' in New Zealand because of a perceived need for specialization associated with the complexity of employment relationships, and a view that a 'continuing relationship' is crucial in employment, and would be harmed by the kind of adversarial conflict resolution that characterizes the general courts.[12] This presupposes that the appropriate role of the courts is, in fact, to provide a running commentary on employment relationships, balancing up interests and assessing fairness, rather than to ensure that basic liberties are protected, and that contracts that reflect them are respected and enforced. As Greenslade argues:

> Industrial parties do not bring employment disputes to employment Courts to get 'continuing' decisions. Just as Jane and John Citizen bring their gripes to conventional Courts to get a ruling on *a problem* which they can't sort out for themselves, *not* (*pace* the popular penchant for everyone to 'counsel' and 'mediate') to get wide-ranging advice – still less, god forbid, decisions – on their 'continuing relationships'. (1988, p. 2, emphasis in the original)

Similarly, Wellington argues (for the United States) that the task of the courts 'is not to impose upon the parties other people's wiser agreement, or its own notion of what would have been an intelligent agreement, or the notions of some other government official on the matter' (1968, p. 28). And in the United Kingdom, Mather argues that:

Re-establishing a Labour Court system would be to build upon some increasingly far-fetched fictions. Fictions that employment contracts are not negotiated between the parties with an intention to be bound by them. The fiction that fundamental breach of a contract by refusing to carry out its main provision, to work, only 'suspends' it. Fictions that economic loss is not caused by industrial action. Pretences that torts have not been committed. (1987, p. 8)

Instead, the main role of the courts, in labour market relationships as in other commercial relationships, should be to preserve competition (to the extent that this enhances efficiency) and to enforce the promises that, in contracting, labour market participants make to each other. These are matters in which the conventional courts are skilled, and which are, for the most part, well served by the 'adversarial' process of examining public evidence, and assessing arguments based on case law and statute to make decisions on the basis of this evidence. Recourse to the courts is in any event likely to be a rarity, being limited to those disputes which cannot adequately be resolved by privately arranged arbitration or other procedures built into contracts.

The constitution in New Zealand of a Labour Court solely responsible for disputes of right in employment relationships (disputes of interest being dealt with by the Arbitration Commission) has in theory moved its activities closer to those of the civil courts than was the case when arbitration and litigation responsibilities in the labour market were merged under a single institution (the Arbitration Court). It would thus be a relatively small step to merge these activities with those of the civil courts.

4.5 Concluding Remarks

Human society and its history are not part of a complete and knowable mechanism that can be controlled and predicted if only humans are sufficiently wise and good. And achieving order in human affairs is not a matter of finding some equilibrium state, some point of rest. Order in this sense is not something that can be confidently planned for. This does not mean that social or economic processes are inherently disorderly, however. Rather, to adopt the language of recent developments in the theory of science, they exhibit a 'spontaneous order', containing both novelties and systematic elements. As Lavoie describes it, '[t]he order we find in a spontaneous order process may be closely akin to a story whose plot we can "follow" without claiming to be able to anticipate it from the outset' (1989, p. 620).

Spontaneity in human affairs and their reliance on widely dispersed and fragmented knowledge, will, and interests means that they do not lend themselves to mechanistic social or economic planning. This is not to say that planning is impossible; it is possible, but it comes at a cost:

> The holistic planner . . . overlooks the fact that it is easy to centralize power but impossible to centralize all that knowledge which is distributed over many individual minds, and whose centralization would be necessary for the wise wielding of centralized power . . . . Unable to ascertain what is in the minds of so many individuals, he must try to simplify his problems by eliminating individual differences; he must try to control and stereotype interests and beliefs by education and propaganda. But this attempt to exercise power over minds must destroy the last possibility of finding out what people really think, for it is clearly incompatible with free thought. Ultimately, it must destroy knowledge; and the greater the gain in power, the greater will be the loss of knowledge. (Popper, 1957, pp. 89-90)

The quality of the outcomes produced by a spontaneous ordering process — and a degree of such 'independent' ordering is inevitable even in the presence of attempts at wholesale planning — will clearly depend on the rules that are imposed upon it. The best results will be those that occur where these rules succeed in facilitating, rather than suppressing or diverting, the ordering process. In order to be 'facilitative', a rule must be designed to ensure the best possible use of many different kinds of knowledge. This makes freedom, and with it a rigorous theory of individual entitlements, central ingredients for any successful system of rules. Freedom in this sense is neither licence nor anarchy; rather it rests on the unbiased application of predominantly 'adverbial' rules — rules that make competing freedoms compatible.

In this chapter it has been argued that such rules have indeed evolved through human history as human interactions, both economic and social, have evolved. These rules find expression both in social mores and traditions and in the basic principles of private law, such as the English common law. Their survival has rested in their protection of the freedoms that make relationships work. This chapter has considered how such rules might be reapplied in the area of employment relationships, where for nearly 100 years in New Zealand they have been largely supplanted by statutory law which has been quite at odds with the protection of individual freedoms and entitlements. Chapter 5 will consider what the effects might be of switching to a system based on freedom of contract, both between employers and workers and between workers and unions, and how a meaningful comparison might be made between such a system and current New Zealand arrangements.

5
The Case for Reform

> The conflict between our instincts — which, since Rousseau, have become
> identified with morality — and the moral traditions that have survived cultural
> evolution and serve to restrain these instincts is embodied in the separation
> now often drawn between certain sorts of ethical and political philosophy
> on the one hand and economics on the other. The point is not that whatever
> economists determine to be efficient is therefore right but that economic
> analysis can elucidate the usefulness of practices heretofore thought to be
> right — usefulness from the perspective of any philosophy that looks
> unfavourably on human suffering . . . . It is a betrayal of concern for others,
> then, to theorize about the just society without carefully considering the
> economic consequences of implementing such views. (Hayek, 1988a, pp.
> 501-2)

Chapter 4 sketched the outlines of a philosophically and theoretically
consistent alternative to New Zealand's current labour market
arrangements. This chapter will show that this alternative is not only
practical, but can reasonably claim to present a means to improved
outcomes for employment relationships, measured in terms of both
equity and efficiency; in other words, that reform is not only feasible
but also justified.

There are inevitably some problems in testing an unfamiliar system
against a familiar one, and in particular in defining the feasible and
likely outcomes of implementing the unfamiliar one. (The
'unfamiliarity' of the proposed system should not, however, be
overstated. Common law governance was never completely ousted
in New Zealand, even for those relationships directly covered by
the Labour Relations Act.[1]) As Cheung emphasizes with regard to
the efficiency effects of what are imagined to be 'perfect' regulations:

> To evaluate economic efficiency by comparing imaginary contracts and
> regulations is futile, for in so doing any divergence between private and social
> costs is simply imagined away. Nor is it fruitful to compare the 'imaginary'
> and the 'actual' . . . . It is the 'actual' compared with the 'actual' that is
> relevant. (1970, p. 69)

This raises the question of how to define the likely effects of
implementing a system of labour market regulation based on
freedom of contract and freedom of association. Once defined some
sensible comparison can be made between the existing system and
the proposed one — and the case for reform can be judged.

The first section of this chapter considers the various sources that can be drawn on in assessing the effects of a system based primarily on voluntary exchanges shaped by common law principles. The second section then discusses what these effects might be, in so far as they can be defined. The final section discusses the case for reform.

5.1   Forming Expectations About Outcomes

A system of labour market regulation based on freedom of contract and freedom of association is by definition targeted at processes rather than at outcomes. If the processes by which relationships between people are formed can be regarded as free of impediments to fairness and efficiency, their outcomes are also likely to be 'fair'. Indeed, they are likely to be superior to those delivered by a more *dirigiste* system, in terms of a more efficient and equitable use and compensation of scarce physical and human resources. (This does not, of course, preclude the use of taxes and transfers to provide a social 'safety net'.)

Assessing Theories

How is the validity of this expectation to be assessed? One answer might be that there is nothing so practical as a good theory. This is neither so glib nor so escapist as it sounds. In all their daily actions, people consciously or unconsciously act on theories; theories about the effects of actions, about the relationship between ends and means—rejecting what does not work in favour of what does, and constantly expanding personal knowledge in an attempt to gain some intellectual control over uncertainties. This, it may be argued, is the very nature of humans as distinct from the rest of creation, and what makes it possible for humans to some degree to shape their environment, rather than simply accommodating themselves to it.

Theorizing about sets of rules for activities that involve the interaction of diverse people is just one manifestation of this kind of process. The basis for accepting or rejecting theories in this context must ultimately be their practicality; their capacity when implemented to improve well-being. Defining this is not limited to an assessment of the results of applying them, although this will certainly be an important element both in winning broad social acceptance and in ensuring the survival of systems of rules or social arrangements based on a particular theory. But the practicality of this kind of theory can also be assessed *a priori* in terms of its relevance to human nature and human interaction.

How well, then, does the argument for a labour market system based on freedom of contract conform with what is known about how people act and interact? There are two human characteristics that are crucial to answering this question. The first is that humans assemble knowledge and act on that knowledge, and do so on an *individual* basis. Humans may participate in groups that act as groups, but these collectives have no independent *persona*; no meaning over and above the individuals who form them. As Buchanan explains:

> Only persons generate values. Specific objectives pursued by collective units or organizations, from the firm to the state, are made legitimate only because these objectives are shared among individuals who are members. Without such shared objectives, there could be no justification for collective action, including that taken by the politically organized unit, the state. (1988, pp. 254-5)

Similarly, von Mises argues that '[s]ociety does not exist apart from the thoughts and actions of people. It does not have "interests" and does not aim at anything. The same is valid for all other collectives' (1978, p. 79).

If it is the thoughts and actions of dispersed individuals that generate 'social' outcomes, the quality of rules in any 'social' sense will depend on their impact at the level of the individual; on their impact on individual rights and capacities. Thus Gewirth writes of 'grounding human rights in the necessary conditions for human action', and argues that:

> All the human rights . . . have as their aim that each person have rational autonomy in the sense of being a self-controlling, self-developing agent who can relate to other persons on a basis of mutual respect and cooperation, in contrast to being a dependent, passive recipient of the agency of others. (1984, p. 24)

And Flathman bases his 'general presumption in favour of freedom' on the human tendency 'to form desires and interests, ends and purposes, and to attempt to satisfy and to achieve them' (1987, p. 5).

The second key characteristic of human interaction is that it is fundamentally co-operative. Humans are the only animals, it is argued, which have learned the superiority of co-operation to competition as a means not only to survival but, further, to progressive improvements in well-being. Thus the serious business of human interactions is conducted primarily on the basis of co-operation for mutual gain. It is the latter which characterizes 'competition' in the economic sense:

> Competition in the market must not be confused with the pitiless biological competition prevailing between animals or plants or with the wars still waged between — unfortunately not yet completely — civilized nations. Catallactic[2] competition on the market aims at assigning to every individual that function in the social system in which he can render to all his fellow men the most valuable of the services he is able to perform. (von Mises, 1978, p. 88)

Society can be seen as the result of the largely co-operative interactions of individuals. The nature of this co-operation (and the likelihood that it will be overtaken by baser competitive instincts, in the sense that we talk of the 'law of the jungle') and the resultant 'spontaneous ordering' will depend on the framework of laws, social mores and moral traditions within which it takes place.

The experience in New Zealand under a labour relations law premised on a belief that the employment relationship is fundamentally adversarial provides an excellent example of how an unhelpful law can undermine both individual control over and responsibility for the effects of actions (by subsuming the interests of the individual to the interests of the collective — in this case the monopoly union), and the otherwise co-operative nature of economic relationships. Put simply, the theory on which it was based — and on which policy initiatives in the labour market by and large continue to be based — is inconsistent with what is known about how individuals behave. A policy based on assuring certain outcomes through some means of collective coercion disregards the importance of the nature of human action — the process of assembling the knowledge that enables means to be selected for achieving desired ends.

A theory that denies the importance of individual incentives and instead looks to impose collective outcomes undermines the role of individuals and the creative use of the information held by individuals in selecting and pursuing their desired outcomes. It also imposes a myth of collectivism; the notion that collectives have meaning over and above the meaning of their members. On both counts, it is unrealistic — it misses the point about the nature of individuals and of society. It is also impractical; it tells not how to understand human actions and relationships, and thus how to facilitate them, but only how to over-rule them.

By contrast, a rule system based on a theory that recognizes the importance of individual human action, both in utilizing knowledge and pursuing preferences, will have some hope of facilitating that action — and the effective (co-operative) functioning of such collective organizations as individuals choose to form. It is reasonable to suggest that a system of rules — whether legal or moral — based on the liberty of individuals to act and to co-operate will be a system with a good chance of working in terms of meeting the ends — both individual and collective — that they desire.

Empirical Analogies

Considering its theoretical consistency or practicality is not the only way of assessing the case for implementing a system such as that proposed in Chapter 4. It is also possible to form expectations about the results that it would yield by drawing analogies with experience in other, less regulated parts of the New Zealand economy and in the New Zealand labour market in the course of reform in other markets, and with the experience of other countries. Two kinds of analogies can be drawn here. The first is between the effects of similarly motivated laws in different markets within a single country. The second is between similarly motivated laws in the same market in different countries. Both analogies are of course to some degree imperfect — labour is not an identical commodity to capital, for example, and the American labour market is set in a rather different social and legal tradition from the New Zealand one. Nevertheless, such comparisons are sufficiently apposite to yield useful insights on the likely effects of adopting a more liberal labour market regime in New Zealand.

The Relevance of Reform in Other Sectors in New Zealand
The present system of labour market law in New Zealand is effectively based on a refusal to acknowledge that an analogy can be drawn between employment and other commercial relationships; this is the essence of the proclamation that 'labour is not a commodity' and that wages should be 'taken out of competition'. The role of co-operation and of voluntary exchange as a means to mutual benefit has implicitly been accepted — if at times warily — in the laws shaping other commercial relationships, but has largely been ignored with respect to employment relationships. New Zealand has not been alone in this. Fischel comments that while corporate law in the United States recognizes that 'it is in the interest of the firm (entrepreneur) to adopt efficient contractual arrangements because the firm pays for inefficiencies through a higher cost of capital', 'labor law generally assumes that unless firms are subjected to direct regulation, they will adopt governance mechanisms that oppress labor' (1984, pp. 1063-4).

In the 1980s in New Zealand there were significant regulatory reforms in product markets and finance markets, as well as extensive structural reforms in the public sector. In each case, the emphasis has been on clarifying the objectives of government legislative or regulatory involvement in economic relationships, and adopting an approach aimed at facilitating these relationships in such a way as to provide incentives for the efficient use of resources, rather than determine their use directly. There is a renewed emphasis on exposure to competition and the threat of competition as a means to fair and efficient outcomes, and there have been concerted attempts to separate out the pursuit of distributional objectives from the pursuit of general efficiency objectives.

This last is particularly clear in the case of the creation of state-owned enterprises to undertake the trading activities previously conducted by government departments, the removal of their regulatory advantages and disadvantages (and hence their increased exposure to competition) and the explicit separation of trading activities from the 'social' policy concerns of these departments. This development has resulted in considerable efficiency gains in such areas as electricity generation and transmission, telecommunications, state-run forests and state-run coal production – gains that might be expected to be further enhanced as privatization exposes these operations to competition in equity markets. The distributional goals formerly woven into the state's involvement in these activities are now more clearly seen as the domain of explicit tax and transfer policies.

In product markets, the removal of production subsidies and export incentives, the elimination of import licensing in favour of tariffs and the progressive reduction of these tariffs have greatly enhanced the responsiveness of industry to the needs and preferences of consumers. Increased exposure to international competition and the erosion or removal of sectoral regulatory advantages have generated an increasing concern with productivity and innovation, focusing on both costs and quality.

It is the developments that have occurred in finance markets, however, that are of most direct relevance to the case for labour market reform. These developments included the removal of interest rate controls and exchange controls and the floating of the dollar, a more rigorous approach to monetary management, liberalization of the banking sector to enable the development of competitive merchant banking and increased competition among trading banks, and changes in prudential policy (including the abolition of reserve ratio requirements and credit guidelines) which aimed at promoting a high degree of self-regulation.[3] The general concern was to enhance competition and improve price signalling in finance markets, and thus to facilitate the direction of financial and thereby physical resources to their best possible uses, raising the average rate of return on investment:

> More specifically, as a wider range of domestic and overseas investments became eligible to compete for the available domestic savings, those activities previously earning a low return might have been expected to phase out and new higher return (higher risk) growth sectors to emerge. Over a sustained period, by shifting resources away from poorly performing sectors towards new growth areas in the economy, this process may be expected to generate an increase in the productive potential of the national economy. (Carey and Spencer, 1989, pp. 65-6)

Early indications are that there have been some significant changes in companies' approaches to financial management, and to the institutional infrastructure in which investment takes place. Carey and Spencer cite the following developments:

> An increasing sophistication in investment management has brought a greater flexibility to the use of funds and a broader perspective to the analysis and selection of investment opportunities. In turn, these developments have imposed a greater discipline on individual enterprises, ensuring that they work to achieve the maximum return on allocated investment funds. In a similar vein, large industrial companies have tended to broaden their horizons so that expertise in a particular industry can be applied to maximise returns in a global market context rather than being limited to the parameters of the small New Zealand marketplace. (1989, p. 68)

This is not to say that people have not made mistakes in learning their way into this new regime; learning the responsibilities that go with relative freedom itself takes time. However, the natural desire to avoid the costs of such mistakes does not necessarily justify the wave of regulatory fervour aimed at creating new 'protections' that followed the share market 'crash' of October 1987. Increased protection for savers and investors must instead be recognized as lodged primarily in the increased investment options offered by the financial reforms of 1984-1985 and the improved investor information afforded by the simplification and clarification of rules surrounding commercial contracts.

There is a direct analogy here with arguments for reform in the labour market, and the concern that in a less regulated system the potential for 'exploitation' would greatly increase. However, the success of a more liberal system does not depend on ubiquitous prudence (although such a system is likely to foster increased responsibility). As Fischel writes:

> It is worth emphasising that I am not claiming that workers will never enter into bargains that do not work well *ex post*; I am not even claiming that all workers will make prudent bargains as judged *ex ante*. Investors do not always make perfect bargains either. My point is that it is extremely unlikely that either workers or investors will be systematically exploited in any meaningful sense. The interest of the firm in minimizing the cost of all inputs in the production process will cause it to adopt the contractual mechanisms that best allay workers' and investors' rational concerns. (1984, p. 1068)

The regulatory reforms in finance and product markets and in the public sector have not only been significant as role models for reform and pointers to the likely effects of reform in the labour market. They have also affected labour market relationships directly.

Increased competition both for consumers and for investment funds, by focusing attention on productivity and success in innovation, has necessarily increased the importance of well-functioning employment relationships and management structures. This in turn has created a need to reconsider how relationships in the workplace should be approached – how they can be developed so as to elicit co-operation, to draw on and reward the diverse skills of all participants in the workplace, and to promote an atmosphere of trust and mutual reliance. There seems to be an increasing recognition that the ability to compete successfully in the long term will depend not on an ability to drive down wages and conditions, but on an ability to raise productivity – and thus remuneration – through a combination of good employment conditions and good management practices. This has been reflected in such developments as the negotiation of site agreements and formal employee participation processes at Mitsubishi and Nissan (the motor vehicle industry being subjected to ongoing reductions in protection) and New Zealand Steel (which was subjected to increased competition as it passed out of government ownership and protection). Blandy and Baker, commenting on a series of case studies of New Zealand companies, note that:

> The majority . . . were responding to trade liberalisation by innovating, trying to improve productivity, and by 'getting close to their people', 'winning the battle for hearts and minds', and so on. In other words, a majority of enterprises had adopted a *dynamic* (and positive) response. This group conceded that 'good old New Zealand' offered little incentive to increase productivity (enterprises settled for a quiet life), to innovate or to 'mix it' in the market place. They also regarded the administered wage system

(through the central institutions), and their own remoteness from their own people, as consistent with their sheltered existence in the product markets.

Virtually all saw the changes in the product market environment brought about by trade liberalisation as the factor which had spurred them towards innovation and changes in management style in industrial and personnel relations. It is interesting to note, then, that changes in approach to the labour market were effected by changes in the product market environment. (1987, pp. 44-5, emphasis in the original)

They also record an emphasis on achieving cost savings through productivity gains. The managers who were interviewed asserted that the alternative of forcing down wages would have been inconsistent with any sound personnel policy, and would have resulted in the loss of much-needed productive workers.

Blandy and Baker's findings indicate that the impact of increased competition on incentives for efficient resource use has had benefits not only in the reformed sectors but also in the labour market, and, further, that there are strong commercial incentives to extend these benefits to workers. However, the capacity of financial and product market reforms to improve the prospects of workers as they have improved the prospects of savers and consumers is currently limited by regulatory barriers to innovation in employment relationships. Such progress as has been made has been hard won, and there are persistent incentives to substitute capital for labour — or to move offshore — instead. Imbalances in the reform process, and in particular the very different approaches adopted in finance and labour markets, have as a result led to a noticeably uneven sharing of the burdens of adjustment, including a dramatic increase in the rate of unemployment. This is not to say that a more liberal approach in the labour market would have meant that financial and product market restructuring would have had no impact on unemployment. However, it can be argued that the level, persistence and severely regressive incidence of unemployment that has accompanied restructuring might have been reduced had labour market institutions been more responsive to the changes that were occurring in industry.

The Experience of Other Countries

Indications of the likely effects of labour market reform in New Zealand can also be inferred from the labour market experience of other countries with more liberal regimes. There are of course dangers in attempting either to transplant another country's regulatory system or to predict domestic outcomes by direct reference to the outcomes that other countries have achieved. As the previous section has illustrated, outcomes in labour markets cannot be separated from the regulatory regime that applies in other markets. Nor can they be separated from the history and evolving institutions and social mores of the country in which they occur.

However, it is possible to learn from the experience of countries where elements of freedom of contract are more pronounced than in New Zealand. Thus, for example, it is possible to draw insights from the experience of the United States, where there has been greater freedom with regard to union membership, so long as it is recognized that the particular outcomes achieved are in part a consequence of a pattern of regulation that New Zealanders might be unwilling to replicate (such as heavy-handed oversight of bargaining or restrictions on company unions). Despite significant cultural differences, there is much to learn from the experience of Japan (with its relatively non-adversarial unions and its strong emphasis on participation mechanisms), as well as from the United Kingdom's attempts to reform employment relationships so as to place increased emphasis on individual rights and reduce union immunities.

The following section draws both on the predictions of theory and on such empirical experience to suggest the kinds of outcomes likely were labour market law to be reformed to emphasize freedom of contract.

5.2 The Practical Implications of Freedom of Contract

One of the crucial reasons for advocating a system based on freedom of contract is the recognition that it is simply not possible to take account of all individual knowledge and preferences so as to make proclamations from on high about welfare-maximizing outcomes or ways of doing things. By similar reasoning, it is not possible to predict what processes and outcomes individuals will come up with in a legal regime that is facilitative rather than directive. However, it is possible to form some general expectations both about the evolution of contracting mechanisms and about the delivery of outcomes that conform with aspirations to fairness and efficiency. This section begins with some general remarks about likely developments in employment relationships. It then discusses the capacity of a system of the kind proposed to deliver desired outcomes in the specific areas of occupational safety and health, the equitable treatment of women and disadvantaged minorities, worker participation, and training and career development, and, more generally, income and employment levels.

Contracting Under a Liberalized Regime

In economic terms, repeal of the labor codes would undermine monopoly in labor markets and facilitate entry into these markets. Opening previously restricted markets tends to punish the guilty and reward the innocent by releasing pressures to equalize rewards. The supra-competitive wage rates of unions will be forced to adjust to competition due to new opportunities for non union workers and the unemployed. The flexibility of the price system, its efficiency in coordinating resource flows, the tendency of markets to fully employ our labor and capital, and our competitiveness in international markets would all improve. The economic pie would expand and redistribution in favor of union officials and members would erode. (Reynolds, 1986, pp. 236-7)

Just as in the financial sector liberalization led to greater diversity of institutional arrangements and of options for savers and investors, so reform in the labour market could be expected to generate increased variety in contracting arrangements, the form and activities of unions, and employment relationships themselves. In each case, there would be increased competitive pressure on those involved to generate arrangements and outcomes that were of genuine mutual benefit — pressure on unions to serve the interests of their members, pressure on employers to offer remuneration and conditions of employment that will attract the kinds of workers that they need, and pressure on workers to acquire needed skills and perform productively. This competitive pressure — in various manifestations — would serve a dual purpose, both facilitating the process of directing labour resources to the most productive uses and the development of effective mechanisms for participation and representation, and providing protections against 'exploitative' or unjustifiably discriminatory behaviour.

One likely result of pressures for increased innovation in employment relationships would be the erosion of the traditional categories of contracts 'of service' and contracts 'for service'. (Mather (1987) argues that this is, indeed, happening in the United Kingdom.) Recent proposals to bring some categories of independent contractors within the ambit of the Labour Relations Act, effectively redefining some contracts for service as contracts of service, may be seen as illustrating the tensions — and power games — created by the false distinction currently made in New Zealand between employment and other commercial contracts. As the New Zealand Business Roundtable argued in its submission on these proposals:

> [V]ariety in itself is not evidence that some workers are more susceptible
> to exploitation than others, or more in need of special protections above
> those provided by a well-functioning labour market and a strong body of
> contractual law . . . [T]he belief that one category of workers, involved in
> what have been termed 'contracts of service', does require special protection
> has given rise to a complex body of industrial relations law, and rules have
> evolved to determine the coverage of this law. Extending this coverage to
> workers deemed 'dependent' on a company would create considerable
> problems of definition and create harmful anomalies, both between
> contractors with different levels of involvement with a single company and
> between individual contractors and contracting companies substantially
> involved with the same company. (1988b, p. 10)

The existing anomalies in the treatment of workers and contractors
may be argued to create unnecessarily rigid categorization of
contracts involving labour. The use of independent contracts by both
workers and companies as a means of escaping coverage by the
Labour Relations Act — rather than purely because such contracts
are the best means of ensuring performance and allocating risk —
may be seen as generating unnecessary inefficiencies in the form of
contracts and work relationships. Some protections may well be lost
in the process — the freedom to choose a form of work relationship
according to how well it suits one's needs and preferences, rather
than how well it avoids regulatory restrictions, is an important means
of ensuring that both workers' and companies' interests are
protected. An erosion of the distinction currently made between
employment contracts and other commercial contracts would remove
much of this problem, and in the process provide scope for increased
innovation in incentive-creation and risk-handling in contracts
involving labour services.

There is an increasing body of theoretical work examining the
kinds of contracts that can emerge in labour markets in response
to the problems of minimizing opportunism, encouraging
performance, promoting a sense of equity and dealing with the risks
that attach to employment relationships.[4] These suggest a high
degree of sophistication both in remuneration structures and in the
form of contracts — including the development of contracts that
emphasize agreement on procedures for the maintenance of
relationships and facilitation of participation as much as on initial
conditions and pay. As Crocker and Masten emphasize, there are
many ways of realizing the performance that both parties seek from
a contract which are not dependent on simply mechanically enforcing
original conditions:

> In that regard, contracts not so much define the terms of trade as establish

the procedures and alter the threat points from which parties compete over the division of transactional surpluses. An important element in designing contracts then becomes economizing on the costs associated with resolving disputes and governing exchange. (1988, pp. 1-2)

Precisely what form a contract takes—its reliance on the provision of structures for the support of ongoing negotiations relative to specific terms and conditions—will vary according to the nature of the employment relationship involved; for example, in the scope for opportunism and the extent of investment required of workers in firm-specific human capital. Precision in terms can be costly to achieve, especially in an uncertain economic environment, but it can help to reduce the scope for opportunism on the part of both employer and employee. More open-ended contracts are less costly to write, but can greatly increase the scope for opportunism, and the costs that this can impose. For this reason, the allocation and reward of labour services over time within a firm will typically be achieved by a combination of contract and personnel policy design and incentive mechanisms. The role of the market is not, however, limited to situations where workers are entering or leaving an employment relationship. Rather the competitive pressure to which firms are subjected in labour markets (as well as in capital and output markets) will act to constrain the contractual options available to employers, and create pressures to develop employment relationships that not only commence with an expectation of mutual benefit, but maintain the mutuality of that benefit over time.

With regard to collective contracting, some change could be expected in the extent of union coverage. Countries where union membership receives less statutory support than in New Zealand typically have a lower level of unionization. Moreover, they have experienced a declining level of unionization over time, as the role of part-time employment, female participation in the labour force and the significance of the service sector have increased. Thus in the United States, for example, unionization of the non-agricultural work-force peaked at around 35% in 1955, but declined to around 15% by 1989. As there was a surge in unionization in the public sector from the early 1960s, this measure of decline understates the reduction in unionization in the private sector, where its level has been more sensitive to structural changes and increasing international competition. This decline is seen by some commentators as largely the result of increased managerial resistance to unions, reflected in the increased number of unfair labour practice charges being brought before the National Labor Relations Board. However, empirical work by Flanagan (1986) suggests that broader economic factors have been a more significant explanator of this decline. Becker emphasizes as well the increasing role of the government in duplicating services formerly offered only by unions:

> [T]he most significant causes of decline in union membership since 1955 are laws that protect workers against unfair dismissal and the growth of unemployment compensation, Social Security payments, medicare, and other government transfer payments. Workers no longer need to rely on unions for protection against job loss and the expense of ill health and old age. (1988b, p. 13)

There has been a similar decline in unionization in the United Kingdom, from around 44% in 1979 to 33% in 1989 — a period in which the Thatcher Government was introducing a series of reforms aimed at individualizing worker rights, reducing union immunities, increasing the internal accountability of unions and reducing the scope for closed shops (Secretary of State for Employment, 1989). Metcalf (1989) attributes the decline to four factors besides these policy changes: high unemployment and above average increases in real wages, structural changes both in industry (including privatization) and in work-force participation, a decreased willingness on the part of employers to recognize unions, and the behaviour of unions themselves. Significant increases in self-employment (Mather, 1987) were arguably also a factor.

The extent of de-unionization that might accompany a move to basing union membership on the free choice of workers cannot, however, be assessed directly from such international experience. In particular, competition between unions and other worker organizations for members under the kind of regime proposed could be expected to yield greater union accountability than yet prevails either in the United Kingdom or in the United States. In these countries unions both retain some significant statutory protections and are submitted to regulatory constraints — such as the prescription of balloting procedures in the United Kingdom and the restriction on company-sponsored unions and cumbersome 'fair representation' requirements in the United States. Such interventions make unions less responsive — and less able to respond — to diverse worker preferences and work situations, and arguably therefore make union membership less attractive than it would be under the kind of system proposed here.

Further, it is possible that more unionization would remain after regulatory reform than would have occurred had there never been intervention in favour of unions:

On the one hand, some amount of collective behaviour is forced by the
regulatory framework and that would disappear with deregulation. On the
other hand, information is now widespread regarding the 'natural' benefits
of collective action; also, one could argue that both employers and employees
would be less resistant to the phenomenon were its currently coercive nature
transformed into voluntary action predicated upon rational self-interest.
Finally . . . deregulation would provide a greater justification for collective
action. Regulation not only forecloses options, but also reduces the amount
of information available about the available options. In short, deregulation
might well increase the benefits of collective action for employees. (Heldman
et al., 1981, pp. 148-9)

Regulatory reform could also be expected to encourage innovation
in the form, organization and functions of unions, and the
development of other kinds of intermediaries and agencies used by
workers and employers in negotiating and maintaining their
relationships with each other.

Some change could be expected in the scope of union coverage
and the level at which collective negotiations take place. In
particular, it is likely that there would be greater use of enterprise-
and workplace-based unions and bargaining, reflecting the common
interests of the employees of a single employer that may well not
extend to other employees in the same occupation or industry, as
well as the greater degree of accountability that may be achieved
in relatively compact union organizations. However, it is possible
that in some situations workers would be better served by unions
operating on a craft or industry basis, and there is no reason why
such union structures should be proscribed. As the New Zealand
Business Roundtable argued in its submission on the 1985 Green
Paper on labour market reform:

It may be that for certain occupational groups there will continue to be a
situation where, even with the rights and freedoms to form enterprise unions
or sign individual contracts, the competitive outcome will still be a craft
union. This situation should, however, be resolved by competitive behaviour
and not by decree or regulation. The real test will be whether there is genuine
competition for places in the professional association or union, or whether,
on the contrary, there are barriers to entry to the craft which are effectively
an attempt to monopolise the activity. (1986, p. 34)

There will also be scope for the development of intermediaries
or workers' organizations that do not conform to traditional union
models. For example, in Japan unionization has fallen from around
35% in 1975 to around 28% in 1989—a decline which has been
attributed at least in part to legal changes that have made it more
difficult to unionize new companies (Clark, 1989). However, a 1988

survey found that while only 20% of newly established firms were unionized in a formal sense, most others had some form of workers' organization or 'Shainkai', providing grievance mechanisms and a channel for worker-management communication. These 'Shainkai' appear to be particularly successful in the service sector:

> In the non-unionized sector, the Shainkai is more likely to hold elections to choose representatives, is more likely to have a function to discuss working conditions and other related issues, and promotes membership for non-regular workers. For these reasons, the Shainkai can serve as an alternative to unions in the growing service economy in Japan, where the traditional unions have fared poorly. (Osawa, 1989, p. 7)

In the United Kingdom, where the reforms since 1979 have led in some companies to employment contracting on an individual basis, there have been some novel collective agreements, including agreements that follow participation-oriented Japanese models.[5] There have also been moves on the part of some unions to modify their approach so as to accommodate increasing self-employment; the Electrical Electronic Telecommunications and Plumbing Union, for example, has proposed the establishment of a labour agency for self-employed workers run jointly with the Electrical Contractors Association. Similar developments have occurred in the unionized sector in the United States, in particular in the form of an increased emphasis on employee involvement (Hoerr, 1989). These privately motivated developments are in strong contrast to attempts to legislate for worker participation, in particular in strategic decision-making, in countries such as West Germany, which have been strongly resisted by employers.[6]

A related possibility is that there would be innovation in the services offered by unions in order to attract workers. The 'Shainkai' in Japan offer one model for this. The early history of unions, in particular in the United Kingdom, also provides some insights on the services that unions might provide in a more competitive environment. The unions that arose in the United Kingdom in the early nineteenth century were informal and club-like, in marked contrast to the unions that were to arise out of political movements in Europe. Their initial role was predominantly as friendly societies; their role evolved only gradually to include the negotiation of pay and conditions, and later pressure for a widened political franchise:

> Indeed, many assumed the name 'Friendly Society' as part of their title as a deliberate strategy to win public support for and to legitimize their activities.

Their supporters successfully built up a picture in the public eye of unions as 'sober insurance societies whose aims were business like and entirely respectable' . . . . Certainly, the benefits they offered were comprehensive, covering not only sickness and funeral expenses, but also 'out-of-work' and 'tool' benefits. (Beenstock and Brasse, 1986, p. 12)

Innovations of this kind, for example, in the creation of union-sponsored medical centres, have already begun to occur in New Zealand. Under a system of increased union accountability and decentralization, considerable further scope for the tailoring of services to the needs of diverse groups of workers could be expected.

Performance in Employment Relations

In the period since the introduction of the Labour Relations Act, there have been a number of policy proposals which have reflected a concern with the capacity of existing employment arrangements to deliver 'socially desired' outcomes, in particular in an environment subject to international competitive pressure. This section considers four of these concerns; health and safety in the workplace, equity for women and disadvantaged minorities, worker participation, and training. The broader question of the impact of reform on incomes and employment is then considered.

Occupational Safety and Health

A frequently voiced concern is that increased competitive pressures, whether in product markets or in the labour market, will induce employers to cut corners in providing for workplace safety and health. At the same time, the burden that can be imposed by rigid safety and health regulations has been recognized, and there have been some important moves to shift the emphasis to performance rather than design standards, and to streamline the regulatory process. There have also been attempts to encourage workplace participation in making decisions about health and safety issues. The low level of adoption of the resulting voluntary code for participation has caused some concern both within the context of health and safety and in terms of a more general desire to encourage worker participation.

Good performance in terms of workplace safety and health may be seen as an important element in promoting productivity. This has both direct physical aspects — the promotion of health and safety can reduce absenteeism, downtime and labour turnover — and less direct psychological aspects, arising from the recognition by workers that their well-being is taken seriously and that their ongoing contribution to the firm is valued. Health and safety programmes thus represent an investment with both tangible and intangible benefits.

Health and safety in the workplace have traditionally been regarded as something delivered by the employer to his or her work-force by conforming to certain designs for equipment, workplace layout or work practices. In practice, there is a varying capacity on the part of workers to affect health and safety outcomes directly, depending on the kind of work in which they are engaged and the way in which this work is organized. An effective health and safety regime will therefore be one that recognizes that health and safety are not only matters of mutual interest for employers and workers, but also to some extent a shared responsibility. This creates a need to draw on the differing capabilities of and information available to workers and management, so as to ensure that all participants in the workplace have incentives to deal with health and safety risks efficiently. In turn, this requires a work environment in which employers and workers are able to negotiate constructively about how health and safety problems should be handled and who should be accountable for handling them — whether through changes in the physical work environment or work practices, or, where it is not feasible to greatly reduce risks by making work safer or healthier, through the purchase of accident or health insurance.[7]

It can be argued that the degree of workplace co-operation and information-sharing required for an efficient health and safety programme within an enterprise or workplace has been discouraged by the current labour relations regime, with its perpetuation of centralized negotiation over relatively limited and stylized aspects of work conditions, and of an adversarial approach to employment relations. The voluntary code of practice for worker participation in resolving health and safety issues represented an attempt to overcome such problems. The low level of adoption of this programme has been regarded by many as reflecting an unwillingness on the part of employers to contemplate worker participation unless coerced into doing so.

However, the low level of compliance may instead reflect the fact that the nature of representation stipulated in the code, and the way in which the responsibilities of health and safety representatives are defined, are unlikely to be the best means of protecting employee interests in all workplaces. For example, some companies have found that a system using employee representatives is inferior to a system involving broader, direct employee participation. But there are also disincentives in the broader regulatory environment, both through the no-fault Accident Compensation Scheme and the labour relations system, to an effective approach to either health and safety or employee participation.

If the kind of labour relations regime proposed in this study were adopted, there would be both greater scope for developing mechanisms at an enterprise, workplace or, where relevant, individual level for negotiating on health and safety issues and developing co-operative solutions. One reason for this is that unions and other representative organizations would be under greater pressure to take account of differences in work environments and worker preferences across workplaces or companies, and even within them, and to become actively involved in providing workers with information about the kinds of risks that they face. A second reason is that employers would face increased competitive pressure to respond to the needs of workers and, for the sake of productivity, to pursue continuously attempts to improve the effectiveness of their investment in health and safety.

The result would be a greater ability to rely on solutions to workplace health and safety issues generated within the workplace or enterprise, rather than on solutions imposed by central organizations — be they unions or government bureaucracies. This does not mean that there would be no remaining role for the government, as situations are likely to continue to arise where workplace hazards have large and privately irresolvable effects on third parties, or where hazards are poorly understood and illness follows only after a long lag. The role of the government in helping to resolve this kind of problem would be primarily facilitative, rather than directive, however, aimed at helping those involved to make better-informed choices. This applies as much, if not more, to more vulnerable workers as to relatively advantaged ones, as Viscusi argues:

> Efforts to promote . . . risk regulations on the basis that they enhance worker rights are certainly misguided. Uniform standards do not enlarge worker choices; they deprive workers of the opportunity to select the job most appropriate to their own risk preferences. The actual 'rights' issue involved is whether those in upper income groups have a right to impose their job risk preferences on the poor. A superior method of expanding worker rights is to provide the risk information that will enable workers to make choices that better reflect their individual preferences. (1983, p. 80)

Equity in Employment
As discussed in Chapter 3, attempts to promote equity in

employment relationships by legislating for 'equitable' outcomes, either through target-based equal employment opportunity programmes or through comparable worth policies, can not only reduce economic efficiency but also impose heavy costs on the most vulnerable members of the groups they are intended to protect. This does not imply that equity should not be a concern in the current system, however. Many current institutions create barriers to entry, to promotion, to the development of work conditions amenable in particular to working mothers, and to improving earnings prospects for women and disadvantaged groups. As Williams argues with regard to continuing barriers to the advancement of blacks in the United States:

> A wide variety of national and state policies — laws setting minimum wages, the national labor law fostering union monopolies, occupational and business licensing laws, and regulatory laws like those administered by the Interstate Commerce Commission — discriminate against whole classes of individuals. Specifically, they discriminate against latecomers, against those without political clout, against those having little skills or capital — which means, almost by definition, disadvantaged minorities . . . . The basic problem that blacks now face in the United States is not one of malevolent racial prejudices *per se*, though it may have been that in the past. It is, rather, one of government restrictions on voluntary exchange . . . . To the extent that emotionally charged words such as exploitation and racism are to have an economic meaning, they should refer to the myriad of collusive agreements, backed up by the government, whereby disadvantaged minorities are subjected to continuing disadvantage. (1979, p. 48)

Reform of the labour market system to place an emphasis on the freedom to contract of individual workers would lead to the erosion of many of these barriers. For example, making union membership a matter of individual choice would place increased pressure on union officials to recognize the differing needs of the workers that they represent — such as the interest of working mothers in flexible or reduced hours, work-sharing and childcare facilities. (This is particularly significant because the 'wage gap' applies primarily to married women. Studies comparing unmarried women and unmarried men in Canada and the United States show only negligible differences in earnings.[8]) Where an existing union was not performing adequately in representing these interests, there would be scope for the women involved to form their own union or to negotiate directly with employers on an individual basis. The scope for union opposition to the advancement of women, as in the case of the Air New Zealand hostesses blocked in their attempts at promotion, would also be greatly reduced.

Increased competition between employers would similarly increase their sensitivity to the needs and preferences of different groups of workers, whether these concerns are cultural (such as the desire by Māori workers for tangi leave), related to physical disability (such as the provision of wheelchair access or the adaptation of work centres to accommodate certain disabilities) or related to the problems of combining work and child-rearing — by both men and women. Thus Gapper (1988), for example, describes a gradual move by British employers, facing increased competition for workers as a result of the tailing off of the baby boom, to make hours and conditions more congenial to working mothers. The practical benefits of doing so are becoming increasingly clear; data from the United States suggest that having a childcare centre on site reduces female absenteeism by around 25% and can cut female staff turnover by as much as 40%. Similar benefits have been estimated in Australia (*National Business Review*, 9 August 1989).

There is also broader-brush evidence of the ability of relatively unfettered markets to enhance the employment and remuneration opportunities of women. Becker points out that while the Reagan administration was criticized by women's groups for its opposition to the Equal Rights Amendment and to comparable worth laws, this was a period in which the unemployment rates of both black and white women declined and the differential between men's and women's median earnings narrowed by seven percentage points (from 39 percentage points in 1980 to 32 percentage points in 1987):

> This strong improvement in the position of women is all the more remarkable since the gender wage gap remained fixed at about 40 percentage points from the late 1950s to the end of the 1970s, and many people believed that the gap would never shrink without extensive government help . . . . The full employment environment, the shift towards a service economy, increased training, and higher labor-force participation all contributed to women's economic advancement. (1988a, p. 12)

For these kinds of reasons, as Paul argues:

> Rather than condemning the market system, feminists ought to be glorying in it, for it has proved remarkably adaptable to women's evolving desire to work full-time, to work throughout their lives, and to work in new and challenging jobs . . . . Why emphasize women's disadvantages — their alleged victimization, their helplessness — when feminism rightly understood should glory in women's remarkable advances? Indeed, it is the opponents of comparable worth, rather than its advocates, who have a positive attitude towards women's abilities, who see women as capable of determining what is in their own best interests and working for these goals in the marketplace alongside men, without any special privileges. (1989, p. 129)

However, in order to facilitate voluntary, market means to women's advancement, and the advancement of other presently disadvantaged groups, there does remain some scope for government action beyond a fundamental reform of labour market law. There may be a role for government collaboration in breaking down sexual or racial stereotypes that are both inaccurate and harmful, for example, through attention to the way in which legislation is worded, public sector activities are conducted, and personnel and remuneration policies in the public sector are operated. In its involvement in compulsory education, it may have a role in breaking down conscious or sub-conscious discrimination on the part of teachers and administrators and encouraging teachers to broaden children's perceptions of the work opportunities available to them. (This is potentially very important in that studies suggest that many children have by the age of eleven formed a firm view of what their future career will be.) Reform of town planning law may also be relevant, for example, to remove restrictive requirements in the provision of childcare facilities that currently serve as a barrier to workplace creches and childcare centres.

Policies aimed at breaking down irrelevant or unfair stereotypes and at widening employment opportunities by reducing labour market barriers to the employment and promotion of women and disadvantaged groups—barriers which have served to protect employers from the consequences of unfair treatment—will need time to take effect. However, the temptation to 'hasten history' by placing what are intended to be transient restrictions on outcomes is to be avoided. There are considerable risks to such interventions, not only in terms of loss of employment and regressive distributional effects. In particular, there is a danger that such short-term measures will divert attention from the causes of inequity, and in so doing perpetuate them.

Worker Participation

Proponents of industrial democracy assert that labor participation in the management of firms would replace conflict with cooperation. The crucial analytical error of this assertion derives from the failure to comprehend the social consequences of weakening the right of ownership. The right of ownership is, in fact, a social rather than a private institution. Its major social consequence is that the guidance of production is transferred from a few individuals (regulators, planners and bureaucrats) with limited knowledge to a social (free market) process that relies upon and uses the knowledge of all. (Pejovich, 1984, p. 6)

Because employment relationships depend crucially on interaction and mutual understanding, they are in their essence co-operative. An important condition for such co-operation to work is the protection of the rights that employers and workers bring to such relationships; in employers' case the property rights of shareholders who bear the residual risks associated with the company's activities, and in workers' case their property rights in their own labour. Effective and sustainable participation by employees in information-sharing, consultation and decision-making within a company will depend on its capacity to enhance the protection of these rights and the mutual benefits of the relationship. Where instead the mechanisms chosen for participation involve the erosion of the rights of shareholders — for example, through worker participation in, but not accountability for, strategic decision-making — the benefits to the work relationship, too, are likely to erode over time, as the incentives for equity investment are eroded.[9]

On the other hand, the quality and productivity of an employment relationship will depend on the success of the partners in making use of their differing abilities and information, and allocating decisions and responsibility for decisions to those most able to undertake them. As the employers surveyed by Blandy and Baker (1987) emphasized, an important response to increased competition in product markets was to 'get closer to the workers', and improvement in the quality of employment relationships was seen as a primary means of increasing productivity and surviving — thus protecting jobs. A number of New Zealand companies, especially, but not exclusively, companies with strong international connections, have developed sophisticated approaches to management and employment relations that afford means of information-sharing, consultation and devolution of responsibility, and elaborate mechanisms for the protection of employee rights. In such commonly cited examples as Nissan and New Zealand Steel, the possibility of enterprise-level bargaining (as opposed to coverage by national awards) has been an important factor in enabling these systems to develop.

There has been a long tradition of such practices in Japan, and they are now being widely copied in such countries as the United Kingdom and the United States — in particular as a means to maintaining the viability of companies involved in heavy industry. Innovation in worker organization, reflected in the emergence of the 'Shainkai', suggests that the 'Japanese' model can, with some modification, be transferred effectively to the services sector; in Western economies longstanding service sector models are also afforded by such companies as IBM and McDonald's.

Under a system based on freedom of contract, the institutional basis for worker participation is likely to vary. In some cases, it will take the form of explicit provision for, say, consultation in an employment contract. In others, it may be developed through a firm's personnel policy, or simply be based on implicit understandings about acceptable behaviour. The success of an employment relationship will depend on the capacity of its combination of contractual terms, explicit and implicit personnel policy, and the incentives that these all create to facilitate welfare-enhancing co-operation between employees and between employees and managers. In such a process, improvements both in productivity and in the self-worth of workers are likely to be complementary.

Training and Career Development
In an economy exposed to international competition and dependent on productivity improvements and innovation for survival, a capacity for continually improving and adapting the skills of workers — both technical skills and skills in decision-making and participation — is crucial. A central authority will scarcely be able to select, produce and allocate these skills. Instead, the impetus for training and signals about the kind of training needed will be generated primarily at a workplace level.

The process of skill and knowledge acquisition needed in a dynamic economy cannot be confined to any one model. Formal training is likely to play an important role, but its significance over the career of a worker may be more in terms of the ability that it creates to learn skills and to adapt than of the specific skills that it transmits. The value of training in tertiary institutions of various kinds *vis-à-vis* training 'on-the-job' is likely to vary from occupation to occupation, as well as over time. Informal on-the-job training, in the form of learning by doing, is likely to play an important role in many occupations.

The balance struck between these different kinds of training will depend not only on the skills and knowledge that they are capable of generating but also on the incentives implicit in the organization and funding of tertiary education and in labour market arrangements. Internationally, there are significant variations. Taking the increase in average earnings that accompanies work experience as a rough approximate for the value of on-the-job training, investment in informal training in New Zealand can be estimated to be around half as important as investment in training at formal tertiary institutions. In the United States, where there is a greater emphasis on student and corporate funding of tertiary education (but nevertheless a far higher level of participation in tertiary education than in New Zealand), and where a less restricted labour market can be argued to facilitate the development of career paths within firms, investment in informal education is estimated to be as large again as investment in formal education. Informal training is estimated to provide all the skills needed in two out of three jobs (Carnevale, 1986).

Employer-worker negotiation which fosters training requires a system of labour market regulation that enables both parties to protect their interests, securing the returns to the investments that they make when they provide or undertake training. Where, for example, pay structures are artificially compressed or competition between employers for actually or potentially highly productive workers is artificially restricted, the attractiveness to workers of investing in training will be reduced. Similarly, where negotiations affecting employment relationships are removed from the workplace, the added difficulty of negotiating workplace or individual approaches to training may reduce the amount and range of training offered, including reducing the potential for 'multi-skilling'.

A labour relations system that enables the interests of individual workers to be protected and facilitates the negotiation of employment arrangements (including training and the development of career structures) that are in the mutual interest of employers and workers is therefore a prerequisite for an efficient approach to training. It will also be a prerequisite for equity in training, in particular enabling those with few or out-dated skills to negotiate arrangements that provide them with both technical knowledge and work experience, rather than condemning them to unemployment or unskilled employment. More generally, it is the strong incentives and greater capacity in a relatively free labour market to draw on and develop existing skills, and find ways of innovating that draw as much on experience as on book-learning, that makes for its superior performance in terms of income and equity over time.

Broader Economic Outcomes

In considering the reform of labour market arrangements and outcomes, there are some more general questions to be answered about its effects on wages and employment.

Proponents of the maintenance of New Zealand's present system of labour market regulation typically depict proponents of reform as working on a hidden agenda of driving down wages and conditions; 'flexibility' in the labour market is depicted as downward flexibility of wages. This emphasis is both biased and inappropriately narrow. Certainly one of the concerns of labour market reform is to enhance firms' performance in minimizing their costs of production and organization. Labour costs are an element in this equation. But wages are only one element in labour costs, and low wages do not necessarily make for low labour costs if productivity is also poor. As Blandy and Baker found in their survey of New Zealand businesses, firms seeking to enhance their ability to adapt to changing economic circumstances are far more likely to emphasize mechanisms for increasing productivity, including more co-operation with and better treatment of their workers. In this context, 'flexibility' is a means to higher productivity, better employment relationships and ultimately *higher*, not lower, remuneration.

This does not necessarily imply, however, that the removal of current union privileges could be achieved without any workers facing reduced incomes, at least in the short run. It is the nature of protected cartels to extract rents for their members at the expense of non-members. Strong, protected unions are no different from protected companies in this; they secure high wages and costly conditions of employment for their members at the expense of workers in relatively weak unions and in non-unionized activities, and of the unemployed. The removal of union privileges could therefore be expected to lead to some redistribution of income among workers in the short to medium term.

How far this redistribution involves actual reductions in nominal incomes for previously privileged workers will depend on the scope for productivity improvements in their activities — wages need not fall, for example, if the more flexible approach to bargaining induced by increased competition enables cost-saving changes in the organization of production. Similarly, how far the incomes available to those workers previously 'priced out' of employment by restrictive union conditions and minimum wages will fall below current wage levels, and for how long, will depend on the flexibility of conditions other than wages. In other words, any reduction needed to price the unemployed into work may be slight if means of reducing barriers to productivity can be found. This does not imply trade-offs between wages and other desirable conditions of employment; instead the concern will be to tailor packages of wages and employment conditions more precisely to the needs of particular workers and workplaces, eliminating costly conditions that are of little benefit to those involved.

In the longer term, the whole point of labour market reform of the kind suggested is that it will enable labour services to be used more effectively and therefore to produce higher incomes (even in times of unemployment, labour is a scarce resource, in the sense that there is a virtually unlimited amount of work that *could* be done); and that it will promote co-operation and fair treatment in employment relationships. The expectation is not equalization of outcomes, but improved incentives for skill acquisition, a fair matching of reward to contribution, and the elimination of those discrepancies in income that are due to regulatory privilege (and the unemployment that such privilege can entail) rather than to economic merit.

A significant part of improved efficiency in the use of labour resources will be a higher level of employment, and lower employment costs of adaptation to changing economic conditions. It is now broadly accepted that unnecessary rigidities in New Zealand's labour market system, enabling wages and conditions to be set by union officials and central employer organizations with little reference to the needs of individual workers or workplaces, has increased the amount of unemployment associated with product and finance market reforms and increased the likelihood that the emerging recovery will involve jobless growth. Bascand, for example, notes that the legal framework of the labour market is a crucial determinant of the level of 'equilibrium' unemployment:

> For instance, compulsory unionism may reduce the ability of unemployed workers to bargain for wage rates at a level which makes it profitable for firms to engage them in employment. Similarly, a national award system . . . can reduce the ability of employers to negotiate lower wages with their employees at times when business is poor, rather than making them redundant. Legislation relating to the terms on which workers can be made redundant is another factor which may have a significant bearing . . . with potential high redundancy payments being a factor inducing firms to employ less labour than they may otherwise. (1988, p. 274)

These sources of rigidity are all the more important given the 'relational' nature of many employment arrangements—the fact that employment is seldom a matter of some discrete market exchange. This makes for the creation of groups of insiders (those employed under relational sorts of contracts) and outsiders (those 'in the market'). This kind of segmentation has been argued to contribute to a 'hysteresis' effect under which equilibrium levels of employment ratchet upwards over time:

> Because the majority of employees and union officials hold secure jobs and control the wage bargaining process on the labour supply side, they have an inherent preference to bargain for higher wage settlements. As a result, marginal 'outside' employees are prevented from bidding to price themselves

back into employment. It is therefore possible that wage growth might
continue in the face of high unemployment . . . . (Bascand, 1988, p. 276)

The availability of individual employment contracts and the
existence of greater competition between unions for the coverage
of workers could be expected to reduce the significance of this effect,
reducing artificial distinctions between workers and artificial barriers
to employment. It would not completely eliminate it because of the
continuing value of developing relational employment contracts to
encourage commitment and investment in skills in some firms and
occupations, and because of the informational and transaction costs
inevitably involved. However, it would enhance competition at the
margin between insiders and outsiders — sharpening employer and
worker sensitivities to the trade-offs between the costs of developing
secure relationships and the costs of entering the market — and it
is such competition at the margin that is important in protecting
the interests of 'outsiders', as well as the interests of firms in
maintaining their ability to adapt to changing circumstances.

5.3   Making the Case for Reform

Comparing a known system with a relatively unknown one is not
a simple process. A number of tools can, however, be brought to
bear on the problem. The philosophical premises of the two systems
can be compared for their compatibility with what is known about
how people behave and how social systems order themselves. In
a similar way, the 'practicality' of the theory on which the
recommended system is based can be assessed (not its realism so
much as its usefulness; unrealistic assumptions can still yield useful
theories).

Empirical evidence can be garnered both from fragments of
systems comparable to the one advocated in this study and from
general economic and social systems that may not conform to it
perfectly, but are based on roughly similar premises. Thus something
can be learned about the practicality and likely benefits of a labour
market system based on freedom of contract from the experience
of countries where freedom of contract has remained an important
basis of economic activity, even if in most such cases it has been
restricted and constrained by governments won over by vaguely
collectivist urges. Looking at the United States, for example, New
Zealand can learn both from the freer employment relationships,
and from the costs of the remaining restrictions which can be

measured by comparing, say, union and non-union firms. Much broader comparisons can also be sketched between systems based on coerced collectivism and systems based, if imperfectly, on individual liberties, and between the levels of income and degrees of equity that they have produced. The general moves throughout the Communist bloc to return, if hesitantly, to some degree of personal freedom in both a political and an economic sense can also cast some light on the importance of freedom at the level of the individual employment relationship.

Both this chapter and Chapter 3 have discussed the implications of the approach to labour market regulation that currently exists in New Zealand and of the kind of system proposed in Chapter 4. In each case, this discussion has to some extent relied on comparisons of the two—the use of one as a counterfactual to the other. In particular, the real economic costs of the present system, its opportunity costs in terms of both efficiency and equity, have been measured by reference to what could be achieved under a feasible reform programme. It is perhaps a moot point as to whether the proposed system based on freedom of contract comes out better in these counterfactual exercises because its intellectual premises are from the outset determined to be more intellectually—and practically—satisfying. A direct analogy can be drawn here with the problems of resolving conflicts between scientific paradigms, as described by Kuhn:

> When paradigms enter, as they must, into a debate about paradigm choice, their role is necessarily circular. Each group uses its own paradigm to argue in that paradigm's defense. The resulting circularity does not, of course, make the arguments wrong or even ineffectual. The man who premises a paradigm while arguing in its defense can nonetheless provide a clear exhibit of what scientific practice will be like for those who adopt the new view of nature. That exhibit can be immensely persuasive, often compellingly so. Yet, whatever its force, the status of the circular argument is only that of persuasion. It cannot be made logically or even probabilistically compelling for those who refuse to step into the circle. The premises and values shared by the two parties to a debate over paradigms are not sufficiently extensive for that. As in political revolutions, so in paradigm choice—there is no standard higher than the assent of the relevant community. (1970, p. 94)

So, too, in the debate about competing regulatory regimes, acceptance of the argument that a more liberal system would, in fact, yield improved outcomes in terms of income levels, efficiency of resource use, fairness and 'industrial harmony' is to some degree dependent on an acceptance of its philosophical and theoretical premises as valid. On the other hand, the validity of these premises is itself to some extent tested by an appeal to observed outcomes, and in particular to evidence that the proposed system would avoid many of the costs imposed by the present system, without creating new, equally important costs.

Making a case for reform thus ultimately rests on making and winning an argument at two levels; in terms of the appropriateness of seeing regulation as facilitating the co-operation of individuals in spontaneous economic and social processes, and in terms of such empirical evidence as can be garnered both about the success of such approaches to regulation and about their suitability in the particular context of employment relationships. The concern of this study has been to illustrate that, at both levels, the case for reform is a convincing one.

For reform to be justified, it must be argued not only that the good effects of reform will outweigh the bad effects in the sense that the proposed regime, once in place, will yield superior outcomes to the existing one, but also that the costs of transition from one to the other will be justified by the ongoing benefits. All change is costly, both in economic and in political terms, as old privileges are eroded and rents are redistributed. Thus Ormond Wilson, commenting on one aspect of the need for a change in approach to New Zealand's labour market regulation, argues that:

> Those orthodoxies, the five-day week and the penal overtime rates to enforce it, may well have been advantageous and beneficial in the conditions of the thirties. They are not suited to the needs of the eighties, and no longer enhance the quality of life of New Zealanders as a whole. But the main present difficulty in bringing about fresh changes in this sphere is that those who were at the vanguard of change in the thirties — the workers — are now among the most reactionary of social groups. (1982, p. 61)

By contrast, Flanagan suggests that in the United States employers have to some extent grown inured to labour market regulation, while unions are increasingly resisting it because of a sense that it is in practice being used more and more to their disadvantage:

> Business opposition to the Wagner Act arose in part from the failure of that statute to regulate union activity. This gap was subsequently filled by the Taft-Hartley Act, which was bitterly opposed by unions. Today, the labor movement's support for deregulation is based on the belief that union organizing will benefit from reduced application of the union 'unfair labor practice' provisions. (1986, pp. 962-3)

In practice, some resistance to change is to be expected in both the union and the employer communities, as some elements in both benefit from the restrictions and certainties of the present system of regulation. An important aspect of attempts to ease a process of transition to a system such as that proposed here would therefore be the winning of acceptance that there would be mutual benefits to such a change.

A remarkable feature of the reforms that have taken place in the finance and product markets in New Zealand in the 1980s has been the acceptance of the need for change, which has greatly reduced the political costs of reform. Indeed, the fall in the opinion poll fortunes of the Labour Government in the later 1980s may be attributed more to its apparent unwillingness to take reforms to their logical conclusions, than to its earlier role in initiating major reforms.

The case for reform in the labour market has in some respects been made easier by acceptance of the need for, and emerging success of, reforms in other markets. This 'success' clearly has philosophical as well as economic elements; while the expected economic benefits of liberalization were clearly a major motivation for reform in these markets, there has also been a clear gain in terms of the greater freedom (and attendant responsibility) accorded to individuals. In this sense, the product and finance market reforms, and corresponding public sector reforms, have reflected a coming-of-age for New Zealanders long inured to repressive, paternalistic government.

The recognition that such freedom will prove both economically and psychologically beneficial if extended to employment relationships now appears to be widespread. Public opinion polls on industrial relations issues, for what they are worth, show consistently strong support for freedom of choice both about whether to join a union and about which union to join — support that is spread across all classes of workers. Employment relationships are widely perceived as based on mutual benefit rather than as adversarial, despite continuing rhetoric to the contrary, and there is strong support for the more decentralized bargaining that would foster the pursuit of such mutual benefits.[10] There is also some recognition that government interventions to set wage minima or restrict job-shedding are in fact harmful to job security (Insight New Zealand, 1988); in other words, that it is not simply the present delivery mechanism — using monopoly unions rather than government bureaucracies — that is wrong, but the underlying policy of restricting opportunities.

The cry of 'political impossibility', Shenfield writes:

. . . is the bane of good government and good social arrangements. To know what ought to be done, whether it is for the time being thought politically possible or not, is an indispensable foundation for the solution of political or social problems. (1986, p. 49)

Emerging popular (as opposed to central union) support for fundamental labour market reform in New Zealand suggests that 'political impossibility' is decreasingly credible as a justification for failing to reform.

6
Conclusion

Freedom, like a recipe for game pie, is not a bright idea; it is not a 'human right' to be deduced from some speculative concept of human nature. The freedom which we enjoy is nothing more than arrangements, procedures of a certain kind . . . . And the freedom which we wish to enjoy is not an 'ideal' which we premeditate independently of our political experience, it is what is already intimated in that experience. (Oakeshott, 1962, p. 120)

[P]erhaps, just perhaps, governmental intrusion into the economic activities of citizens is slowing down. With the romance of politics gone, rational constitutional discrimination between the legitimate and illegitimate exercise of legislative authority may at last emerge. (Buchanan, 1988, p. 261)

New Zealand's system of labour market legislation was built on a genuine and legitimate concern to promote the quality of employment relationships and the access of workers, through employment, to high and improving incomes. These concerns are as important today as they were when the Industrial Conciliation and Arbitration Act was passed in 1894. But experience over the last ninety-six years has taught that good intentions in labour market policy are not enough. If well-intentioned, even visionary, policy is not based on a sound understanding of the nature of human action and interaction, and of the dynamics of social processes, it risks undermining individual autonomy and self-determination, and thwarting the co-operation between individuals that is essential for social cohesion and prosperity.

The failure of New Zealand's labour market arrangements does not lie in the detail of the Labour Relations Act or other legislation constraining employment relationships. Certainly, as is shown by comparisons with other countries, such as the United States, Japan or Switzerland, where labour market law is less resolutely collectivist, the relative restrictiveness of these arrangements has been an important factor in New Zealand's poor economic performance. As a result, some streamlining of the law could be expected to yield improvements both in the quality of employment relationships and in broad macroeconomic outcomes.

The real problem, however, lies in the legislation's fundamental mistreatment of individuals; its subordination of the individual to the mythical 'collective good'. To emphasize the individual is not to deny the value of co-operation among individuals, collective effort and, ultimately, social order, but to provide them with a firm and sustainable basis; to make co-operation robust and meaningful — and genuine.

If individuals are to pursue the ends that are valuable to them, and co-operate with one another in the pursuit of mutual benefit, they must be free. This 'freedom' is not a vague, open-ended ideal, but a practical matter. It is a freedom against exploitation — the erosion of valuable opportunities — by either the state or other citizens:

> Value-enhancing voluntary exchanges must be free from interference by special-interest and protectionist pressure groups. Value-reducing restrictions must be effectively proscribed, whether instituted by private or by public agency. (Buchanan, 1988, p. 255)

In employment relationships, the crucial freedom is the freedom of workers and employers to contract with one another, by whatever means and towards whatever outcomes they consider to be of mutual benefit. This does not necessarily imply a system based on individual contracting; in many situations there will be benefits to both workers and employers in collective bargaining, the use of a union to assist in arbitration on grievances, or union involvement in supplying social services to employees. In such cases, again, the guiding principle will be one of freedom of contract between unions and their members, and freedom on the part of employers in deciding whether or not to enter a relationship with a union.

These freedoms are constrained in that they are essentially freedoms to increase welfare, not to diminish it. The strongest pressure to ensure that employment and union relationships are in fact beneficial, both to the direct participants and to society as a whole, will come from competition between employers for workers, workers for employment, and unions for members. It is economic competition, not coercive collective action, that minimizes opportunities for exploitation of workers (and consumers), whether by employers or by unrepresentative unions. Common law principles of property, contract and tort provide guidance on the kinds of constraints that will provide an effective legal basis for such competition — enabling contracts and ensuring that voluntarily-formed contracts are enforced, outlawing the use of force or fraud, providing protection for those incompetent to contract for themselves, and providing third parties with remedies against significant spillover effects.

To protect the freedom of workers, and thus their material and psychic well-being, policy-makers must relinquish the desire to control the outcomes of the relationships they form. Also to be resisted is the temptation to assume that because employment relationships are complex and important, a complex and paternalistic law is needed to coerce workers and employers into acting in each other's interest. It is, indeed, the complexity and significance of employment relationships that makes heavy-handed, blanket regulation so damaging, and damaging above all to the most vulnerable members of the work-force.

An interest in the welfare of workers, individually and in aggregate, therefore requires the removal of those labour market regulations that restrict the freedom of workers to form the kinds of employment relationships that are in their interest, and that restrict the freedom of employers to offer employment, and to tailor the conditions of employment to the preferences and circumstances of would-be employees. Similarly, it requires the removal of barriers to accountability on the part of unions, and to the formation of relationships between unions and workers that reflect and accommodate widely differing needs and interests. It is by removing such barriers to opportunity that the greatest present protections *for* exploitation will be destroyed.

It is for this reason that, for example, the New Zealand Council of Trade Unions proposals for reform of labour market institutions to create mega-unions arranged on industrial lines, while based on a commendable recognition of the need for reform, are inappropriate. The point here is not that an industry union will *never* offer the best means of organizing bargaining or serving the interests of workers, but that to *impose* such unions on all firms and workers, without regard for individual choice, is both ethically offensive and likely to be economically damaging.

Industry-based awards are likely to be as unresponsive to regional variations, differences in technology and differences in worker preferences as the current national craft and occupational awards. They would certainly do little to foster the co-operation and trust between employers and workers that is essential to good working relationships, to innovation and, in some cases, to survival. They would if anything discourage information-sharing between employers and workers, for fear that shared information would find its way to competitors. They would continue to restrain competition between employers for workers, and thus substantially weaken one of the main protections that a well-functioning labour market can offer to workers. And they would limit employers' ability to devise schemes to price the low-skilled, or the unemployed in relatively depressed regions, into jobs and on-the-job training.

As argued in Chapter 4, a primary reliance on competition in labour markets and the legal principles contained in private law as means of enhancing employment relationships and protecting the participants does not imply that there will be no need for a labour statute. However, the role of any such statute should be *facilitative*; concerned with reducing the costs to workers and employers, and workers and unions, of forming mutually satisfying relationships. There is a need for further research to assess just what such a statute should contain — for example, whether and how non-prescriptive standard contracts might be set out, whether there are informational services that the government has a relative advantage in funding or providing, how labour market relationships should be subjected to the Commerce Act, and whether any need remains for a specialist bureaucracy to advise on or administer labour market law.

There is also a need to consider how transition from the present system to the proposed one should be managed. New ways of doing things will need to be learned; new freedoms (and accompanying responsibilities) explored. However, the importance of this learning process does not necessarily mean that reforms should be introduced only gradually, especially if some substantial increases in freedom are required for such learning to proceed. Nor does it indicate a case for the introduction of special transitional incentives, for example, for moves towards enterprise bargaining (a structure that is in any event unlikely to be universally appropriate).

In considering the management of transition to a new system, it must be recalled that the labour market is by its nature slow to adjust. At least in part, this is a result of the relational nature of many employment contracts, and the potentially high information costs associated with adjustment. Even dramatic reforms will therefore need some time to take effect — a point that should if anything serve to ease the learning process for employers, workers and unions. The most immediate changes are likely to occur in companies currently under strong competitive pressure, which have used the present capacity for enhancing productivity and protecting jobs to the absolute limit, and which therefore have much to gain from any increase in flexibility. The workers most immediately affected will be those who are currently in particularly insecure employment (or unemployed), or who are strongly in conflict with the unions currently charged with representing them. Companies and workers facing less immediate problems under the current regime might be expected to adapt to a new regime more gradually, as competition from other companies adopting more productive and, from the point of view of workers, more attractive employment policies compelled them to do so. As the New Zealand Business Roundtable argued in its submission on the 1985 Green Paper:

> The process is . . . one of facilitating change where the parties express a preference for change, and this process is expected to be popular precisely because the changes are seen as increasing incomes, equity and efficiency in labour markets, and therefore in all other markets. (1986, p. 44)

Relatively rapid, decisive change has benefits in terms of the greater certainty it creates for firms in planning employment and related policies, and for workers making decisions about employment and career plans. As such, it can significantly reduce the potentially large information costs of adjustment, and reduce the risks of 'bad' decision-making based on faulty expectations about the extent and direction of future reforms. It will also reduce the risk, typically associated with gradual reforms, that impediments to opportunity will be removed in an unbalanced way so that the burdens of adjustment are unfairly distributed. On a grander scale, this was illustrated by the distributional effects of substantially reforming finance and product markets and the public sector, while leaving significant impediments in the labour market to adapting to these changes.

The case for reform in New Zealand's labour market arrangements does not rest on the wild pursuit of some elusive utopia, or on an insistence that change is due because the principles on which our current system is based have been outmoded. Rather, it rests on a recognition that human dignity and human happiness depend on the championing of freedom and individual responsibility. This freedom is not some vague, unconstrained ideal but a practical principle; a principle that is essential if a society is to be created that draws its order and prosperity from the way in which it empowers its individual members.

Notes

Introduction
1. See, for example, Braun (1986).

Chapter 1
1. See, for example, Horwitz in Kronman and Posner (1979) and Merritt (1982).
2. See, for example, Sowell (1987) on the views of such diverse writers as Jean-Jacques Rousseau and George Bernard Shaw.
3. As in the International Labour Organisation's 1948 Philadelphia Declaration.
4. It is, however, the *relevance*, rather than the *presence*, of such competition that would be denied by socialist writers. Thus Beatrice and Sidney Webb write: '[T]he monopoly of which [workers are] here impatient is not that of any *single* individual, but that of the *class itself.* What the workers are objecting to is . . . a . . . feudal system of industry . . . of domination of the mass of ordinary workers by a hierarchy of property owners, who compete, it is true, among themselves, but who are nevertheless able, as a class, to preserve very real control over the lives of those who depend on their own daily labour . . . [the worker is] free only to choose to which master he would sell his labour — free only to decide from which proprietor he would beg that access to the new instruments of production without which he could not exist.' (Quoted in Dickman, 1987, p. 104)
5. See, for example, Williams (1989).

Chapter 2
1. As a judicial innovation rather than a requirement of the Act, granting of preference clauses was subject to some variation. From around 1913 onwards, the Arbitration Court began to grant 'unqualified preference' clauses, requiring workers to join a union within some fixed period of starting employment. This may have been an attempt to win greater union support for the system in a period of strong opposition from the Red Federation of Labour (see Walsh, 1983). However, the granting of unqualified preference clauses was ruled to be outside the authority of the Arbitration Court in a 1916 Court of Appeal ruling. Qualified preference clauses then became the prevailing form of membership requirement until the introduction of compulsory unionism legislation in 1936.
2. The Labour Relations Amendment Bill introduced in mid-1990 provided for a limited return to compulsory final-offer arbitration in situations where awards were being restructured and employers had displayed an unwillingness to bargain in 'good faith'. At the time of writing, this Bill had yet to be passed into law.
3. The 1990 Labour Relations Amendment Bill provided for the ability to opt out of awards to be extended to employers, but in strictly limited circumstances. In particular, this provision was to be applicable only in workplaces with over 50 workers, which would effectively preclude its use in 98 per cent of all enterprises, employing 65 per cent of the total work-force.
4. See Dickman (1987).
5. See, for example, Rideout (1966).
6. Under the National Labor Relations Act, it is an unfair labour practice to 'interfere with, restrain, or coerce employees' in the exercise of their rights to form, join or assist unions, to 'dominate or interfere with the formation or administration of any labor organization or contribute financial aid or other support to it' — a provision that precludes company unions — or to dismiss or fail to hire a worker on account of his or her union affiliation.
7. See Section 2.3 below.

8. See Williams (1989).
9. See Anderson and Tollison (1984).
10. See Brook (1988c).
11. Brosnan and Wilkinson (1989), p. 19.
12. See, for example, Sutton (1988) on this trend in the New Zealand context. This issue will be discussed at greater length in Chapter 4.

Chapter 3
1. The leading exponents of this theory are the Harvard-based economists Richard Freeman and James Medoff (see, for example, Freeman and Medoff (1979); also Allen (1984) and Brown and Medoff (1978)).
2. A detailed exposition of these ideas in the New Zealand context can be found in Barker and Chapman (1989).
3. See Moorhouse (1982).
4. Research by Blanchflower and Oswald, cited in Metcalf (1988).
5. For a relatively brief critique, see Addison (1985).
6. See, for example, Hirsch and Link (1984), Maki (1983) and an overview of British research in Metcalf (1988).
7. This would seem to have been the case with the Victorian employers described by Brown (1983) as willingly accommodating the formation of unions at the workplace level. It is also suggested by the adoption of 'Nissan'-style collective agreements in the United Kingdom in the 1980s, when union protections were being progressively reduced. In New Zealand, a recent public opinion survey suggests that, while a move to voluntary unionism would be widely supported, the majority of workers would still elect to join a union were they given the choice (Insight New Zealand, 1988).
8. For example, a case was recently taken to the Labour Court contesting a compulsory unionism ballot among farmworkers which was decided by a vote of 102 for, 46 against, from a total membership of over 20,000. This decision was ultimately disallowed.
9. See, for example, Heylen Research Centre (1984) and (1987), and Insight New Zealand (1988).
10. *National Business Review*, 31 October 1989.
11. A detailed analysis of labour relations problems on the waterfront in New Zealand is provided by Trebeck (1989).
12. *NZ Storeworkers, Packers, Warehouse Employees IOUW* v *Tulloch Road Limited and Mogal Freight Services Limited*, Christchurch Labour Court, 62/89.
13. At the time of writing, it is unclear whether proposed legislative changes to redundancy law will eliminate this problem.
14. *NZ Cleaners, Caretakers etc. Union* v *Ferrymead Historic Trust*, Christchurch Labour Court, 1 December 1989.
15. *NZ Food Processing Chemical Related Union* v *ICI Limited*, Wellington Labour Court, 98/89.
16. Cited in Heldman *et al.* (1981), p. 88.
17. For empirical evidence, see, for example, Hashimoto (1982).
18. See Monetary and Economic Council (1962), which records that New Zealand performed worse than any other OECD country over the 15 years to 1962.

Chapter 4
1. There are direct parallels here with developments in the theory of science, and in particular contemporary work on 'chaos theory' that finds 'spontaneous order' and intelligibility in phenomena that are disorderly by classical Newtonian standards (Gleick, 1988; Prigogine and Stengers, 1984). Lavoie describes some of the implications for political economy in the following manner: 'A machine is understood when it is fully under the control of its user. A philosophy that sees everything as a machine will naturally put the idea of control at the very center of its view of reason and science. By contrast, spontaneous order analysis prefers a notion such as cultivation. A spontaneous order is not designed and never really under our control, since it evolves according to a logic all its own. This does not mean, however, that we are utterly helpless to exert influence

over the workings of such ordering processes. Its order may be intelligible in terms of general principles, and these principles may well show us that some environments are more conducive to its self-ordering process than others. Understanding a spontaneous order may enable us to tailor the general conditions for its flourishing. But if we persist in trying to control the detailed working of this kind of process, we are more likely to interfere with its own logic and obstruct its self-ordering, than to intelligently "guide" it in any sense. Attempting to control a spontaneous order is like trying to fix a complex machine, whose detailed workings we do not know, by throwing a monkey wrench at it.' (1989, p. 621)

2. See, for example, Posner (1973).
3. From a legal perspective, the allocation of authority to the employer or his or her managers reflects the fact that the employer is liable for all that employees do on firm business. Epstein points out that this 'vicarious liability' in practice ensures that 'the firm's need for internal control is the same for both potential litigation and forgone profits' (1985a, p. 129), the latter arising from the scope for opportunistic behaviour on the part of employees at the expense of the firm.
4. St Antoine (1988), for example, in advocating a 'just cause' regime for the United States, suggests that it should *not* apply to managers and supervisors (for whom the threat of being fired 'at-will' may be an important means of controlling performance), public employees with specific civil service or tenure provisions, probationary employees and employees in small companies — say, those with less than ten to fifteen employees. It is this last exception which is perhaps most telling, in that St Antoine justifies it on the basis that 'we feel uneasy about intruding too hastily into the sometimes intensely personal relationships of small, intimate establishments' (1988, p. 73). He does, however, favour extending its coverage to unionized workers, for whom guards against 'unjust' dismissal are already typically supplied by collectively negotiated contracts — 'one might ask why the state should shield nonunion workers gratis, and force unionized workers to expend bargaining chips to obtain the same safeguards' (1988, p. 75). 'For-cause' clauses are, however, effectively *necessary* for unionization, not because they are a service to workers that unions must provide in order to survive, but because they are a means to the kind of institutional stability necessary for the survival of union structures (and hierarchies). In so far as they become an important means of protecting union officials and the hold of a union in a workplace, it is unclear why they should be bestowed as a matter of 'right'.
5. See also Williamson (1979) and Williamson, Wachter and Harris (1975) for an economic perspective of internal governance structures.
6. See Hansmann (1988).
7. Hanson and Mather (1988) note in the British context, however, that the requirement that new employees join a union is in contravention of the European Declaration of Human Rights. They propose actively deterring closed shops by means of penalties. For this proposal to stand, it must be assumed that *any* closed shop will by definition infringe the rights of some workers. This would not seem to be the case in competitive industries, however, where employment opportunities for workers with industry-specific skills will have a variety of employment options.
8. See McCallum (1987).
9. Hanson and Mather suggest that a strike may be seen as a means of bypassing malfunctioning contracting mechanisms: 'Strike action in this sense can be seen as the result either of a mismatch of employment objectives from the outset between the parties to the contract, or the consequence of a "mistake" in bargaining, which may be the result of bargaining on too large a scale or on terms influenced by outside parties like national unions.' (1988, pp. 24-5) The potential for malfunctioning of either sort would appear to be greatly reduced by making the form and activities of unions more directly a matter of worker choice than has historically been the case in both the United Kingdom and New Zealand.
10. See, for example, Moore (1983) on an attempt to apply antitrust to the activities of the Screen Actors' Guild and the American Federation of Television and Radio Artists in allegedly prohibiting advertising agencies from using non-union subcontractors in making radio and television commercials.

11. See Wilson (1988); also Hyman and Clark (1987).
12. Sir Ivor Richardson, quoted by Greenslade (1988).

Chapter 5
1. Thus, as McCallum (1987) argues with respect to Australia, the machinery for conciliation and arbitration 'by and large left the common law intact'. (In this, New Zealand and Australia differ from the United Kingdom, where unions were immunized against the common law, and the United States, where union certification under the Wagner Act effectively ousted the common law.) Exercise of common law remedies for illegal industrial action is a relatively recent event in Australia (see, for example, Costello, 1989, and Evans, 1989). The extent to which comparable remedies are available in New Zealand is as yet largely untested.
2. Von Mises uses 'catallactics' as a more precise term for the human actions and interactions with which the discipline of economics is concerned.
3. It is notable that the direction and magnitude of these reforms has not been matched in markets for equity. While a review of companies legislation by the Law Commission offered the opportunity for broadly based reforms centred on clarifying and liberalizing the relationship between shareholders and their companies, the reform process appears to have disintegrated into ill-designed forays into insider trading and takeovers legislation, re-regulation of shares and futures trading, and the creation of unusual — and arguably economically damaging — powers for statutory managers.
4. See, for example, Carmichael (1983), Huberman and Kahn (1988), Klein (1984), Lazear (1989), Lazear and Rosen (1981), Malcolmson (1986), and Rosen (1986) and (1987).
5. See Roberts (1987), and Wickens (1987) on developments at Nissan.
6. See Pejovich (1984).
7. In New Zealand the latter incentives are blunted by the monopoly of the Accident Compensation Corporation in providing accident insurance and prescribing its form, and by the funding of health care primarily through taxes rather than through an insurance mechanism. For an elaboration of the interaction of the no-fault accident compensation regime, health and safety regulations and labour market law, see Brook (1988b).
8. See, for example, Block and Walker (1985).
9. See, for example, Jensen and Meckling (1979).
10. See Heylen Research Centre (1984) and (1987), and Insight New Zealand (1988).

References

Addison, J.T. (1982), 'Are Unions Good for Productivity?', *Journal of Labor Research*, 3, pp. 125-38.

———— (1985), 'What Do Unions Really Do? A Review Article', *Journal of Labor Research*, 6, pp. 127-46.

———— and Burton, J. (1984), *Trade Unions and Society: Some Lessons of the British Experience*, Vancouver, Fraser Institute.

Advisory Council for Occupational Safety and Health (1988), *Occupational Safety and Health Reform*, Wellington.

Alchian, A.A. and Demsetz, H. (1972), 'Production, Information Costs and Economic Organization', *American Economic Review*, 62, pp. 777-95.

———— and Woodward, S. (1988), 'The Firm is Dead; Long Live the Firm: A Review of Oliver E. Williamson's "The Economic Institutions of Capitalism"', *Journal of Economic Literature*, 26, pp. 65-79.

Allen, S.G. (1984), 'Unionized Construction Workers are More Productive', *Quarterly Journal of Economics*, 99, pp. 251-74.

Anderson, G.M. and Tollison, R.D. (1984), 'A Rent-Seeking Explanation of the British Factory Acts', Alexandria, mimeo.

Atiyah, P.S. (1986), *Essays on Contract*, Oxford, Clarendon Press.

Baldwin, C.Y. (1983), 'Productivity and Labor Unions: An Application of the Theory of Self-Enforcing Contracts', *Journal of Business*, 56, pp. 155-85.

Barker, G.R. and Chapman, R.B. (1989), 'Evaluating Labor Market Contracting and Regulation: A Transaction Costs Perspective with Particular Reference to New Zealand', *Journal of Institutional and Theoretical Economics*, 145, pp. 317-42.

Barry, N.P. (1988), *The Invisible Hand in Economics and Politics*, London, Institute of Economic Affairs.

———— (1989a), *The Crisis in Law*, St Leonards, Centre for Independent Studies.

———— (1989b), 'Ideas and Interests: The Problem Reconsidered', in Veljanovski, C. (ed), *Ideas, Interests and Consequences*, London, Institute of Economic Affairs, pp. 53-74.

Bartel, A.P. and Thomas, L.G. (1985a), 'Direct and Indirect Effects of Regulation: A New Look at OSHA's Impact', *Journal of Law and Economics*, 28, pp. 1-26.

Bartel, A.P. and Thomas, L.G. (1985b), 'Predation through Regulation: The Wage and Profit Impacts of OSHA and EPA', Working Paper No. 1660, Cambridge (Mass.), National Bureau of Economic Research.

Bascand, A. (1988), 'The Persistence of Unemployment: Lessons from Overseas Experience', *Reserve Bank Bulletin*, 51, pp. 273-8.

Lord Bauer (1981), *Equality, the Third World and Economic Delusion*, Cambridge (Mass.), Harvard University Press.

—————— and Burton, J. (1983), *On the Power of Britain's Organized Labour: Sources and Implications*, Vancouver, Fraser Institute.

Baxt, R. and Franks, S.L. (1988), *Submission to the Law Commission on Company Law*, Wellington, New Zealand Business Roundtable.

Becker, G.S. (1971), *The Economics of Discrimination* (2nd edition), Chicago, University of Chicago Press.

—————— (1980), *Human Capital: A Theoretical and Empirical Analysis, with Special Reference to Education* (2nd edition), Chicago, University of Chicago Press.

—————— (1988a), 'Contrary to Popular Belief, The Economic Boom did Trickle Down', *Business Week*, 19 September, p. 12.

—————— (1988b), 'It's Time to Scrap a Few Outmoded Labor Laws', *Business Week*, 7 March, p. 13.

—————— (1989), 'The Courts Shouldn't Become Pink-Slip Police', *Business Week*, 28 August, p. 8.

Bedford, D.J. (1989), 'Current Industrial Relations Policies: Their Effect on Managing Change', Paper presented to an Institute for International Research Conference on Managing Change in Industrial Relations, 17-18 August, Auckland.

Beenstock, M. and Brasse, V. (1986), *Insurance for Unemployment*, London, Allen and Unwin.

Benn, S.I. (1988), *A Theory of Freedom*, Cambridge, Cambridge University Press.

—————— and Peters, R.S. (1959), *The Principles of Political Thought: Social Foundations of the Democratic State*, New York, Free Press.

Bennett, J.T. and Johnson, M.H. (1980), 'The Impact of Right-to-Work Laws on the Economic Behaviour of Unions: A Property Rights Perspective', *Journal of Labor Reseach*, 1, pp. 1-27.

Blandy, R. (1988a), 'Efficiency and Productivity in the Workplace: Where to Now?', *Australian Bulletin of Labour*, 15, pp. 20-8.

—————— (1988b), *Reforming Tertiary Education in New Zealand*, Wellington, New Zealand Business Roundtable.

172   **References**

Blandy, R. and Baker, M. (1987), *Industry Assistance Reform and the Labour Market: The New Zealand Experience*, Adelaide, National Institute of Labour Studies.

────── and Sloan, J. (1986), *The Dynamic Benefits of Labour Market Deregulation*, Canberra, Westpac Banking Corporation.

Block, W. *et al.* (eds) (1985), *Morality of the Market: Religious and Economic Perspectives*, Vancouver, Fraser Institute.

────── and Walker, M.A. (1985), *Focus on Employment Equity*, Vancouver, Fraser Institute.

Bonnell, S.M. (1987), 'The Effect of Equal Pay for Females on the Composition of Employment in Australia', *Economic Record*, 63, pp. 340-51.

Bounine-Cabale, J. *et al.* (1989), *Japan at Work: Markets, Management and Flexibility*, Paris, Organization for Economic Co-operation and Development.

Braun, A.R. (1986), *Wage Determination and Incomes Policy in Open Economies*, Washington, International Monetary Fund.

Brook, P.J. (1987), 'A Study of the Creation of Firms as Vehicles for Product Innovation', DPhil Thesis, Oxford, University of Oxford.

────── (1988a), *Employment Equity: Issues of Competition and Regulation*, Wellington, New Zealand Business Roundtable.

────── (1988b), *Regulating for Occupational Safety and Health*, Wellington, New Zealand Business Roundtable.

────── (1988c), *The Regulation of Shop Trading Hours*, Wellington, New Zealand Business Roundtable.

────── (1989a), *Industrial Democracy: A Case for Regulation or Deregulation?*, Wellington, New Zealand Business Roundtable.

────── (1989b), 'Reform of the Labour Market', in Walker, S. (ed), *Rogernomics: Reshaping New Zealand's Economy*, Auckland, New Zealand Centre for Independent Studies, pp. 183-207.

────── (1989c), 'Safety and Health within a Deregulated Society: The Case for a Unified Approach', Paper presented to the New Zealand Institute of Safety Management, 29 June, Palmerston North.

────── (1990), *The Pursuit of Fairness: A Critique of the Employment Equity Bill*, Wellington, New Zealand Business Roundtable.

────── (forthcoming), *The Inequity of 'Pay Equity': Comparable Worth Policy in New Zealand*, Auckland, New Zealand Centre for Independent Studies.

Brosnan, P. (ed) (1983), *Voluntary Unionism, Proceedings of a Seminar 5 October 1983*, Wellington, Industrial Relations Centre, Victoria University of Wellington.

Brosnan, P. and Wilkinson, F. (1989), *Low Pay and the Minimum Wage*, Wellington, New Zealand Institute of Industrial Relations Research.

Brown, C. and Medoff, J.L. (1978), 'Trade Unions in the Production Process', *Journal of Political Economy*, 86, pp. 355-78.

Brown, E.H.P. (1983), *Origins of Trade Union Power*, Oxford, Clarendon Press.

Brunhes, B. (1989), 'Labour Flexibility in Enterprises: A Comparison of Firms in Four European Countries', *Labour Market Flexibility: Trends in Enterprises*, Paris, Organization for Economic Co-operation and Development, pp. 11-36.

Buchanan, J.M. (1975), *The Limits of Liberty: Between Anarchy and Leviathan*, Chicago, University of Chicago Press.

——— (1986), *Liberty, Market and State: Political Economy in the 1980s*, Brighton, Wheatsheaf Books.

——— (1988), 'Constitutional Imperatives for the 1990s: The Legal Order for a Free and Productive Economy', in Anderson, A. and Bark, D.L. (eds), *Thinking About America: The United States in the 1990s*, Stanford, Hoover Institution Press, pp. 253-63.

Burton, J. (1987), 'Australia Reconstructed: Some European Reflections', Centre for Independent Studies Policy Report, 3/5, pp. 1-5.

——— et al. (1978), *Trade Unions: Public Goods or Public 'Bads'?*, London, Institute of Economic Affairs.

Business Council of Australia (1986), 'Industrial Relations in Sweden', *Business Council Bulletin*, 28, pp. 1-19.

Butterfield, H. (1931), *The Whig Interpretation of History*, London, G. Bell and Sons.

Caenegem, R.C. van (1988), *The Birth of the English Common Law* (2nd edition), Cambridge, Cambridge University Press.

Calabresi, G. and Melamed, A.D. (1972), 'Property Rules, Liability Rules and Inalienability: One View of the Cathedral', *Harvard Law Review*, 85, pp 1089-128.

Calmfors, L. and Driffill, J. (1988), 'Centralization of Wage Bargaining', *Economic Policy*, April, pp. 13-61.

Campbell, I.B. (1987), *Legislating for Workplace Hazards in New Zealand: Overseas Experience and Our Present and Future Needs*, Palmerston North, Massey University.

Campbell, T.J. (1986), 'Labor Law and Economics', *Stanford Law Review*, 38, pp. 991-1064.

Carey, D. and Spencer, G. (1989), 'Financial Policy Reform', in Walker, S. (ed), *Rogernomics: Reshaping New Zealand's Economy*, Auckland, New Zealand Centre for Independent Studies, pp. 49-92.

Carmichael, H.L. (1983), 'The Agent-Agents Problem: Payment by Relative Output', *Journal of Labor Economics*, 1, pp. 50-65.
—— (1984), 'Reputations in the Labour Market', *American Economic Review*, 74, pp. 713-25.

Carnevale, A.P. (1986), 'The Learning Experience', *Training and Development Journal*, January, pp. 18-26.

Cheung, S.N.S. (1970). 'The Structure of a Contract and the Theory of a Non-Exclusive Resource', *Journal of Law and Economics*, 13, pp. 49-70.
—— (1974), 'A Theory of Price Control', *Journal of Law and Economics*, 17, pp. 53-71.
—— (1983), 'The Contractual Nature of the Firm', *Journal of Law and Economics*, 26, pp. 1-21.

Clark, K.B. (1984), 'Unionization and Firm Performance: The Impact on Profits, Growth and Productivity', *American Economic Review*, 74, pp. 893-919.

Clark, L. (1989), 'Japan's Sinking Unions', *Asian Wall Street Journal*, 1 August, p. 6.

Coe, D.T. (1989), 'Hysteresis and Insider-Outsider Influences on Industry Wages: Evidence from Fourteen Industrialized Countries', Paper presented to the American Economics Association meetings, December 1988 (revised).

Cohen, Y. and Pfeffer, J. (1984), 'Determinants of Internal Labor Markets in Organizations', *Administrative Science Quarterly*, 29, pp. 550-72.

Coleman, J.L. (1988), *Markets, Morals and the Law*, Cambridge, Cambridge University Press.

Collins, H. (1986), 'Market Power, Bureaucratic Power, and the Contract of Employment', *Industrial Law Journal*, 15, pp. 1-14.

Cooke, R. (1989), 'Fairness', Paper presented to the Australasian Universities Law Schools Association Annual Conference, Wellington.

Costello, P. (1989) 'The Dollar Sweets Story', *Proceedings of the H R Nicholls Society*, 5, pp. 27-32.

Cox, J. (1988), *Unemployment Income Support in New Zealand: Options for Policy Reform*, Wellington, New Zealand Business Roundtable.

Crocker, K.J. and Masten, S.E. (1988), '*Pretia ex Machina*? Prices and Process in Long-term Contracts', Working Paper No. 588, University of Michigan School of Business Administration.

Demsetz, H. (1969), 'Information and Efficiency: Another Viewpoint', *Journal of Law and Economics*, 12, pp. 1-22.

Dennison, S.R. and Forrest, D. (1984), *Low Pay or No Pay?*, London, Institute of Economic Affairs.

Department of Labour (1989), *Submission to the Committee of Inquiry into Industrial Democracy*, Wellington, Department of Labour.

De Soto, H. (1989), *The Other Path: The Invisible Revolution in the Third World*, New York, Harper and Row.

Dickman, H. (1987), *Industrial Democracy in America: Ideological Origins of National Labor Relations Policy*, La Salle, Open Court.

DiLorenzo, T.J. (1988), 'Property Rights, Information Costs, and the Economics of Rent Seeking', *Journal of Institutional and Theoretical Economics*, 144, pp. 318-22.

Doeringer, P.B. (1986), 'Internal Labor Markets and Noncompeting Groups', *American Economics Association Papers and Proceedings*, 76, pp. 48-52.

—— et al. (1986), 'Capitalism and Kinship: Do Institutions Matter in the Labor Market?', *Industrial and Labor Relations Review*, 40, pp. 48-60.

Dorsey, S. and Walzer, N. (1983), 'Workers' Compensation, Job Hazards and Wages', *Industrial and Labor Relations Review*, 36, pp. 642-54.

Douglas, K. (1989), 'Industrial Democracy: Trade Union Perspective', Paper presented to a Seminar on Industrial Democracy, 11 May, Wellington.

Douglas, R.O. (1988), 'Government's Briefing on the Economy to the 1988 Tripartite Wage Conference', Wellington, mimeo.

—— (1989), 'The Ends and the Means', in Walker, S. (ed), *Rogernomics: Reshaping New Zealand's Economy*, Auckland, New Zealand Centre for Independent Studies, pp. 22-9.

Dunn, S. and Gennard, J. (1984), *The Closed Shop in British Industry*, London, Macmillan.

Elliott, R.D. and Huffman, J.R. (1984), 'The Impact of Right-to-Work Laws on Employer Unfair Labor Practice Charges', *Journal of Labor Research*, 5, pp. 165-76.

Epstein, E. (1986), 'The Share Economy: An Idea Whose Time Came Long Ago', *Challenge*, January/February, pp. 62-4.

Epstein, R.A. (1975), 'Unconscionability: A Critical Reappraisal', *Journal of Law and Economics*, 18, pp. 293-315.

—— (1983a), 'A Common Law for Labor Relations: A Critique of the New Deal Labor Legislation', *Yale Law Journal*, 92, pp. 1357-408.

—— (1983b), 'Common Law, Labor Law, and Reality: A Rejoinder to Professors Getman and Kohler', *Yale Law Journal*, 92, pp. 1435-41.

—— (1984), 'In Defense of the Contract at Will', *University of Chicago Law Review*, 51, pp. 947-82.

Epstein, R.A. (1985a), 'Agency Costs, Employment Contracts, and Labor Unions', in Pratt, J.W. and Zeckhauser, R.J. (eds), *Principals and Agents: The Structure of Business*, Boston, Harvard Business School Press, pp. 127-48.

—— (1985b), *Takings: Private Property and the Power of Eminent Domain*, Cambridge (Mass.), Harvard University Press.

—— (1987a), 'Affidavit' (on Province of Ontario labour statutes), Chicago, mimeo.

—— (1987b), 'Beyond the Rule of Law: Civic Virtue and Constitutional Structure', *George Washington Law Review*, 56, pp. 149-71.

—— (1988), 'AIDS, Testing and the Workplace', *University of Chicago Legal Forum*, pp. 33-56.

Evans, N.R. (1989), 'Trade Unions and the Common Law', *Proceedings of the H R Nicholls Society*, 5, pp. 85-90.

Faith, R.L. and Reid, J.D. (1987a), 'An Agency Theory of Unionism', *Journal of Economic Behaviour and Organisation*, 8, pp. 39-60.

—— 'Right-to-Work and Union Compensation Structure', *Journal of Labor Research*, 8, pp. 113-30.

Fama, E.F. and Jensen, M.C. (1983), 'Agency Problems and Residual Claims', *Journal of Law and Economics*, 26, pp. 327-49.

Fane, G. (1981), 'Employment Contracts, Specific Training and Liability Rules', Working Paper No. 58, University of Victoria.

Farber, H.S. (1984), 'Right-to-Work Laws and the Extent of Unionization', *Journal of Labor Economics*, 2, pp. 319-52.

Finkin, M.W. (1986), 'The Bureaucratization of Work: Employer Policies and Contract Law', *Wisconsin Law Review*, pp. 733-53.

Fischel, D.R. (1984), 'Labor Markets and Labor Law Compared with Capital Markets and Corporate Law', *University of Chicago Law Review*, 51, pp. 1061-77.

Fisher, M. (1985), 'Regulation and the Labour Market', Working Paper No. 85-021, Australian Graduate School of Management, University of New South Wales.

Flanagan, R.J. (1984), 'Wage Concessions and Long-Term Union Wage Flexibility', *Brookings Papers on Economic Activity*, pp. 183-221.

—— (1986), 'NLRA Litigation and Union Representation', *Stanford Law Review*, 38, pp. 957-89.

—— (1989), 'Compliance and Enforcement Decisions under the National Labor Relations Act', *Journal of Labor Economics*, 7, pp. 257-80.

Flathman, R.E. (1987), *The Philosophy and Politics of Freedom*, Chicago, University of Chicago Press.

Freed, M.G. *et al.* (1982), 'Unions, Fairness and the Conundrums of Collective Choice', *Southern California Law Review*, 56, pp. 461-525.

Freeman, R.B. and Medoff, J.L. (1979), 'The Two Faces of Unionism', *Public Interest*, 57, pp. 69-93.

Friedman, M. and Friedman, R.D. (1988), 'The "Tide in the Affairs of Men"', in Anderson, A. and Bark, D.L. (eds), *Thinking About America: The United States in the 1990s*, Stanford, Hoover Institution Press, pp. 455-68.

Fuchs, V.R. (1988), *Women's Quest for Economic Equality*, Cambridge (Mass.), Harvard University Press.

Fulton, H. (1987), 'The New Labour Court: Window Dressing or Substantive Change', Paper presented to the New Zealand Law Conference, Christchurch.

―――― (1989), 'The Nature of the Labour Court', Working Paper, Wellington, New Zealand Business Roundtable.

Furubotn, E.G. (1979), *The Economics of Industrial Democracy: An Analysis of Labor Participation in the Management of Business Firms*, College Station, Texas, Center for Education and Research in Free Enterprise.

―――― and Pejovich, S. (1972), 'Property Rights and Economic Theory: A Survey of Recent Literature', *Journal of Economic Literature*, 10, pp. 1137-62.

Gamble, A. (1989), 'Ideas and Interests in British Economic Policy', in Veljanovski, C. (ed), *Ideas, Interests and Consequences*, London, Institute of Economic Affairs, pp. 1-21.

Gapper, J. (1988), 'Market Forces Fuel Drive to Recruit Women', *The Dominion*, 19 October, p. 24.

Garner, C.A. (1986), 'Equity in Economic Relationships', *Journal of Behaviour and Organisation*, 7, pp. 253-64.

Gewirth, A. (1984), 'The Epistemology of Human Rights', in Paul, E.F. *et al.* (eds), *Human Rights*, Oxford, Basil Blackwell, pp. 1-24.

Gjerdingen, D.H. (1983), 'The Coase Theorem and the Psychology of Common-Law Thought', *Southern Californa Law Review*, 56, pp. 711-60.

Gleick, J. (1988), *Chaos: Making a New Science*, London, Sphere.

Goetz, C.J. and Scott, R.E. (1981), 'Principles of Relational Contracts', *Virginia Law Review*, 67, pp. 1089-150.

Goldberg, V.P. (1976), 'Regulation and Administered Contracts', *Bell Journal of Economics*, 7, pp. 426-8.

Gorringe, P.A. (1987a), 'A Contracting Theory View of Industrial Relations', Paper presented to a Conference of the H R Nicholls Society, 8 June, Mooloolaba, Queensland.

Gorringe, P.A. (1987b), 'Hostages, Asset Dependence and the Enforcement of Labour Market Contracts', Paper presented to a Conference of the Australian Association of Economists, 25 August, Surfers Paradise.

Gould, W.B. (1988), *Japan's Reshaping of American Labor Law*, Cambridge (Mass.), MIT Press.

Gray, J. (1989), *Limited Government: A Positive Agenda*, London, Institute of Economic Affairs.

Gray, W.B. (1987), 'The Cost of Regulation: OSHA, EPA and the Productivity Slowdown', *American Economic Review*, 77, pp. 998-1006.

Greenslade, B. (1988), 'An Employer View: Strikes: Injunctions and Compliance Orders: Labour Relations Act 1987', Wellington, mimeo.

Greenwald, B.C. (1986), 'Adverse Selection in the Labour Market', *Review of Economic Studies*, 53, pp. 325-47.

Gregory, R.G. and Duncan, R. (1981), 'Segmented Labour Market Theories and the Australian Experience of Equal Pay for Women', *Journal of Post-Keynesian Economics*, 2, pp. 403-28.

Haakonssen, K. (ed) (1988), *Traditions of Liberalism: Essays on John Locke, Adam Smith and John Stuart Mill*, St Leonards, Centre for Independent Studies.

Haigh, J. (1987), 'Industrial Relations: Will They Survive the Labour Relations Act 1987?', *New Zealand Journal of Industrial Relations*, 12, pp. 119-21.

Hall, R.E. and Lazear, E.P. (1984), 'The Excess Sensitivity of Layoffs and Quits to Demand', *Journal of Labor Economics*, 2, pp. 233-57.

Hansmann, H. (1988), 'Ownership of the Firm', *Journal of Law, Economics, and Organization*, 4, pp. 267-304.

Hanson, C.G. and Mather, G. (1988), *Striking Out Strikes: Changing Employment Relations in the British Labour Market*, London, Institute of Economic Affairs.

Hart, O.D. (1988), 'Incomplete Contracts and the Theory of the Firm', *Journal of Law, Economics, and Organization*, 4, pp. 119-39.

———— (1989), 'Bargaining and Strikes', *Quarterly Journal of Economics*, 114, pp. 25-43.

Hashimoto, M. (1981), 'Firm-Specific Human Capital as a Shared Investment', *American Economic Review*, 71, pp. 475-82.

———— (1982), 'Minimum Wage Effects on Training on the Job', *American Economic Review*, 72, pp. 1070-87.

Hatton, T.J. (1988), 'Institutional Change and Wage Rigidity in the UK, 1880-1985', *Oxford Review of Economic Policy*, 4/1, pp. 74-86.

Haworth, N. (1989), 'Economic Restructuring and Industrial Relations in New Zealand', Department of Management Studies and Labour Relations, University of Auckland, Auckland, mimeo.

Hayek, F.A. (1944), *The Road to Serfdom*, Chicago, University of Chicago Press.

————— (1945), 'The Use of Knowledge in Society', *American Economic Review*, 35, pp. 519-30.

————— (1948), *Individualism and Economic Order*, Chicago, University of Chicago Press.

————— (1988a), 'Central Planning: The Fatal Conceit', in Anderson, A. and Bark, D.L. (eds), *Thinking About America: The United States in the 1990s*, Stanford, Hoover Institution Press, pp. 501-5.

————— (1988b), *The Fatal Conceit: The Errors of Socialism*, Chicago, University of Chicago Press.

Heldman, D.C., *et al.* (1981), *Deregulating Labor Relations*, Dallas, Fisher Institute.

Hess, J.D. (1983), *The Economics of Organisation*, Amsterdam, North-Holland.

Heylen Research Centre (1984), *Public Opinion Survey on Compulsory Unionism*, Wellington, Heylen Research Centre.

————— (1987), *Public Opinion Survey of Industrial Relations Issues*, Wellington, Heylen Research Centre.

Hince, K. (1989), 'Industrial Democracy: Historical Perspectives', Paper presented to a Seminar on Industrial Democracy, 11 May, Wellington.

Hirsch, B.T. and Link, A.N. (1984), 'Unions, Productivity, and Productivity Growth', *Journal of Labor Research*, 5, pp. 29-37.

Hirschman, A.O. (1970), *Exit, Voice, and Loyalty*, Cambridge (Mass.), Harvard University Press.

Hobson, M.J. and Maurice, S.C. (1983), *Minimum Wages: Who Benefits, Who Loses?*, College Station, Texas, Center for Education and Research in Free Enterprise.

Hodgson, G.M. and Jones, D.C. (1989), 'Codetermination: A Partial Review of Theory and Evidence', *Annals of Public and Cooperative Economics*, 60, pp. 329-40.

Hoerr, J. (1989), 'The Payoff from Teamwork', *Business Weekly*, 10 July, pp. 36-42.

Holt, J. (1976), 'The Origins of Compulsory Arbitration in New Zealand', *New Zealand Journal of History*, 10, pp. 99-111.

Horn, J.R.P. *et al.* (1989), *Report of the Committee of Enquiry into Industrial Democracy*, Wellington.

Horsfield, A. (1988), *Women in the Economy*, Wellington, Ministry of Women's Affairs.

Huberman, G. and Kahn, C. (1988), 'Two-sided Uncertainty and 'Up-or-Out' Contracts', *Journal of Labor Economics*, 6, pp. 423-44.

Hutt, W.H. (1973), *The Strike-Threat System: The Economic Consequences of Collective Bargaining*, New Rochelle (NY), Arlington House.

—— (1975), *The Theory of Collective Bargaining 1930-1975*, London, Institute of Economic Affairs.

—— (1986), 'The "Power" of Labour Unions', in Anderson, M.J. (ed), *The Unfinished Agenda: Essays on the Political Economy of Government Policy in Honour of Arthur Seldon*, London, Institute of Economic Affairs, pp. 41-63.

Hyman, P. and Clark, A. (1987), *Equal Pay Study: Phase One Report*, Wellington, Department of Labour.

Insight New Zealand (1988), *Industrial Relations Issues in New Zealand: A Survey of Public Attitudes*, Auckland, Insight New Zealand.

Jantsch, E. (1980), *The Self-Organizing Universe: Scientific and Human Implications of the Emerging Paradigm of Evolution*, Oxford, Pergamon Press.

Jensen, M. and Meckling, W. (1979), 'Rights and Production Functions: An Application to Labor-Managed Firms and Codetermination', *Journal of Business*, 52, pp. 469-506.

Kahn-Freund, O. (1977), 'Blackstone's Neglected Child: The Contract of Employment', *Law Quarterly Review*, 93, pp. 508-28.

Kelman, M. (1979), 'Choice and Utility', *Wisconsin Law Review*, pp. 769-97.

Kirkbride, P.S. (1985), 'The Concept of Power: A Lacuna in Industrial Relations Theory?', *Journal of Industrial Relations*, pp. 265-82.

Klein, B. (1984), 'Contract Costs and Administered Prices: An Economic Theory of Rigid Wages', *American Economic Review*, 74, pp. 332-8.

—— *et al.* (1978), 'Vertical Integration, Appropriable Rents and the Competitive Contracting Process', *Journal of Law and Economics*, 21, pp. 297-326.

—— and Leffler, K.B. (1981), 'The Role of Market Forces in Assuring Contractual Performance', *Journal of Political Economy*, 89, pp. 615-41.

Kniesner, T.J. and Leeth, J.D. (1987), 'Can We Make OSHA and Workers' Compensation Insurance Interact More Effectively in Promoting Workplace Safety? A Numerical Analysis of Hedonic Labor Market Equilibrium', Working Paper, Department of Economics, University of North Carolina.

Knox, W.J. (1986), *Looking Ahead: A More Just Industrial Relations System*, Wellington, New Zealand Federation of Labour.

———— (1987), *FOL Submission to the Labour Select Committee on the Labour Relations Bill*, Wellington, New Zealand Federation of Labour.

Kosters, M. and Welch, F. (1972), 'The Effects of Minimum Wages on the Distribution of Changes in Aggregate Employment', *American Economic Review*, 62, pp. 323-32.

Kronman, A.T. and Posner, R.A. (1979), *The Economics of Contract Law*, Boston, Little, Brown and Company.

Kuhn, T.S. (1970), *The Structure of Scientific Revolutions* (2nd edition), Chicago, University of Chicago Press.

Kukathas, C. (1989), 'The Fraternal Conceit', Paper presented to the Mont Pelerin Society Pacific Regional Meeting, 30 November, Christchurch.

Kurth, M.M. and Reid, J.D. (1984), 'The Contribution of Exclusive Representation to Union Strength', *Journal of Labor Research*, 5, pp. 391-411.

Lande, R.H. and Zerbe, R.O. (1985), 'Reducing Unions' Monopoly Power: Costs and Benefits', *Journal of Law and Economics*, 28, pp. 297-310.

Landes, E.M. (1980), 'The Effect of State Maximum-Hours Laws on the Employment of Women in 1920', *Journal of Political Economy*, 88, pp. 476-94.

Lang, K. (1989), *Trade Liberalisation and the New Zealand Labour Market*, Wellington, New Zealand Institute of Economic Research.

Lave, L.B. (1987), 'Injury as Externality: An Economic Perspective of Trauma', *Accident Analysis and Prevention*, 19, pp. 29-37.

Lavoie, D. (1985), *National Economic Planning: What is Left?*, Cambridge (Mass.), Ballinger.

———— (1989), 'Economic Chaos or Spontaneous Order? Implications for Political Economy of the New View of Science', *Cato Journal*, 8, pp. 613-35.

Lazear, E.P. (1983), 'A Competitive Theory of Monopoly Unionism', *American Economic Review*, 73, pp. 631-43.

———— (1988), 'The Labor Market and International Competitiveness', in Anderson, A. and Bark, D.L. (eds), *Thinking About America: The United States in the 1990s*, Stanford, Hoover Institution Press, pp. 367-81.

———— (1989), 'Pay Equality and Industrial Politics', *Journal of Political Economy*, 97, pp. 561-80.

Lazear, E. P. and Moore, R.L. (1984), 'Incentives, Productivity, and Labor Contracts', *Quarterly Journal of Economics*, 94, pp. 275-96.

—— and Rosen, S. (1981), 'Rank Order Tournaments as Optimum Labor Contracts', *Journal of Political Economy*, 89, pp. 841-64.

Leadbeater, C. (1989), 'A Charter for Casual Labour', *Financial Times*, 17 April, p 25.

Leslie, D.L. (1980), 'Principles of Labor Antitrust', *Virginia Law Review*, 66, pp. 1183-234.

—— (1984), 'Labor Bargaining Units', *Virginia Law Review*, 70, pp. 353-418.

Lomasky, L. (1984), 'Personal Projects as the Foundation for Basic Rights', in Paul, E.F. *et al.* (eds), *Human Rights*, Oxford, Basil Blackwell, pp. 35-55.

McCallum, R.C. (1987), 'Trade Unions, Collective Bargaining and the Law: Present Trends and Future Options', Paper delivered for the Parliamentary Library of Australia, 2 November, Canberra.

Lord McCarthy (1987), 'The Case for a More Balanced Framework of Labour Law', Warwick Paper in Industrial Relations No. 14, Industrial Relations Research Unit, School of Industrial and Business Studies, University of Warwick.

McCloskey, D. (1986), *The Rhetoric of Economics*, Brighton, Wheatsheaf.

McKenzie, R.B. (ed) (1984), *Plant Closings: Public or Private Choices?*, Washington, Cato Institute.

—— (1987), *U.S. Employment Opportunities in a Competitive World Economy: Positive Approaches to a New Labor Policy Agenda*, Washington, Center for the Study of American Business.

—— (1988), *The American Job Machine*, New York, Universe.

MacNeil, I.R. (1978), 'Contracts: Adjustment of Long-Term Economic Relations under Classical, Neoclassical, and Relational Contract Law', *Northwestern University Law Review*, 72, pp. 854-905.

Maki, D.R. (1983), 'The Effects of Unions and Strikes on the Rate of Growth of Total Factor Productivity in Canada', *Applied Economics*, 15, pp. 29-41.

Malcolmson, J.M. (1986), 'Work Incentives, Hierarchy, and Internal Labor Markets', in Akerlof, G.A. and Yellen, J.L. (eds), *Efficiency Wage Models of the Labor Market*, Cambridge, Cambridge University Press, pp. 157-78.

Maley, B. (1985), 'Industrial Decay and Democratic Illusions: The Dead End of Industrial Democracy', Paper presented to the Pacific Regional Meeting of the Mont Pelerin Society, 19-23 August, Sydney.

Marvel, H.P. (1977), 'Factory Regulation: A Reinterpretation of Early English Experience', *Journal of Law and Economics*, 20, pp. 379-402.

Masten, S.E. (1988), 'A Legal Basis for the Firm', *Journal of Law, Economics and Organization*, 4, pp. 181-98.

—— *et al.* (1989), 'The Costs of Organization', Working Paper No. 603, Division of Research, Graduate School of Business Administration, University of Michigan.

Mather, G. (1987), 'The Future Shape of Labour Legislation', Warwick Papers in Industrial Relations No. 14, Industrial Relations Research Unit, School of Industrial and Business Studies, University of Warwick.

—— (1988), 'Time for a Pay Revolution', *Sunday Telegraph*, 23 October.

Meltzer, B. D. (1963), 'Labor Unions, Collective Bargaining, and the Antitrust Laws', *Journal of Law and Economics*, 6, pp. 152-223.

Merritt, A. (1982), 'The Historical Role of Law in the Regulation of Employment: Abstentionist or Interventionist?', *Australian Journal of Law and Society*, 1, pp. 56-86.

Metcalf, D. (1988), 'Trade Unions and Economic Performance: The British Evidence', Discussion Paper No. 320, Centre for Labour Economics, London School of Economics.

—— (1989), 'Can Unions Survive in the Private Sector? The Implications of the Impact of Unions on Pay, Productivity, Profits and Jobs', Paper presented to an Employment Institute Conference on Trade Unions and the Economy: Into the 1990s, 21 March, London.

Mincer, J. (1976), 'Unemployment Effects of Minimum Wages', *Journal of Political Economy*, 84, pp. S87-S104.

Minkler, A.P. (1989), 'Property Rights, Efficiency and Labor-Managed Firms', *Annals of Public and Cooperative Economics*, 60, pp. 341-57.

Minogue, K. (1989), *The Egalitarian Conceit: False and True Equalities*, St Leonards, Centre for Independent Studies.

Mirrlees, J. (1976), 'The Optimal Structure of Incentives and Authority within an Organisation', *Bell Journal of Economics*, 7, pp. 105-31.

Mises, L. von (1978), *The Ultimate Foundation of Economic Science* (2nd edition), Kansas City, Sheed Andreas and McMeel.

Monetary and Economic Council (1962), *Economic Growth in New Zealand*, Wellington, Government Printer.

Moore, T.G. (1971), 'The Effect of Minimum Wages on Teenage Unemployment Rates', *Journal of Political Economy*, 79, pp. 897-902.

Moore, W.J. (1980), 'Membership and Wage Impact of Right-to-Work Laws', *Journal of Labor Research*, 1, pp. 349-75.

—— (1983), 'FTC Probes Labor Antitrust Exemption', *Legal Times*, 3 October, p. 1.

—— *et al.* (1985), 'The Effect of the Extent of Unionism on Union and Nonunion Wages', *Journal of Labor Research*, 6, pp. 21-44.

Moorhouse, J.C. (1982), 'Compulsory Unionism and the Free-Rider Problem', *Cato Journal*, 2, pp. 619-35.

Morrall, J.F. (1986), 'A Review of the Record', *Regulation*, November/December, pp. 25-34.

Muir, P. (1989), 'Contracts of Employment: Industrial Relations and Employment Law Issues', Paper presented to a Seminar on Workforce Structure and Executive Remuneration, 5 July, Auckland.

Mulgan, M.A. (1987), 'Toward a Uniform Law of Dismissal in New Zealand', *New Zealand Universities Law Review*, 12, pp. 384-433.

Murray, C. (1988), *In Pursuit of Happiness and Good Government*, New York, Simon and Schuster.

New Zealand Business Roundtable (1986), *New Zealand Labour Market Reform: A Submission in Response to the Green Paper 'Industrial Relations: A Framework for Review'*, Wellington, New Zealand Business Roundtable.

—— (1987), *Submission to the Labour Select Committee: The Labour Relations Bill*, Wellington, New Zealand Business Roundtable.

—— (1988a), *Labour Markets and Employment*, Wellington, New Zealand Business Roundtable.

—— (1988b), *Submission to the Committee Inquiring into 'Dependent' Contracting*, Wellington, New Zealand Business Roundtable.

—— (1989a), *Review of the Operation of the Labour Relations Act in the 1988/89 Wage Round*, Wellington, New Zealand Business Roundtable.

—— (1989b), *Submission to the Working Party on Employer Funding Contribution to Training*, Wellington, New Zealand Business Roundtable.

New Zealand Council of Trade Unions (1988), *The Need for Change: Challenges for the Trade Union Movement of Today*, Wellington, New Zealand Council of Trade Unions.

New Zealand Employers Federation (1989), *Future Directions for New Zealand: An Agenda for Change and Choice*, Wellington, New Zealand Employers Federation.

New Zealand Federation of Labour and Combined State Unions (1985), *Occupational Health and Safety in New Zealand*, Wellington, FOL/CSU.

New Zealand Treasury (1984), *Economic Management*, Wellington, Government Printer.

―――― (1987), *Government Management*, Wellington, Government Printer.

Niland, J. (1989), *Transforming Industrial Relations in New South Wales: A Green Paper*, Sydney, Government Printer.

Oakeshott, M. (1962), *Rationalism in Politics*, London, Methuen.

―――― (1983), *On History*, Cambridge, Cambridge University Press.

Oi, W.Y. (1962), 'Labor as a Quasi-fixed Factor', *Journal of Political Economy*, 50, pp. 538-55.

O'Neill, J. *et al.* (1989), 'Effects of Comparable Worth Policy: Evidence from Washington State', *American Economics Association Papers and Proceedings*, 79, pp. 305-9.

Organization for Economic Co-operation and Development (1986a), *Flexibility in the Labour Market: The Current Debate*, Paris, Organization for Economic Co-operation and Development.

―――― (1986b), *Labour Market Flexibility*, Paris, Organization for Economic Co-operation and Development.

Orr, D. (1980), 'The Free Rider and Labor Law', *Journal of Labor Research*, 1, pp. 285-93.

Osawa, M. (1989), 'The Service Economy and Industrial Relations in Small and Medium Size Firms in Japan', *Japan Labor Bulletin*, 28/7, pp. 4-8.

Pally, T.I. (1988), 'The Effect of Unemployment Among Union Members on Union Wage Contracts', *Atlantic Economic Journal*, 16/3, pp. 19-30.

Palomba, N.A. and C.A. (1971), 'Right-to-Work Laws: A Suggested Economic Rationale', *Journal of Law and Economics*, 14, pp. 475-83.

Parsley, C.J. (1980), 'Labor Union Effects on Wage Gains: A Survey of Recent Literature', *Journal of Economic Literature*, 18, pp. 1-31.

Parsons, D.O. (1980), *Poverty and the Minimum Wage*, Washington, American Enterprise Institute for Public Policy Research.

Paul, E.F. (1989), *Equity and Gender: The Comparable Worth Debate*, New Brunswick, Transaction.

Pejovich, S. (1984), *Industrial Democracy: Conflict or Cooperation?*, College Station, Texas, Center for Education and Research in Free Enterprise.

Polanyi, M. (1958), *The Study of Man*, London, Routledge and Kegan Paul.

Popper, K. (1957), *The Poverty of Historicism*, London, Routledge and Kegan Paul.

Porter, M.G. (1989), 'Getting On Top Internationally: The Centrality of Labour Market Reforms', Paper presented to the New Zealand National Marketing Conference, Rotorua, 26-28 April.

Posner, R.A. (1973), *Economic Analysis of the Law*, Boston, Little, Brown and Company.

—— (1979), 'Some Uses and Abuses of Economics in Law', *University of Chicago Law Review*, 46, pp. 281-306.

Prigogine, I. and Stengers, I. (1984), *Order Out of Chaos: Man's New Dialogue with Nature*, New York, Bantam.

Raphael, D.D. (1976), *Problems of Political Economy* (revised edition), London, Macmillan.

Rees, A. (1963), 'The Effects of Unions on Resource Allocation', *Journal of Law and Economics*, 6, pp. 69-78.

Reserve Bank of New Zealand (1987), *Post-Election Briefing Paper to the Minister of Finance*, Wellington, Reserve Bank of New Zealand.

Reynolds, M.O. (1984), *Power and Privilege: Labor Unions in America*, New York, Universe.

—— (1985), *The History and Economics of Labor Unions*, College Station, Texas, Center for Education and Research in Free Enterprise.

—— (1986), 'The Case for Ending the Legal Privileges and Immunities of Trade Unions', in Lipset, S.M. (ed), *Unions in Transition*, San Francisco, Institute for Contemporary Studies, pp. 221-38.

—— (1987), *Making America Poorer: The Cost of Labor Law*, Washington, Cato Institute.

—— (1988), 'Labor Reform: A Blip on the Radarscope', in Boaz, D. (ed), *Assessing the Reagan Years*, Washington, Cato Institute, pp. 321-32.

Rideout, R.W. (1966), 'The Contract of Employment', *Current Legal Problems*, 1966, pp. 111-27.

Riechel, K.-W. (1986), 'Labor Market Disequilibrium and the Scope for Work-Sharing', *International Monetary Fund Staff Papers*, 33, pp. 509-40.

Roback, J. (1986), *A Matter of Choice: A Critique of Comparable Worth by a Skeptical Feminist*, New York, Priority Press.

Roberts, B. (1987), *Mr Hammond's Cherry Tree: The Morphology of Union Survival*, London, Institute of Economic Affairs.

———— (1989), 'The Social Dimension of European Labour Markets', in Dahrendorf, R. *et al.*, *Whose Europe: Competing Visions for 1992*, London, Institute of Economic Affairs, pp. 39-49.

Rodger, S. (1985), *Industrial Relations: A Framework for Review*, Wellington, Government Printer.

———— (1986a), *Government Policy Statement on Labour Relations*, Wellington, Government Printer.

———— (1986b), *Industrial Relations: A Framework for Review – Summary of Submissions*, Wellington, Government Printer.

———— (1986c), *Pay Fixing in the State Sector: A Review of Principles and Procedures in the Fixing of Pay and Associated Conditions in the New Zealand State Sector*, Wellington, Government Printer.

———— (1989), 'Industrial Democracy/Employee Pariticpation: Prospects and Plans for New Zealand', Paper presented to a Seminar on Industrial Democracy, 11 May, Wellington.

Rosen, S. (1985), 'Implicit Contracts: A Survey', *Journal of Economic Literature*, 23, pp. 1144-75.

———— (1986), 'Prizes and Incentives in Elimination Tournaments', *American Economic Review*, 76, pp. 701-15.

———— (1987), 'Transactions Costs and Internal Labor Markets', Working Paper No. 2407, Cambridge (Mass.), National Bureau of Economic Research.

Rottenberg, S. (ed) (1980), *Occupational Licensure and Regulation*, Washington, American Enterprise Institute for Public Policy Research.

Routley, V.C. (1989), 'Enterprise Unions: The Alternative', *Proceedings of the H R Nicholls Society*, 6, pp. 87-90.

Royal Commission on Social Policy (1988), *The April Report, 2: Future Directions*, Wellington, Royal Commission on Social Policy.

Sah, R.K. and Stiglitz, J.E. (1986), 'The Architecture of Economic Systems: Hierarchies and Polyarchies', *American Economic Review*, 76, pp. 716-27.

St. Antoine, T.J. (1988), 'A Seed Germinates: Unjust Discharge Reform Heads Toward Full Flower', *Nebraska Law Review*, 67, pp. 56-81.

Samuels, W.J. (1971), 'Interrelations Between Legal and Economic Processes', *Journal of Law and Economics*, 14, pp. 435-50.

Savage, J. (1989), *Internal Labour Markets: Labour Adjustment within Firms*, Wellington, New Zealand Institute of Economic Research.

Schmidt, E.P. (1973), *Union Power and the Public Interest*, Los Angeles, Nash Publishing.

Secretary of State for Employment (1989), *Removing Barriers to Employment: Proposals for the Further Reform of Industrial Relations and Trade Union Law*, London, Her Majesty's Stationery Office, Cm 655.

Sen, A.K. (1977), 'Rational Fools: A Critique of the Behavioural Foundations of Economic Theory', *Philosophy and Public Affairs*, 6, pp. 317-44.

——— (1984), *Resources, Values and Development*, Oxford, Basil Blackwell.

Shapiro, C. (1986), 'Investment, Moral Hazard, and Occupational Licensing', *Review of Economic Studies*, 53, pp. 843-62.

Sharp, A. (1986), 'The "Principle" of Voluntary Unionism in New Zealand Political Debate, 1983-1985', *Political Science*, 38, pp. 1-26.

Shenfield, A. (1986), *What Right to Strike?*, London, Institute of Economic Affairs.

Simons, H.C. (1944), 'Some Reflections on Syndicalism', *Journal of Political Economy*, 52, pp. 1-25.

Smith, A. (1974), *The Wealth of Nations*, Harmondsworth, Penguin.

Smith, R.S. (1988), 'Comparable Worth: Limited Coverage and the Exacerbation of Inequality', *Industrial and Labor Relations Review*, 41, pp. 227-38.

Soltwedel, R. and Trapp, P. (1987), 'Labor Market Barriers to More Employment: Causes for an Increase of the Natural Rate? The Case of West Germany', in Giersch, H. (ed) *Macro and Micro Policies for More Growth and Employment*, Tubingen, J.C.B. Mohr, pp. 181-225.

Sowell, T. (1982), 'Weber and Bakke, and the Presuppositions of "Affirmative Action"', in Block, W.E. and Walker, M.A. (eds), *Discrimination, Affirmative Action and Equal Opportunity*, Vancouver, Fraser Institute, pp. 37-63.

——— (1987), *A Conflict of Visions: Ideological Origins of Political Struggles*, New York, William Morrow & Company.

——— (1989), '"Affirmative Action": A Worldwide Disaster', *Commentary*, December, pp. 21-41.

Spence, A.M. (1974), *Market Signalling: International Transfer in Hiring and Related Screening Processes*, Cambridge (Mass.) Harvard University Press.

Stewart, M.B. (1987), 'Collective Bargaining Arrangements, Closed Shops and Relative Pay', *Economic Journal*, 97, pp. 140-56.

Stigler, G.J. (1976), 'The Xistence of X-Efficiency', *American Economic Review*, 66, pp. 213-6.

Stigler, G.J. (ed) (1988), *Chicago Studies in Political Economy*, Chicago, University of Chicago Press.

Stockton, W. (1988), 'Tearing Apart Eastern Airlines', *New York Times Magazine*, 6 November.

Sutton, R.J. (1988), 'Undue Influence, Fiduciary Duty and Unconscionability', Paper presented to the Judges' Conference, 1 May, Wellington.

Taskforce to Review Education Administration (1988), *Administering For Excellence: Effective Administration in Education*, Wellington, Government Printer.

Thurow, L.C. (1975), *Generating Inequality*, New York, Basic Books.

Tollison, R.D. (1982), 'Rent-Seeking: A Survey', *Kyklos*, 35, pp. 575-602.

Toogood, C.H. (1989), 'Update on the Labour Relations Act 1987', Paper presented to an Institute for International Research Conference on Managing Change in Industrial Relations, 17-18 August, Auckland.

Trebeck, D. (1989), *Ports and Shipping Reform in New Zealand: Current Developments and Future Requirements*, Wellington, New Zealand Business Roundtable and Federated Farmers of New Zealand.

Tully, C. (1983), 'Note: Challenging the Employment-at-Will Doctrine through Modern Contract Theory', *Journal of Law Reform*, 16, pp. 449-64.

Ungern-Sternberg, T. von and Weizsacker, C.C. von (1985), 'The Supply of Quality in a Market for "Experience" Goods', *Journal of Industrial Economics*, 33, pp. 531-40.

Viscusi, W.K. (1983), *Risk by Choice: Regulating Health and Safety in the Workplace*, Cambridge (Mass.), Harvard University Press.

Vranken, M. (1989), 'Institutionalised Forms of Worker Participation: Some European Experiences', Paper presented to a Seminar on Industrial Democracy, 11 May, Wellington.

Walker, D. (1984), *Value and Opportunity: Comparable Pay for Comparable Worth*, College Station, Texas, Center for Education and Research in Free Enterprise.

Walker, G. de Q. (1989), 'In the Shadow of the Law', *Proceedings of the H R Nicholls Society*, 6, pp. 81-4.

Wallis, J.J. (1989), 'Towards a Positive Economic Theory of Institutional Change', *Journal of Institutional and Theoretical Economics*, 145, pp. 98-112.

Walsh, P. (1983), 'Union Membership Policy in New Zealand: 1894-1982', in Brosnan, P. (ed), *Voluntary Unionism, Proceedings of a Seminar 5 October 1983*, Wellington, Industrial Relations Centre, Victoria University of Wellington, pp. 15-21.

Walzer, M. (1983), *Spheres of Justice: A Defense of Pluralism and Equality*, New York, Basic Books.

Lord Wedderburn (1988), 'Labour Law: Autonomy from the Common Law?', *Comparative Labor Law Journal*, pp. 219-52.

Weitzman, M.L. (1984), *The Share Economy*, Cambridge (Mass.), Harvard University Press.

Weizsacker, C.C. von (1980), *Barriers to Entry: A Theoretical Treatment*, Berlin, Springer-Verlag.

Wellington, H.H. (1968), *Labor and the Legal Process*, New Haven, Yale University Press.

Wickens, P. (1987), *The Road to Nissan: Flexibility, Quality, Teamwork*, London, Macmillan.

Williams, W.E. (1979), 'Preference, Prejudice and Difference: Racial Reasoning in Unfree Markets', *Regulation*, March/April, pp. 39-48.

────── (1989), *South Africa's War Against Capitalism*, New York, Praeger.

Williamson, O.E. (1975), *Markets and Hierarchies*, New York, Free Press.

────── (1979), 'Transaction Cost Economics: The Governance of Contractual Relations', *Journal of Law and Economics*, 22, pp. 233-61.

────── (1982), 'Efficient Labor Organization', Discussion Paper No. 123, Center for the Study of Organizational Innovation, University of Pennsylvania.

────── (1985), *The Economic Institutions of Capitalism*, New York, Free Press.

────── (1988), 'Internal Economic Organization', Berkeley, mimeo.

────── (1989), 'Operationalizing the New Institutional Economics: The Transaction Cost Economics Perspective', Berkeley, mimeo.

────── *et al.* (1975), 'Understanding the Employment Relation: The Analysis of Idiosyncratic Exchange', *Bell Journal of Economics*, 6, pp. 250-78.

Wilson, M. (1988), *Towards Employment Equity: Report of the Working Group on Equal Employment Opportunities and Equal Pay*, Wellington, Government Printer.

Wilson, O. (1982), *An Outsider Looks Back: Reflections on Experience*, Wellington, Port Nicholson Press.

Winter, R.K. (1963), 'Collective Bargaining and Competition: The Application of Antitrust Standards to Union Activities', *Yale Law Journal*, 73, pp. 14-73.

Woodbury, S.A. (1987), 'Power in the Labor Market: Institutionalist Approaches to Labor Problems', *Journal of Economic Issues*, 21, pp. 1781-807.

Wooden, M. (1989), 'Trade Unions and Productivity: Can Australia Learn Anything from the U.S. Research?', National Institute of Labour Studies, Adelaide, mimeo.

Young, S.D. (1987), *The Rule of Experts: Occupational Licensing in America*, Washington, Cato Institute.

Index